Table of Contents

IV. Doctors, Nurses, And Health Professionals

V. Pharma, Biotech, Device Companies

VI. Patients And Consumers

VII. Employers, Insurers, Regulators

VIII. Gadgets, Apps, Technology

IX. Behavior, Design, And Translation

x. Big Data, Measurement, and Metrics

XI.   VCs And Other Investors

XII.   Innovation

Dedications

David:

This book is for...

... my parents, Bennett and Sally, who've inspired me;

... my brothers, Jonathan and Adam, who've sustained me;

... my wife, Diana, who's indulged me;

... my children, Juliet, Amelia, and Mirielle, who've blessed me.

Lisa:

This book is for many who care about and support me—family, friends, and colleagues who I love dearly—but is principally for my daughter, Maddy, who teases me mercilessly about my attempts to be a writer but whom I know is secretly proud of me.

Become a Hyperink reader. Get a special surprise.

Like the book? Support our author and leave a comment!

II.

Preface

Health matters.

"When you have your health, you have everything," wrote memoirist Augusten Burroughs. "When you do not have your health, nothing else matters at all."

Health can also be very expensive, and reducing costs isn't easy, since as Stanford health policy expert Victor Fuchs famously observed, "Every dollar of waste is income to some individual or organization."

One key challenge healthcare faces today is figuring out how to maintain health and deliver better care for patients while somehow keeping in check the overall costs associated with these activities.

The good news is that there is now the massive potential for healthcare transformation. Data-driven analysis has called into question many traditional healthcare assumptions, and permits us to view the challenges in a fresh light. For instance, there seems to be little correlation between healthcare cost and quality—and great care can be delivered at lower cost if we can improve the alignment of incentives among patients, payers, and providers.

Key drivers of healthcare change are the intense economic pressure of healthcare costs, the impact—to be determined—associated with the implementation of the Affordable Care Act, and the advent of inexpensive and widely accessible technologies; together these have created a platform for industry transformation the likes of which has not been seen since the dawn of modern surgery.

And it's about time. Technology has been used to optimize and redefine virtually every key industry except healthcare. Manufacturing has gone from human assembly lines to robotics; banking has gone from tellers to home banking; travel has gone from agents with brochures to Travelocity; and yet the practice of medicine, in many ways, hasn't changed in decades.

Improved assessment technologies and analytics have enabled many other industries to improve efficiency and ensure resources are spent as effectively as possible; now, perhaps, it's healthcare's turn. The explosion of mobile technologies has dramatically empowered customers and redefined the way they make choices and conduct business; now, perhaps, it's healthcare's turn.   Upstart entrepreneurs willing to think differently have completely reshaped the way we enjoy music, read books, retrieve information, and communicate with friends; now, perhaps, it's healthcare's turn.

Many of today's most passionate entrepreneurs are trying to bring the dazzle and real promise of technology innovation to the challenges of healthcare, resulting in an explosion of companies focused on everything from wearable sensors and weight-loss apps to big data analytics and GPS-tagged hospital equipment—the "internet of things." These technologists are hoping to apply the lessons from other other industries and other successes—Facebook, Uber, Google, Apple, Yelp, Open Table—to health and medicine.

As a whole, these approaches—which include information technologies, mobile capabilities, and sophisticated analytics—might just allow us to re-conceptualize healthcare in a fashion that is more patient-focused and democratic. Importantly, these approaches are also being used to help shift healthcare towards a mindset that is focused on maintaining wellness as well as treating illness, that recognizes health is experienced, and deserves to be assessed in a fashion that is continuous rather than episodic, that uses data to drive better decisions, and that helps avoid the costly mistakes and waste that make up over 30% of healthcare spending.

These emerging tools and promising technologies—which collectively comprise "digital health"—offer a promising path forward, and entrepreneurs and innovators are forging forward seeking to make a real difference in a field which we all need but which is sorely in need of its own tender loving care if it is to flourish in tomorrow's world. As Hippocrates once said, "Healing is a matter of time, but it is sometimes also a matter of opportunity." And technology—if judiciously applied—may be just the tonic to help reinvigorate the health of our healthcare industry.

The key challenge faced by would-be disruptive technologists is not only recognizing potentially useful analogs from other industries, but also understanding the ways in which health remains fundamentally different. Success in healthcare requires a nuanced understanding of the problems to be solved, since these problems are often less obvious and more personal than may be initially apparent.

Amid the clamor to disrupt healthcare, we should also take care to preserve and augment what may be right about medicine—the doctor/patient relationship for example, or the drive of inquisitive physicians, especially within academic centers, to continuously push and challenge the limits of what is known and what is possible.

In *Tech Tonics*—a distillation of our writing and thinking over the last several years—we introduce the reader to the fascinating digital health space, including a ground-level view of the landscape, the structural challenges, the players, and the progress.

From our perch in Silicon Valley, we've sought to chronicle the recent trials and tribulations of digital health, capturing the energy, passion, hope, and hype, the ambition —occasionally misguided—of wildly smart technologists trying to grapple with some of the most difficult challenges of the modern era. We hope you enjoy the ride as we have.

III.

Entrepreneurs & Startups

SXSW: Woodstock For Geeks

Turns out there are all different kinds of techno geeks out there. At HIMSS not long ago I was feeling semi-hip among the healthcare uber-nerd crowd that worries about how to make big hospital and healthcare enterprises function with big data. It's a festival of old-school techno weenies recognizable in the wild by their big company expense accounts and the blue and gray suits that barely cover their pocket protectors. It also felt like a group desperately trying to catch the back of the social networking wave into the world where Mark Zuckerberg and Biz Stone are Gods, not men. In fact, Biz Stone, founder of Twitter, was a keynote speaker at HIMSS and it seemed like the proverbial fish in need of a bicycle. One audience member actually leaned over and said to me, "I have no idea what these young social networking people are talking about." Poor guy could not have been more than 50 but he was definitely his father's Oldsmobile. I didn't want to tell him that by failing to recognize social networking as a meaningful phenomenon he had one foot in the healthcare IT grave and the other on a banana peel.

Fast forward two weeks and I found myself, too uncool for school and entirely overdressed, among the techno glitterati at South By Southwest (SXSW) in Austin, TX. Not a suit to be found there at that gathering, which would blanche at the thought of being called a conference. SXSW is more of a happening. Rather than suits (the costume is old jeans and rock and roll t-shirts), the primary thing that comes in blue is hair. I also saw pink, green, and purple hairstyles, none of which were evident at HIMSS. More than anything, sensory stimulation is the big difference between HIMSS and SXSW; the former is conducted in black and white while the latter is conducted in riotous technicolor.

Don't get me wrong, SXSW (or "South By" as the locals call it, sending the hipster meter to its limit) is loaded with techno weenies, they are just of an entirely different species than the kind that are native to HIMSS. These guys are all about their iPhones and Pinterest and lord knows they have got the Twitter thing down. There was a program being promoted at SXSW called "Tweet a Beer" where you could pay-it-forward by sending your favorite nerd or nerdess a beer through Twitter if you were in the SXSW orbit. In stark contrast to the crowd who works 9-5 in a glass tower, this is the live fast, die young, work at a Starbucks crowd that thrives on 4-hour energy drinks, double lattes and stock options. And beer I guess.

SXSW is such a phenomenon that there are even Twitter feeds about NOT being there. Witness one tweet from the deluge called #notatsxsw from @vielmetti: if you're not at #sxsw let me summarize: utilikilt, ukulele, startup, kickball cancelled by rain, barbeque. However, I have to say my favorite Twitter post on the subject was from humorist Andy Borowitz @borowitzreport.com: I'm here at North By Northwest. Where the hell is everybody? #nxnw Note: I still feel like an idiot when I say the word "tweet" and thus I'll never truly be one of SXSW's natural leaders.

SXSW has traditionally been about music and film. There are massive festivals of both within the SXSW program and as I sat in the lobby of my hotel I saw celebrities of both worlds milling about. Coolest sightings were ?uestlove (pronounced Questlove) of the band the Roots (bandleader on the Jimmy Fallon show… Fallon was there too), Australian stud-muffin Chris Hemsworth (star of Thor) and badass actor Danny Trejo, although the place was crawling with the people who fill the pages of People and Rolling Stone. Of course, I wasn't there for the cool stuff. No one is asking me to come and play Bohemian Rhapsody on the ukulele or sing with Jay-Z, probably because it would empty out Austin faster than Drano in a kitchen sink, but I got asked to show up and speak nonetheless, courtesy of the kind people at Health 2.0 and the Office of the National Coordinator. Why you ask? Well, SXSW is diversifying beyond music and film. They now have another track called SXSW Interactive that is focused on other fields where technology can make a difference, particularly healthcare and education.

The day before I was to speak at SXSW's Startup Bootcamp session I got a call from a Bloomberg reporter asking me what I thought about this SXSW diversification strategy. To quote the article (which liberally quoted me, which was nice) I offer the following:

Dubbed "Woodstock for geeks," South by Southwest is no longer just about creating buzz for the latest social-networking tools like Twitter and Foursquare Labs Inc. The 19-year-old conference is expecting about 20,000 entrepreneurs, investors and executives searching for the next big thing across the technology landscape, seeking to bring industries such as healthcare and education further into the digital realm.

"There are more and more applications for social and mobile technologies in the healthcare world," said Lisa Suennen, a co-founder at San Francisco-based venture capital firm Psilos Group, who is going to the conference for the first time. "To the extent you can bring it into the hip and exciting opportunity area it is a wonderful thing."

I was also quoted saying this, "I'm not sure if I'm groovy enough to be there. I guess I'll find out." I now know the answer: um, no. I did not come clad in either skinny jeans or an ironically ancient Bob Dylan concert t-shirt, and I will never be seen at a public speaking event wearing a hoodie a la Mark Zuckerberg. Call me square. I can live with that, confidently knowing I will never show up on People Magazine's Worst Dressed List. Of course, not having green hair and visible tattoos probably keeps me out of the coolest parties. Go figure. Credibility is in the eye of the beholder. On the other hand, I had some extremely great times in my short visit at SXSW, and for those of you responsible, you know who you are and thanks!

Anyway, back to the point, which is that the SXSW events in which I participated were part of the Social Health Startup Bootcamp, which was sponsored by Health 2.0 and Boehringer Ingelheim with much coordination by the incredibly upbeat and sharp Shwen Gwee of Edelman. I had two tasks: first was to give an opening, stage-setting presentation about the state of healthcare IT investing; the second was to participate in a fireside chat with recent past Chief Technology Officer of the United States, Aneesh Chopra (fyi, at the conference it was announced that Todd Park will replace Chopra as the new U.S. CTO).

The gist of my presentation was to explain why healthcare IT ("HIT") is suddenly hot as an investment area and the various issues that both advance and detract from this reality. I have written extensively on this topic so won't rehash it all here, but suffice it to say that just two years ago HIT wasn't even measured as its own investment category by those who track venture capital investments—it was just buried in the life sciences categories and dwarfed by biotech, pharma, and medical device money. Since those particular segments have fallen on somewhat harder times, money is flowing fast to HIT and, in fact, venture investment in HIT as measured by number of deals doubled in 2012 as compared to 2011, which had been up 26% as compared to 2010. In contrast, both biotech and medical device investing were down in the period. Only about $600 million went into HIT in 2011, however, a number less than 1/5 of what went into each of the other sectors, but still up 22% over the prior year. By 2012 it was up to $1.2 billin.

There is a concept in psychology called the "operational diagnosis." This is the idea that, despite the fact that you have had a lifetime of misery and that your parents didn't love you enough, it takes one final thing to get you to finally decide to start therapy. That reason—the specific impetus that led you to seek help today—is the "operational diagnosis." It answers the question, "why now?" So while we have long and desperately needed healthcare IT solutions to help correct the unmitigated disaster that is our healthcare system, the reason that HIT is finally getting attention today, the "why now" is, in my humble opinion, the fact that the national economy tanked.

We could all blithely pretend that the ridiculous inflationary costs of our healthcare system weren't at red alert level as long as the economy was growing like crazy, but the minute the economy collapsed and you are Starbucks and you realize you are literally spending more money on employee health care than on coffee, you have probably had enough. Moreover, as employers have eaten over 113% in health insurance premium cost increases in the last 10 years, employees themselves have borne 134% increases over that same period. With annual health insurance premiums rising literally 4-5 times faster than wages and general inflation, consumers are taking it where the sun don't shine and they are beginning to engage in a more significant way in their own healthcare experience. This is, of course, being further driven by numerous other insurance industry dynamics, such as the growing phenomenon of healthcare insurance exchanges, but the result is the same. Providers are also feeling the heat as market forces and government regulation force them to accept reductions in reimbursement and more financial accountability for the care they provide. A plethora of new healthcare-focused regulations and laws are the cherry on top, making greater healthcare system productivity a necessity.

The good news is that in the last 10-15 years there have been such significant advances in technology, including the near ubiquity of the Internet, broadband, Smart Phones, and software as a service ("SAAS") models that there is a kind of harmonic convergence of experiences making it the best time we have ever had to let a thousand HIT-shaped flowers bloom.

The recognition of the importance of HIT to the healthcare system's health was what led to the formation of the Office of the National Coordinator for HIT and, in part, what led to Aneesh Chopra's role as the first U.S. Chief Technology Officer, a role founded in 2009. Chopra had broad IT experience, but he had very specific healthcare experience having worked at the hospital-focused organization The Advisory Board.

If you have never met Aneesh Chopra, it helps to know that he has more energy than Justin Bieber and loves to talk HIT policy and process in a way that the Biebs has been heard to talk his cool Fisker sports car. Chopra has an infectious enthusiasm that makes people actually want to listen to him talk about the Open Government Initiative and data security and other things that typically prove more effective than Ambien in curing the average sleep disorder. There were real live rock stars crawling all over SXSW but to the HIT crowd, this guy is Adam Levine—or maybe I should say Blake Shelton, in that we were in Texas.

In our fireside chat at SXSW, Aneesh and I covered a wide range of topics including initiatives to bring data transparency to government, how IT can change the healthcare business and how HIT is, as he put it, "a job grower, not a job killer." One of the things he pointed out that was quite interesting (if not surprising) is that our HIT industry has historically been great at innovating around things that further increase volume to the healthcare system, such as billing and scheduling software. Of course, this just leads to more cost, not more efficacy, which is where innovation needs to be focused. On the other hand the system has been historically lousy at innovation that improves outcome and reduces costs. That's where today's opportunities lie.

We also talked about the interesting dichotomy of patient privacy, which is a very squirrely concept in the age of social networking. On the one hand, federal law (HIPAA) requires very strict handling of patient data and each state further legislates on this issue. On the other hand, you see all kinds of patients out there putting their own healthcare data into the public domain, whether they are tweeting their weight (what the hell? I don't even tell myself my weight), Facebooking about their pharmaceutical side-effects or communicating with friends about their cancer experience on Caring Bridge. Privacy is clearly a complex issue which means different things to different people at different times for different reasons, but is "the most important thing we have to get right," according to Chopra. "We have to earn people's trust." And then he was mobbed in the hall like he had just headlined with Kanye West at Madison Square Garden.

It is an interesting time in healthcare IT, and I think that the incredible gulf between HIMSS and SXSW is a perfect metaphor for the challenge. We have to figure out a way to engage legions of young innovators who really understand next generation technology in channeling their energy into healthcare solutions. The old school enterprises who have the biggest presence at HIMSS are unlikely to be the leaders of the future if they don't come up the social networking ubergeek learning curve. On the other hand, too many of the new kids on the block can program a sophisticated piece of software in their sleep while eating a pizza with the other hand, yet don't really understand the intricacies of how money moves through the healthcare system and where all the privacy, security, and financial incentive bodies are buried.

What we really need is some Spock-style mind-melding, which should be appealing to the SXSW crowd, many of whom look like they just left a Star Trek convention. In a perfect world, the ideal HIT gathering would be somewhere psychologically between HIMSS and SXSW: fewer gray suits, less purple hair, more next generation technology, more business models that work. If we could do a little cross breeding between species here, we just might make it work. Or we could accidentally end up with the Monster from Young Frankenstein. Wait a minute, my God it's brilliant! He might actually be perfect! The Monster had both a gray suit AND a green head. If he knows how to code, we have a winner. Oh, sweet mystery of life at last I've found you! – LS

America's Healthy Infatuation With Entrepreneurs

At large, established companies, doing old things more efficiently becomes more important than doing new things. That's the problem.

America has fallen hard for entrepreneurs.

The aesthetic appeal is easy to understand. Compare the Fortune 500 CEOs interviewed on the HBR IdeaCast talking about Campbell's Soup or Coca-Cola (podcast here) with the entrepreneurs at the Stanford Entrepreneurial Thought Leader Seminar Series discussing Pandora and Instagram (podcast here). The big company CEOs sound just like you'd expect. They are competent, factual, and in control. But while most of them presumably have strong interpersonal skills and a high EQ, they come across as dry, unemotional, and focused on the "core business."

In contrast, the entrepreneurs presenting at Stanford wear their hearts on their sleeves. They are vividly passionate. They exude emotion. They are selling themselves, with a kind of animated desperation. They tell students to "do what you love." It's an appealing message, and you can see why it catches on.

These two personalities generally reside at opposite ends of the business spectrum, presumably reflecting two very different business needs. It's essential to be brash and irrationally exuberant to start a business. But to sustain a large multinational corporation, you've got to be calculating and rational. It's also a well-described phenomenon that as start-ups evolve into progressively larger companies, their character changes, and their needs evolve, or "mature." Mature organizations are supposed to act predictably, responsibly, unemotionally. The qualities embraced (or at least tolerated) at the start-up level can become liabilities. Many start-up CEOs hand over the reins at this stage, or at least share them (as Google did for years when Brin and Page hired Eric Schmidt), explicitly acknowledging the need for an "adult in the room."

While many large organizations might similarly benefit from having a kid in the room— someone who is energetic, passionate, emotional, excitable—it's hard to envision a corporate phenotype that would be more doomed: the environment just doesn't support it. Sure, companies trot out bromides about "cultivating entrepreneurship," while HR departments sponsor group training sessions on innovative thinking. But the reality is that the culture of most big companies is geared to performing established activities in increasingly efficient ways. Simply stated: doing the old things better takes precedence over doing new things well enough. Most employees (and certainly the ones who last) figure out extremely quickly how you're supposed to act at work (Sir Joseph wasn't far off). You could say most large organizations have elected to trade the passion of young love for the predictability of adult relationships.

And perhaps this is why we look so wistfully at entrepreneurs. They seem to exude the raw passion that experience has taught us to modulate, the vivid emotion that we've learned to suppress, the intense energy that we learn must be channeled, the unreasonable audacity that has been replaced by sensible objectives. We cheer for them because they represent our youthful hopes, our idealism, our ambitions, and our dreams. And when these entrepreneurs defy the extraordinary odds, and succeed, we rejoice, for at the moment we can sense, if only fleetingly, the exceptional untapped potential within each of us. We rejoice, and wonder: what if?

It would be easy to dismiss our infatuation with entrepreneurs as misty-eyed revisionism, the way we might selectively recall and invoke treasured childhood memories while forgetting the many painful challenges of youth and adolescence. The day-to-day reality of getting a new company off the ground is generally far less glorious than the inspirational experiences trotted out by the small minority of ultra-successful entrepreneurs who are routinely invited to share their stories. There's a significant selection bias here, to say nothing of the urge to write oneself into a heroic cultural narrative.

But I'd argue that if we had to find a group of people to admire and admittedly idealize—and you know we're going to—we could do a lot worse than taking our inspiration from impassioned, dedicated individuals seeking against all odds "to make a dent in the world."
– DS

What The Healthcare Industry Can Learn From Technology Startups— And Vice Versa

In the development of drugs, it's too difficult to change things on the fly, and to rapidly pivot in response to an appreciation of customer need

A couple of years ago, I heard a young design entrepreneur named Aza Raskin talk about his idea for a consumer health company, MassiveHealth, built around the concept of providing rapid feedback. For example, if you had a skin dye that faded a certain amount each time you took a dose of your antibiotic, you would be more likely to complete the full course.

Skip ahead not very far. MassiveHealth launched its first, free app (dubbed an experiment), called the Eatery. The idea was that you take a picture of your meal and rate its healthiness, which is then shared with other users. You would benefit, as I understood it, by thinking more about your food and by getting input on your food from other users. What the company itself got was not immediately clear. They shared some pretty maps of San Francisco and New York City showing where people are eating more vs. less healthy foods, and they drey some fairly general conclusions about how the supposed healthiness of our food changes during the day (good at breakfast, bad during the day, partial recovery at dinner).

At least as important, I'd imagine, they engaged group of users who seemed (at least at this early stage) interested in interacting with the platform, and thus contributing to the development of the emerging data set; after their first week, more than one million food ratings were reportedly received.

As I followed the evolution of MassiveHealth (subsequently enfolded into Jawbone), I was struck by some of the profound differences between a tech start-up (even one ostensibly in the healthcare space) and a biopharma start-up. In the standard biopharma model, you spend years developing a product, without having any real idea of (a) whether it will work, (b) whether it will be safe and well-tolerated, and (c) whether by the time you've demonstrated (a) and (b), anyone will care, or pay you for your efforts. When you develop a new drug, most of the relevant properties of the product are pretty much baked in at a fairly early stage; you can tweak the formulation a little bit (to make it longer-lasting, say), but otherwise, you have what you have, and the challenge is figuring out just what this something is, and determining who might benefit most from it. Many have compared the process to an unforgiving lottery: Make a mistake at any point (choose the wrong indication, the wrong study design, or the wrong study sites) and you're out of the game; execute flawlessly and you buy yourself only a chance to see whether or not your number is drawn.

Unfortunately, getting to the drawing takes a lot of time and money: most of the cost of drug development (which generally exceeds $100 million for an individual program—and this figure doesn't include the cost of all the failures) isn't from coming up with the particular molecule, but rather in putting it through the increasingly expensive series of clinical studies required to see if it's actually going to work. Of course, once you've successfully run this gauntlet, not only do you have something that's demonstrably effective (at least in the setting of clinical trials—see here), but there's also a pretty high barrier for potential competitors, at least until your patents expire.

In contrast, MassiveHealth managed to get a product in customer hands after a few months of work. True, they probably had not yet made any money, and (not insignificantly) it's entirely unclear whether they had, or would ever impact anyone's health, massively or otherwise. Nevertheless, they had an extraordinarily powerful opportunity, at a very early stage, and after spending (I suspect) very little money, to learn, gather feedback, iterate, and explore: In an organismic sense, they could carefully assess their environment and respond adaptively—evolve their product based on demonstrated customer needs. And they could do this very rapidly so that even if just one aspect of their platform was interesting, they could rapidly pivot and exploit it (similar to the way Twitter developed).

The ability to make cost-effective exploratory efforts is a powerful enabler of innovation, as Peter Sims has highlighted in *Little Bets* (my *Wall Street Journal* review here, implications for pharma discussed here and here), and the need for successful start-ups to rapidly collect data and adjust course is more the rule than the exception, as John Mullins and Randy Komisar thoughtfully discuss in *Getting to Plan B* (listen to this interesting podcast of Komisar at Stanford).

Unfortunately, drug development is far less conducive to this sort of exploration; as I've discussed elsewhere, the cycle times tend to be far too long, and the costs are way too high. As a result, it's a lot more difficult to change things on the fly, and to rapidly pivot in response to a new appreciation of customer need.

Not surprisingly, there's been a lot of interest in ways to streamline the drug development process. One especially attractive way is to identify new uses for existing drugs (as these have already been carefully vetted), an approach I've previously argued might be especially amenable to a crowdsourcing model. More detailed patient segmentation—more comprehensive phenotyping—could also be helpful, as many clinical studies could be smaller and in many cases shorter if you could more precisely target your intervention to the patients more likely to benefit, and thus boost your effect size. The development of new, highly predictive models, including in silico, preclinical (i.e. animal), and especially experimental measurements in healthy human volunteers, would be especially valuable, and would allow for more rapid iteration and optimization.

The challenge for consumer health companies, on the other hand, is somewhat different: the question for them is whether will they actually improve health, in a robust, measurable fashion, offering the disruptive innovation their founders usually promise, or will they essentially be the Vitamin Shoppes and Whole Foods Whole Body departments for tech-oriented Millennials, offering what I would characterize as generally benign placebos at extremely profitable margins.

My guess is that to the extent consumer health tech companies can make money delivering a vague notion of wellness, they will. For example, I can imagine startups like MassiveHealth generating significant revenue by selling geographically-targeted advertisements from restaurants promoting healthy alternatives—a business model that wouldn't require them to mess around with prickly medical product regulatory requirements.

I'm most excited, however, by the opportunity to bring consumer health products to bear in a serious way, and ask whether they can deliver measurable health care value, which I'd provisionally define as improving health while removing costs from the system within a five-year period—a standard I cribbed from Stanford health care guru Arnold Milstein, and thus I dub the "Milstein Metric." (Milstein directs Stanford's innovative "Clinical Excellence Research Center," focused on developing better and cheaper health delivery models—see here.)

What I like about the Milstein Metric (obviously not the only way to evaluate a new medical innovation) is that it represents a surprisingly high bar, and has a way of immediately focusing our thinking on impactful healthcare innovations. Prioritizing innovations that remove costs from our system makes sense given the urgent national need to rein in healthcare costs, a bipartisan ambition. The time period selected (five years) is admittedly somewhat arbitrary, and reflects not only the fact that patients switch payers frequently (so an investment not recouped before patients switch out is difficult to justify on financial terms), but forecasting is an inherently fragile business, and projecting years into the future is tenuous to the point of rarely being credible. An intervention that maybe kinda sorta pays off in 50 years is usually too speculative to be useful.

So the question—highlighted in this *Washington Post* article—is: can you make money by saving money? Phrased differently: There are literally hundreds of new devices, apps, and companies jumping into the consumer health space (see here and here); some will succeed simply because they delight users, but will any deliver real health benefits, measured by the Milstein Metric?

In general, I suspect the answer is no; Most consumer health companies are unlikely to deliver measurable health benefits. Thousands of apps will be downloaded, perhaps used for a week, and then abandoned in favor of the latest snazzy offering.

My suspicion is that it might take an entirely different set of people, and a very different mindset to start thinking seriously about how to deploy some of these new technologies in a fashion that actually impacts health. These technologies represent the raw tools, and it will require additional insight and effort to rigorously apply these tools to the practice of medicine and the delivery of health, and use them to extract measurable value.

That's OK. I'm grateful for these tools. As I've advocated frequently (see here and here), improved patient measurement is the single most important mechanism we have to improve health, both in the short term (essentially by providing physicians and patients with more immediate feedback and enabling just the sort of iterative learning described earlier) and in the long term (by providing an extensively annotated view of human physiology, yielding fundamental new insights and enabling the development of powerful new therapeutics).

My guess is that the integration of consumer health and patient health will be driven by innovators in both the public and private sectors. Academic medical centers—a precious source of both inquisitive physician and involved patients—can play a critical role in orchestrating and driving this process. (Disclosure: I am co-founder of one such non-profit institute, the Center for Assessment Technology and Continuous Health.) I also imagine some of the most important advances will continue to come from the private sector, extending from the start-ups I see all around me in the Bay Area, advancing promising technologies and data-analysis platforms, to the large medical products companies seeking to sharpen their focus and improve their offerings, to the payors always on the hunt for the elusive "cut costs but improve care" program, to regulators, who to their credit were among the first to recognize the need for improved patient-associated measurements (as noted here and here).

I am inspired by this integrative vision of the future, motivated by our urgent unmet healthcare needs, stimulated by the energy and passion of the entrepreneurs and inquisitive physicians and scientists I meet, and driven by the patients whose endurance has been sorely tested. It's time to deliver consumer health—consumer health we can believe in. – DS

Hey East Coast Entrepreneurs: We Fail Better Than You. XO—Your Friends In The Valley

Apparently, the secret to Silicon Valley's success isn't just the good weather and smart people—turns out, the secret to our region's entrepreneurial preeminence just may be the way we embrace failure.

According to KPCB life-science (devices) partner Dana Mead—who notes he hails from the northeast—there's a world of difference between Palo Alto and Cambridge (MA).

In Cambridge, he contends in an informative lecture/podcast at the Stanford Technology Ventures Program, if you tell people your last three businesses failed, "they'll look at you sideways" and shake their heads, presumably with a mixture of sadness and pity. In Palo Alto, by contrast, the reaction will be "that's awesome! I'm sure your next company will be a world-beater."

OK—three points:

(1) Cue obvious throw away comments about what a truly "awesome" time the last five years have been for life-science VC (Bruce Booth's anticipated objections are noted for the record).

(2) Agree failure is important—after all, wasn't it Mark Zuckerberg who originally said "success is going from failure to failure with undiminished enthusiasm?"—oh, wait, that was Churchill. Perhaps the basic concept here didn't originate in the Valley—although I suppose it's possible we've done the best job of appropriating it.

(3) Is there a chance Mead's actually right here? This deserves some comment:

On the one hand, I think there's a mystique in the Bay Area that goes way beyond anything reasonable, and leads to all sorts of outlandish errors of attribution.

At the same time, I've certainly seen in large companies how fear of failure absolutely inhibits innovation—and in academia, how fear of failure has led many promising academic physicians to pursue safe but uninspired research questions, rather than questions that were riskier but more important. As I've discussed elsewhere (actually, my favorite piece), it's likely (and, to me, rather sad and disappointing) that many of the most successful companies and most successful people (including academics) got there through careful, deliberate, incremental advances rather than via breakthrough innovation.

Certainly, it makes sense that entrepreneurs would benefit from a culture that accepts failure as part of growth. My question is whether Cambridge is as different from Palo Alto as Mead suggests?

As a relatively recent West Coast arrival who spent more than 20 years in Cambridge and vicinity, and who remains an ardent Red Sox fan—I suspect Mead's impression is off, and beyond that, I certainly hope it's not what the Sand Hill crowd is counting on to beat back the east coast competition.

As a Boston resident in the fall of 2004, I had the chance to bear joyful, immersive, witness to what can happen when a perennial favorite counts on historical trends and a sense of manifest density. The results speak for themselves. -DS

Reid Hoffman Connects Four Themes For Would-be Innovators (And Tomorrow's Healthcare Companies)

Reid Hoffman's captivating talk at Stanford (podcast and video available here) touched on several themes that collectively seem to comprise the Silicon Valley innovator ethos; most are relevant to healthcare and biopharma, and I agree with all his assertions except one.

(Hoffman, for those tuning in late, is a Silicon Valley superstar: he was a major part of PayPal, a co-founder of LinkedIn, and currently a partner at Greylock.)

Theme 1: Breakout success requires risk. This is, of course, the defining credo of entrepreneurs, and initially may seem a bit obvious. However, I'd argue that the most radical part of this statement is not the notion of taking risk, but rather the assumption that one aspires to achieve breakout success.

Many people go to the office each day, aspire to do their jobs well and earn a good living, and generally hope to get a measure of satisfaction from their work and their colleagues. But the yearning for breakout success—whether this reflects colossal ambition, haughty arrogance, deep insecurity, or a desperate need for external validation—seems a trait that isn't shared by everyone. Arguably, a worthy goal of entrepreneurship programs is to awaken this drive in more people. (For more about the entrepreneur meme, see here.)

Theme 2: Adaptation, resilience, iteration. I've grouped these three essential traits together because they seem to be fundamentally related, and connect to the idea of a flexible mindset.

Entrepreneurs commit to a central paradox. In order to get a new enterprise off the ground, you need a remarkable amount of chutzpah, a conviction that you are embarking on something worthy and important and likely to be successful; at the same time, you need to somehow also recognize that almost certainly, your initial ideas will be off, and will need continuous refinement. You may also fail entirely.

Somehow, you need the ability to learn from all of your endeavors, and gain wisdom without sacrificing ambition and courage—an approach to experience that seems more the rule in the valley than the exception.

Hoffman also discussed the importance of optimizing ideas through a rapid succession of iterations—though I found it amusing that, as a consumer internet guy accustomed to instant feedback, he found a waiting period of several months uncomfortably long. Presumably, he would find the timelines in pharma unbearable (an extended feedback loop that I've previously argued is a true barrier to innovation in the industry).

Theme 3: Manage your education, training, and career development with an entrepreneurial mindset. Hoffman argued persuasively that life isn't a linear track, and encouraged audience members to more aggressively manage their careers; for instance, he believes employees should view their current job as a "tour of duty" rather than a lifetime commitment, and should unapologetically consider a range of options after a substantive piece of work is accomplished.

He also expressed profound enthusiasm for the American education system, and in particular called out its relative lack of rigidity; there are clearly many important life qualities that are not reflected by a given standardized test nor reducible to a single number, a lesson most entrepreneurs viscerally appreciate (even if some testing agencies do not). (Further discussion of our obsession with dubious metrics available here.)

Hoffman, like several previous STVP speakers, also highlighted the importance of recognizing what you don't do well: for instance, Warren Packard's experience at Baxter working alongside noted product innovator Dean Kamen helped him realize that he didn't have Kamen's skills, and encouraged him to shift his focus to an area where he felt he could be world-class. Hoffman describes a remarkably similar experience with coding. Fortunately for them, both Hoffman and Packard were not only able to recognize their own limitations but were also able to find other areas of strength that they could develop and effectively leverage.

Theme 4: If it's not 10x, don't bother. This message—seek profound change not incremental improvement—is yet another common expression among successful entrepreneurs, and it's a sentiment with which I resonate deeply, yet I worry it may be somewhat misleading.

What I love about this aspiration is the ambition, the goal of wanting to change the world, and make a dent in the universe. I also agree that you can spend as much energy doing trivial or incremental tasks as doing work that's truly revolutionary and impactful.

My disagreement is with how we get there. I'm not sure it's always possible to sort the world into 1x and 10x opportunities, and there's an extensive literature on the incremental nature of profound innovations (a topic I've addressed here and here).

Most new ideas—even the ones Silicon Valley tends to fetishize endlessly—didn't emerge either fully-formed or obviously brilliant; eBay is one of the few exceptions that come to mind. In many more cases, a great idea evolved progressively, often through a succession of more modest innovations or improvements, so that while the final product may be overtly better, its evolution was more gradual than punctuated.

Consequently, though I especially resonated with Hoffman's critique of incremental innovation, and his distaste for slight improvements, I also suspect these iterations ultimately may be more valuable than his talk might suggest. Perhaps, progress requires both the ability to opportunistically deliver incremental improvements as well as the capacity to retain the big picture view, and never losing sight of the grander ambition.

Lessons for healthcare companies?

Can healthcare companies learn from Hoffman's ideas? You have to hope so. Clearly, it is an industry in need of breakout ideas, where adaptation to a rapidly-changing environment is essential, and where profoundly improved products could fundamentally reshape the human condition.

As for the human capital—I suspect it would have no trouble identifying and migrating to the most exciting and innovative companies in the healthcare space, the way aspiring medical scientists were drawn to Genentech 20 years ago, or the way top developers descended upon Google five years ago, and flocked to Facebook plus a range of small start-ups more recently.

Who will be the innovative healthcare companies of tomorrow? Follow the talent. – DS

The Real Appeal Of Entrepreneurs, From Ira Glass To Zuck: Authorship Of Life

Even as we are beset by coverage providing up-to-the-second updates of Mark Zuckerberg's estimated net worth, I suspect that our fascination with entrepreneurship, and our celebration of entrepreneurial achievement, has less to do with money, or even business itself, and more to do with the joy we feel in seeing someone successfully author their own life, rather than simply being carried along by it.

The enterprise is the creative accomplishment, the money (as noted in this NYT article and elsewhere) is simply a way of validating the achievement, and keeping score.

Two inspirational examples of auteurs immediately come to mind, individuals who perhaps might be thought of as leading an entrepreneurial life not focused on business: Woody Allen and Ira Glass.

Allen has not only created some of the most memorable moments in cinema, but has managed to write and direct a movie every year or so for the last forty years, films that encompass a remarkable range of styles and subjects. While he typically affects a nebbish on screen, his real life persona, as evident from a range of recent interviews (e.g. here and here), is far more competent and calculating than Fielding Mellish , Virgil Starkwell, or Alvy Singer might suggest—if anything, he evokes the famous Ronald Reagan Mastermind sketch from Saturday Night Live.

Allen's movies, while generally not blockbusters, do well enough to allow him to continue to do exactly what he loves to do, the way he loves to do it—and leave an indelible imprint on the world in the process.

I've discovered Ira Glass only recently, through podcasts of his weekly radio show, This American Life, an hour-long treatment of a specific theme, in three acts, and with the assistance of talented contributors such as David Sedaris, Dan Savage, and Sarah Vowell. What's most striking to me about This American Life, however, is not just how extraordinarily well done it is, but how deliberate it must be. It definitely isn't the sort of program that just comes to pass, but rather clearly reflects an impassioned and deliberate vision, executed week after week with inspiration and grace. (It can occasionally veer towards the precious, as The Onion captures perfectly here).

What an incredible program to have thought of and created—an assessment presumably shared by the thousands of listeners who've regularly made it the most downloaded audio podcast on iTunes

(An interesting side note: you could probably add another popular radio personality, Howard Stern, to the auteur list; certainly, Glass has frequently expressed his deep admiration for Stern, telling Time Magazine Stern's program represents "The Happiest Show in Broadcasting.")

It's probably important to recognize that even in film and radio, a significant measure of the success accorded to standouts such as Allen and Glass reflects not just the breadth of their vision, but their ability to attend to the practical details—delivering a product on time and on budget, and attracting an audience large enough to justify continued investment.

Clearly, the expressive visions of Allen and Glass stand out even in the arts—I doubt most productions are informed by such a deep-seated personal passion (but perhaps there's a subtlety in The Wonder Pets I've managed to overlook).

In business—as David Brooks has highlighted, and as I have lamented—the opportunity for such meaningful personal expression, unfortunately, is rarer still, and all the more wonderful when we encounter—or even better—create it. – DS

Is There A Purity Test For Innovators?

Silicon Valley is based on idea of cultivating a culture of entrepreneurship—we now raise kids to think they should go out and change the world (perhaps even before, or instead of, going to college). Work—especially entrepreneurship—is viewed as an opportunity to author your own life, and large companies (and middle managers) are eager to grab hold of this concept, and this meme.

At the same time, it turns out that many people (I call them "jobbers") go to work—by choice, it seems—not to change the world, but to put in a good day's effort, to get paid fairly, and to go home. This quaint mindset is likely shared by most CEOs, and is probably responsible for the majority of industrial accomplishment.

The convenient assumption, of course, is that as you grow up, you go down one of two paths—become an innovator, and come up with brilliant new disruptive ideas, or become a jobber, and dutifully execute.

The small problem with this tidy model: while some of our most remarkable entrepreneurs and business innovators grew up knowing they wanted to pursue original ideas ("Formative From Birth"—FFBs), an awful lot of innovation in the world, including some of the most creative and disruptive ideas, has been developed by individuals ("Beyond Traditional—BTs) who started off as jobbers, then at some point along the way found themselves pursuing, with passion, a grander ambition. On the other hand, many who start on the FFB track ultimately wind up creating little value (at least as measured by payment for services rendered or goods sold).

Arguably, the BT folks, the ones who at some point recognize an intrinsic passion and aptitude for entrepreneurship, may be more likely to be successful because they actually understand how grown-up companies really work, and may be more grounded by their life experiences.

I worry a lot about the fate of BTs, because it seems that popular culture is increasingly consolidating around a disappointingly rigid idea—really, a coarse caricature—of what "real" innovation, and "real" innovators, look like—i.e. FFBs, hunched over an iPad at Philz, not BTs, staring at a PC in the midst of some corporate cubicle farm or a small family business. FFBs are glamorized as "authentic," while BTs risk being regarded as *poseurs*.

The increasingly purist, exclusionary view of innovation inevitably will underestimate— significantly—the broader innovative potential in our nation, in our people, and in our companies, that might be awakened and cultivated.

Admittedly, innovation may be harder to realize in some environments than in others— few places are as hospitable to new ideas, and creative thinkers, as the sun-drenched streets of Palo Alto—but that just makes it all the more important to look.

Ultimately, if there is, in effect, a purity test for innovators, we'll be leaving a lot of value on the table—just the sort of missed opportunity enterprising minds of all stripes—FFBs and BTs alike—strive so intensively to avoid. – DS

Medicine And Silicon Valley: Two Cultures With More In Common Than You Think

As a recent arrival to Silicon Valley and its unique culture, I've had the opportunity to consider how it contrasts with the culture of medicine, with which I'm deeply familiar.

I've been especially struck by the excessively reductive view many Silicon Valley engineers seem to have of medicine, a practice many see as fundamentally an exercise in algorithm optimization currently performed rather badly by physicians who are locked in an antiquated mindset, and who are unwilling to relinquish their traditional elevated status, even though it's no longer warranted or relevant.

For their part, physicians view many Silicon Valley engineers as frivolous, Tolkien-quoting, unrepentant Trekkies who don't appreciate the gravitas of illness, who underestimate the human element of medicine, and who promote consumer-focused health applications because they're too ignorant and fearful to meaningfully engage a system that may be imperfect, but which still manages to do far more good than often appreciated—and arguably a lot more good than Farmville, Angry Birds, or the latest photo-sharing app.

Other than that, Mrs. Lincoln, how was the play?

While it's important to acknowledge and understand the legitimate differences in perspective that exist, I'd argue it's at least as important to recognize the remarkable degree of alignment between Silicon Valley culture and medicine as I've experienced it. Consider these five domains:

Drive: Entrepreneurs, of course, are driven by their desire to have an impact, and famously, "make a dent in the universe." Most entrepreneurs who participate in the Stanford Entrepreneurial Thought Leader (ETL) seminar series frame their accomplishments in this context. A passionate commitment to making a difference was also a defining element of most of the med school applicants I interviewed over the years when I was in Boston, and constitutes an enduring character trait of the physician role models I admire most (including in particular, full disclosure, both my parents). While it may remain a bit of a stretch to compare the accomplishments of Paul Farmer and Judah Folkman, two more heroes of mine, with those of the founders of Dropbox and Instagram, their underlying passion to leave the world different than they found it seems an important common quality.

Autonomy: Perhaps the most appealing and resonant aspect of entrepreneurship is the opportunity to author your own life—the autonomy to select what you do, and to figure out how best to do it, within certain constraints. Traditionally, the opportunity for a similar degree of autonomy attracted many to clinical medicine; while such autonomy has been progressively constrained in most clinical practices, physicians still enjoy considerable flexibility—much to the consternation of many critics, including technologists, who cite this as the source of many of our health care woes. The resistance of most physicians to even the most basic attempts at standardization highlights the value they place on doing medicine their own way.

Empathy: Many of the most successful technology entrepreneurs, from Bezos to Jobs to Hsieh—excelled at understanding what the customer wanted(whether or not the customer was even aware). A feel for the voice of customer is vital for the success of most Silicon Valley startups—and equally important for the success of most doctors, with deep roots in medicine's best traditions. In the words of Sir William Osler, "The good physician treats the disease; the great physician treats the patient who has the disease."

All-in: The hours entrepreneurs put into the business and their commitment to its success are the stuff of Silicon Valley legend—yet follow around a medical resident one (long) day, or a trauma surgeon, or a devoted primary care physician whose pager beeps constantly, and I suspect you'll be struck by both the schedule and the devotion. Most physicians that I know (and I acknowledge my sampling, deeply rooted in academic medicine in general and MGH in particular, may not be representative) are absolutely "all-in," and their lives revolve are the calling they have chosen.

Disruption: To the extent technologists in Silicon Valley have thought about medicine, they are attracted by the idea that the system is broken, and is "ripe for disruption"— easily the most common phrase I hear. Funny thing is, most doctors I know agree. Almost everyone I know in medicine believes that the way care is delivered, and monitored, could and should be so much better, more complete, and more continuous, with much better feedback mechanisms in place, and considerably more patient focus and patient involvement—and much less duplicative paperwork.

I wouldn't want to gloss over the very significant differences that remain—most notably, physicians are looking for innovations that help them solve problems, while many technologists believe doctors themselves are the problem.

Even so, I find myself aligning with the view I've heard most eloquently and relentlessly articulated by Geoff Clapp: constructive engagement is good, already happening, and the best way to make a difference.

I agree. I've long believed that medical schools should provide greater exposure to entrepreneurship and to entrepreneurs—see this 2005 op-ed (co-written with my MGH colleague Denny Ausiello) entitled, "Entrepreneurs: Missing Link in the Training of Medical Scientists." As medical trainees increasingly fret about the world they're preparing to enter, it's difficult to think of seminars more relevant or inspiring than the Stanford ETL series, or a more uplifting and humane world view than that offered by tech VC Brad Feld's blog and associated publications (then again, what do you expect? His father is an endocrinologist).

Yes, the challenges we face are daunting—but I believe in the power and the passion of physicians and tech entrepreneurs, and the extraordinary impact they can have working to solve problems—important problems—together. – DS

How Dave McClure Captures Perfectly The Agony And The Ecstasy Of Silicon Valley

A must-read blog post about entrepreneurship is "Late Bloomer, Not a Loser" by Silicon Valley tech entrepreneur-turned-VC Dave McClure (who I don't know and have never met). It's short and amazingly raw, a frank assessment of the gap he sees between what he's already accomplished and where he hopes (and had hoped) to be.

"So here I am," he writes, "still standing in the arena, in hand-to-hand combat with demons mostly of my own making, aiming to make a small dent in the universe. Nowhere near a great success story, yet fighting the good fight and perhaps helping others to achieve greatness as I attempt a bit of my own. I'll be 46 in a month, well past the age when most folks have already shown what they're made of. But I'm still grasping for that brass ring."

McClure's post, which seems to have taken on a life of its own, cuts to the quick, and speaks directly and plaintively to the grandest hopes and most agonizing fears experienced by so many ambitious, highly-trained men and women in their (our) 30s, 40s, and 50s, strivers all too aware they've not quite lived up to their own expectations (and often that of others), but who at the same time are so close that it feels unbearably painful. They could so easily see themselves as the next Andreessen, Thiel, Feld, or Wilson (all of whom McClure cites), but realize this may never happen—and what to do then? (Answer: continue trying.)

As McClure is the first to acknowledge, these are of course absurdly privileged problems to have, and he appropriately recognizes how fortunate he is. Based on the outpouring of affection for his comments, it seems he's not the only one wrestling with these demons.

The other striking thing about McClure's post is that its very rawness captures what I love most about the Silicon Valley entrepreneur environment (not that it's specific to either Silicon Valley or entrepreneurs).

I've actually been thinking recently about what makes the environment out here so unique and so compelling. I've decided it's this: the belief in the ability of an impassioned individual driven by the power of an idea to make a difference in the world.

Few other businesses are like this; most corporate cultures I've seen (HR platitudes aside) seek to domesticate passion and dampen individuality—or at least, intentionally or not, this is what happens. The most successful people I know at large companies have a phenotype conspicuously different from the entrepreneurs Silicon Valley elevates. Traditional corporate culture tends to place less emphasis on raw intensity and vision, and to teach instead the art of discreet manipulation and the tireless gamesmanship of process.

But Silicon Valley celebrates the struggling visionary—and is one of the few places where a heartfelt *cri de coeur* like McClure's could be both so courageously voiced and so empathetically welcomed. Even—particularly—those who have truly "made it" appreciate how unbelievably fortunate they are, and how uncertain about their continued success they remain. – DS

Folly To Forecast Startup Performance?

Paul Graham, co-founder of noted Silicon Valley accelerator Y-Combinator (YC), has written an exceptional post, "Black Swan Farming," observing how crazy difficult it is to predict success in the startup space, and noting that just two companies—Airbnb and Dropbox—account for about 75% of the total value created by all YC-associated companies.

Subsequently, Dave McClure (the white-hot seed-stage Silicon Valley investor, familiar to readers of this column—see this discussion of his small bets style in connection with digital health) responded in a post titled (what else?) "Screw the Black Swans" that his investment model (at 500 Startups) is slightly different.

While most VCs are looking for the big score, McClure said, he's deliberately seeking singles and doubles, which he basically expects will result in a similar expected value for his portfolio but reduce the chances of getting shut-out. He anticipates and is hoping for a greater number of successes (albeit more modest ones) than achieved by other VCs.

This will be a familiar dialog not only to investors but also to those in biopharma (who perhaps should be thought of as investors as well), as they continuously need to decide whether to go for a risky potential blockbuster or more of a sure-thing that ostensibly may be associated with a smaller market.

I've been fascinated with this exact question for a while (see here and here), and I've always looked at the problem a bit differently than McClure—which, if I'm right, may actually be good news for him.

While robust data are difficult to come by, so much of what I've seen in the two exception-dominated spaces with which I'm most familiar—startups and drug development—suggest that Paul Graham (and Nassim Taleb—see this WSJ piece arguing most successful investors are lucky not good, nicely summarized here by Business Insider) are right: success, and particularly the magnitude of success, is virtually impossible to predict.

The folly of forecasting, if taken seriously, is a mind-blowing concept that is at once viscerally uncomfortable and operationally nearly impractical; as a result, most investors and businesses effectively ignore it, and basically (as I've discussed in perhaps my favorite piece) "assume a can opener."

Now add to the mix the well-described tendency of startups to pivot like mad, and you have a situation where I suspect it's not at all clear whether you have a potential single or homerun on your hands, even if McClure (who usually acknowledges the limitations of forecasting) believes he can accurately predict this. Yet (as McClure certainly recognizes), many incredibly successful companies in the valley started off focused on a very narrow problem, then subsequently realized their solution or approach could be applied or redirected to a larger opportunity.

Sure, I appreciate that the idea of trying to solve huge problem seems more likely to be massively successful than if you're trying to solve a trivial problem, and I also believe that while you can't predict the magnitude of success, you can certainly increase the probability of failure—wrong team, wrong problem, even wrong advice from investors. And let's be honest—there are a large number of entrepreneurial efforts that are overtly, painfully trivial; it's just that I don't see McClure going after them.

Having highlighted the problems with predictions, let me go ahead and make a counter-intuitive one: in 10 years, the best performers in McClure's portfolio could very well create more value (to use Graham's standard—and note this value may or may not be realized by the seed-stage investor) than the top performers at YC. – DS

Silicon Valley: Work-Life Balance Is For Losers, Not Closers

The latest shot in the work-life balance debate was fired by Mukund Mohan, a Bangalore-based serial entrepreneur with roots in Silicon Valley, and author of the "Be a Force of Good" blog.

Mohan's entry, "My discipline will beat your intellect," argues that the key to start-up success is to recognize that it's necessary both to "work smart" and to "work hard"—really, really hard.

He writes,

"Some 'older' entrepreneurs (usually over 35 years of age) will share their ability to 'strike a balance' between work and life. Practically speaking (I hate to break this to them) that does not exist in a startup. If you have that balance, you are not serious enough about your startup.

"I understand they have families and kids, but I have come to the realization that both smart work and hard work are necessary (but not sufficient) to run a successful startup."

I took a similar message from a recent David Brooks column discussing a Bloomberg profile by Ashlee Vance of noted Silicon Valley entrepreneur Elon Musk. Vance reports that Iron Man director Jon Favreau "has called Musk the basis for his version of comic book hero Tony Stark, the playboy inventor who builds a flying weaponized suit."

While the Brooks piece focuses mostly on Musk's many professional accomplishments, and doesn't discuss his five sons (twins plus triplets), Brooks also notes,

"Many employees love him, but there has been at least one blog set up to catalog his mistreatment of those he deems mediocre. He's run through two marriages already, and his first ex-wife wrote a brutal but not necessarily persuasive takedown of him in Marie Claire. He's taken a grand total of one vacation in four years, and his romantic life has faltered. As he told Vance, 'I would like to allocate more time to dating, though. I need a girlfriend. How much time does a woman want a week? Maybe 10 hours?'"

Between the Mohan blog and the Vance and Brooks articles about Musk, there's a fairly coherent version that emerges of the consummate Silicon Valley entrepreneur, and it's pretty intense.

Two questions come to mind:

(1) Are there other models of entrepreneurial success? Are there entrepreneurs who've been amazingly successful while also maintaining a sense of work/life balance? In other words, are most highly successful entrepreneurs basically like Musk, or is it that Musk fits our preconceived vision, so we remember (and discuss) examples that fit the mold, and perhaps overlook other examples who don't.

(2) Even if we assume, for argument's sake, that most successful Silicon Valley entrepreneurs do fit the Musk mode, perhaps this is an accident of history or of the particular technology and sort of people who've driven much of the innovation in the Valley. Going forward, you'd think that other examples might still be possible.

I'm not going to react to the first question, or rather, I'd prefer to crowdsource that response—I'd be very interested in hearing in the comments section below about examples of wildly successful entrepreneurs who either fit or contradict the Musk model.

I will offer an initial, and perhaps somewhat personal response to question two, from the perspective of someone who both loves to be with his family and who, while not an entrepreneur, has definitely experienced the sense of Csikszentmihalyi "flow" associated with total immersion in an activity about which I've been passionate.

My honest answer is that I think there are few experiences more amazing than "flow," when you are so at one with your activity that you lose almost all sense of time and life outside the thing you're working on. You are exceptionally productive. And other commitments do slip—you really are so much less available for others.

I suspect that most (perhaps not all) creative and successful people, whether Silicon Valley entrepreneurs or not, probably do need the time to detach and focus, to put their head down and selfishly think about their work and no one else.

The thing is, when you're so immersed, you also tend to be far more fulfilled, more excited about life, and thrilled and enthusiastic by what you're working on—a phenotype that I suspect may at some level be easier for your friends and family than the opposite. I'm not sure how much of a treat it is to be with someone who feels deeply unfulfilled at work, simply clocking in and clocking out.

I'm also not sure states of flow are a constant for anyone, even successful entrepreneurs. I see even the most creative and involved work as a series of sprints, with essential respites in between, recovery periods valuable not only because they restore the mind and enable you to dive in again, but also because it's the time you spend with the people you care so much about that gives both work and life meaning.

Right?

The uncomfortable question is whether in embracing and taking pleasure from personal commitments, we are subtly eroding our potential to do something really, really big.

I want to believe our efforts to achieve work/life balance reflect our sophisticated recognition that happiness and fulfillment result from integrated involvement across a range of domains, with family being by far the most significant.

At the same time, there's a part of me that worries that work/life balance simply represents a hedge, a rationalization, an acknowledgement that we'll probably never write the great American novel, or start the next Google.

Most of us pursue work/life balance because we believe this represents the most fulfilling expression of our human potential; let's hope that we've not instead stumbled upon a devastatingly effective way to constrain it. – DS

In Praise Of Late Bloomers And Unconstrained Thinkers

In a society constantly searching for the new, new thing, it's hardly surprising we seek and celebrate innovation in the young. Peter Thiel's legendary fellowship program seeks to encourage young creatives under 20 to defer college and pursue their passions (notably, Thiel himself is a graduate of Stanford and Stanford Law School). Forbes publishes lists of 30 under 30, "young disruptors, innovators, and entrepreneurs" who "are impatient to change the world." Fortune has a 40 under 40 list of "business's hottest rising stars."

These are all good things; we should do all we can to nurture young innovators.

My worry, however, is that we risk conflating innovation with youth, risk institutionalizing a dangerous cognitive shortcut that may significantly underestimate the potential contribution of the over-40 crowd—the demographic in which, full disclosure, I comfortably reside.

The extent of the problem here was poignantly captured in a powerful feature by Sarah McBride in Reuters, "Silicon's Valley Dirty Little Secret: Age Bias." McBride describes the absurd contortions of highly qualified middle-age entrepreneurs as they struggled to come across as younger than they were, in order to be employable in the Valley.

McBride effectively surfaces quotes from legendary Valley VCs, such as this gem from Sequoia Capital's Michael Moritz (age 49 at the time):

"I am just an incredibly enthusiastic fan of very talented 20-somethings starting companies. They have great passion. They don't have distractions like families and children and other things that get in the way of business."

(When contacted by McBride, Moritz [now 58] wrote, "Unfortunately, I don't think the quote you have selected is very representative of what I think.")

Similarly, McBride reports that Vinod Khosla, 57, told conference attendees last year that "People over 45 basically die in terms of new ideas." Khosla subsequently told McBride he was simply pointing out young people tend to be more experimental; McBride notes Khosla Ventures has invested in several companies with leaders over 45.

McBride also shares several other arresting examples, including Benchmark Capital's stated intention of keeping the average age of its most active partners under 40, and Mark Zuckerberg's comment that "Young people are just smarter."

Yet 500 Startups founder Dave McClure, 46, challenges this conventional wisdom, both through his writing and his accomplishments. McClure's "late bloomer, not a loser" (discussed here) is my single favorite essay of the year, and discusses in an incredibly personal way the challenges of a career path that evolves slower than the apparent Silicon Valley standard. Meanwhile, McClure's impassioned globetrotting evangelizing would challenge the cardiovascular reserve of even the fittest twentysomething.

I resonate deeply with McClure's description of an elongated career path, and share his optimism, energy and profound underlying confidence that a lengthy journey can provide critical skills, valuable life experiences, and a heightened sense of urgency—all vital, enabling qualities for an impact player.

There's a larger lesson as well: whether the barrier is an unorthodox career path or a different learning style (see this WSJ review of *Outliers*, and this WSJ review of *The Rare Find*), biases of gender, ethnicity, or sexual orientation (see here), a reflexive antipathy towards industry (see here), or the ageism described by McBride, our ability to succeed and change the world for the better can be limited by our own preconceived notion of what success looks like.

Meanwhile, McClure's relatively late success, and that of many others, demonstrate what can be achieved by removing artificial constraints, maintaining an open mind, and focusing only on building the best team possible.

How quaint. – DS

Massive Hype—And Hope—For Digital Health In Silicon Valley

The initial reports from the Valley were breathless: upstart digital health company led by accomplished and charismatic design-focused entrepreneur (Forbes 30 under 30; 2012 invitee to exclusive Founders Fund Hawaii retreat) was acquired for "tens of millions of dollars," according to the (original) TechCrunch headline, conservatively reflecting a 10x return to the company's gold-plated VC investors. Exultant congratulatory tweets (including from partners at some of these VCs) were joyfully exchanged. Another Silicon Valley success story.

Very shortly after the original news broke, however, I started to hear another story: in this version, a brilliant design team (that part doesn't change) struggled for a few years to figure out what they wanted to do, launched a much-anticipated, well-designed but fairly trivial app along the way, made some elegantly designed graphics, was unable to raise additional capital, and ultimately were tucked into another portfolio company of one of its leading investors, in a "big talent acquisition," as the revised TechCrunch headline stated.

While it's unclear to me which version is right (if either), I strongly suspect the second version is much closer to the truth.

The details of the individual company seem less important than the two key lessons I propose taking away from this experience.

First, the Silicon Valley hype machine is unbelievable, and you really have to be careful about what you read. For all the talk about celebrating failure, it's perhaps not surprising to learn that VCs and other stakeholders are far more interested in pumping up their big wins (see this NYT story from today) than in talking about the vast majority of struggling portfolio companies.

I wouldn't fault either a struggling small company or a VC backer for focusing on the bright side, and the new potential opportunity, but at some point, the disconnect between the reality and the massive hype seems almost absurd. It's easy to understand how aspiring entrepreneurs following the field could get a warped view of both the success achieved by others (often lower than you'd think) and the risk of failure (almost certainly higher than you'd imagine).

Second, while it's important not to overgeneralize from a single case, it's hard for me not to look at the challenges faced by this design-focused health company and see it as more symptomatic of Silicon Valley's overall bias in digital health towards cool, consumer-facing technology, rather than pragmatic solutions to defined medical problems.

I was reminded of this contrast during a recent experience I had as a digital health advisor for a team within a UCSF program whose focus includes stimulating innovation from front-line clinicians. While I'm not sure whether the idea proposed will turn into any kind of business (though frankly, I hope it does), the problem the physician was trying to solve was both real and pressing, and the innovation, developed by a real clinical expert in the field, focused squarely on helping out a specific group of afflicted patients. (Disclosure: I'm also co-founder of the Center for Assessment Technology and Continuous Health [CATCH], a MGH/MIT digital health initiative that also seeks to link front-line clinicians with sophisticated technologists, in effort to turn improved phenotypic measurement into better care and deeper science.)

I'm also following the efforts of Rock Health graduate Reify Health with interest; their goal is to bring the technologies of digital health to the sort of folks Judah Folkman would call "inquisitive physicians." While it's hard to see this as a significant, scalable business at the moment, it wouldn't surprise me if this initial focus on motivated, front-end users ultimately enabled them to discover a particularly compelling opportunity that they could subsequently pursue—an opportunity less visible to other would-be entrepreneurs.

My takeaway: while Silicon Valley adores design and technology (and adores itself for adoring design and technology), there's a critically important role for field discovery in medical innovation; imagine how powerful it would be if the Valley's most elegant design principles were brought to bear on a specific, compelling clinical need. – DS

Rock Health's New Class: Daring To Be Useful

If the Rock Health demo day for its fourth class is a representative guide, it would appear that digital health is starting to gain some real traction, focusing on discrete pain points and delivering potentially useful, appropriately-scoped solutions. There's clearly been some excellent coaching and helpful guidance received along the way.

While I experienced a modest degree of regret at what might be described as an overall lack of grand ambition, I also thought these companies (nicely summarized by Rebecca Grant over at VentureBeat) were generally much more grounded than some efforts I've seen in the past.

One theme was that improved coordination and increased patient engagement could lead to reduced medical costs by payors (and at-risk providers); Wildflower Health focused on reducing pregnancy complications, for example, while Wellframe looked at cardiac rehab. The key proof point for both companies will be whether investment in their product will quantifiably reduce costs in the way they project.

While Open Placement also ostensibly focused on care coordination (discharge planning), their service was much more like an online traveling booking service, but involving secondary care facilities, and geared to the needs of hospital discharge coordinators. Key challenges for the company include the ability to achieve (and maintain) a critical mass of care centers, and the need to successfully, and durably, provide accurate information and ratings. But if well-executed, Open Placement could be a big story—there's a real need for this kind of service (notably, other companies are also looking at this space, e.g. Boston-based CarePort).

The trendiest company to present (and presumably the fittest) was Wello, who also boasted the simplest operating model (basically, "webcam with a trainer"), but involves a business model that reminded me most of Uber. Essentially, they realized, or discovered, that there's a tremendous number of fitness trainers who have a lot of downtime, and hence, unused capacity; Wello connects (by video) "select" trainers with users (individuals or groups) who want to exercise at home, in a hotel, or pretty much anywhere but a gym.

Users pay, Wello collects, gives 80% to the trainer, and keeps the balance.

I even liked some of the fairly specialized niche plays. For example, Eligible reportedly integrates effortlessly with almost any IT system used by providers and enables them to easily check whether a patient is covered by insurance. Not earthshattering, but useful. Meanwhile, KitCheck places RFID tags on the individual components of medical kits used by hospitals, to enable them to rapidly evaluate and update contents (a process which evidently costs hospitals a huge amount of time and money); this seems a clever use of this much-discussed "internet of things" technology.

One of the more ambitious companies to present was Zipongo, which aims to enable healthy eating by pairing a behavior engagement platform with discounts on selected "healthy" foods. There seemed to be a lot of moving parts in the grand vision, and it's unclear to me whether the whole thing will actually function as an integrated unit (with personalized eating plans, employer involvement, etc.), as envisioned, or whether it will essentially morph into a service that provides "healthy coupons."

LabDoor also focuses on healthy choices, seeking to chemically test common supplements such as vitamins and energy drinks, to determine their actual content. I'm not sure how many supplement users are likely to actually care about this information, and thus it's hard to know what the revenue model will be; however, it's encouraging to hear that some supplement manufacturers have reported offered to pay to have their products tested, evidently believing a good result from a trusted source could represent an important competitive advantage.

Improved health through user engagement was a theme of SuperBetter (applying gaming to health challenges such as depression; this model of small goals is very popular these days—cf Lift, Everest); MangoHealth (gamification of medication and supplement management); and the Beam Brush (toothbrush with sensor so you can monitor usage on your mobile device). The revenue model of the first two companies (still in "stealth mode," as were Benefitter and Moxie Health) was not clear. I'm also not sure how much real world interest there will be in the Beam Brush—although dental insurers are evidently very interested in it as a research tool to understand real-world toothbrush use.

Perhaps the most intriguing idea discussed at demo day was advanced by Clinicast, an analytics company that aspires to develop an industry-standard health risk score, analogous to the FICO credit score. Clinicast also offers a panel of services and clinical decisions support tools similar to that of other leading analytics companies, and it's unclear how they (or anyone else) is going to stand out from the crowd—though Clinicast is savvy enough to recognize and acknowledge the importance of workflow integration.

(See here for recent overview of data challenges in digital health.)

Closing Thoughts

Almost all of the companies here are working on some aspect of operational improvement, or else (like Wello) are completely in the consumer space. Several of the companies (especially those focused on cost savings) are counting on the ACO movement to swell—though this must still be viewed as an assumption. (See this related WSJ commentary.)

As Denny Ausiello and I discussed in a Boston Globe Op-Ed, it would be great to see digital health move beyond operational improvement, and focus not only on ensuring more care is up to our highest standards, but also on finding ways to ensure this standard is substantially elevated. Within this graduating class of companies, only one—Clinicast— seems to harbor even the potential to deliver such truly profound change, and I'm not sure their sights are set this high.

Even so, the companies presenting today seem to have responded enthusiastically to Rock Health's motto, "build something useful." They have—and so has Rock Health. – DS

Hype, Hope, And Health In Silicon Valley

My experience as a healthcare guy in Silicon Valley seems well described by the technology "hype cycle," beginning with a jolt of excitement triggered by the thrill of arrival. Progressive immersion led me up the "peak of inflated expectations," followed by descent into the "trough of disillusionment" as I became better at distinguishing mythology from achievement.

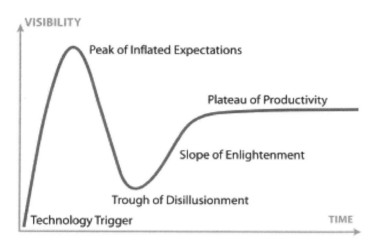

Now, perhaps enlightened, I've reached what I can only hope is the "plateau of productivity." I've an even deeper belief in the power that Silicon Valley technology and thinking could have if applied to healthcare problems, as well as an equally strong belief that while success may be enabled by technology, it will be driven by a sophisticated, nuanced, and (yes) humanistic understanding of the complex healthcare problems that need to be solved.

Hope

From my first moments in the Valley, I was struck—I remain struck—by the incredible energy and sense of possibility that seems to be in the air out here, the bedrock conviction that with some inspiration and hard work, you can change the world, make a dent in the universe, and potentially earn millions of dollars for your effort. It wasn't surprising to learn from a recent WSJ article that a relatively large number of LinkedIn profiles from the Bay Area include the words, "change the world."

The Entrepreneurial Thought Leader podcasts from Stanford, the tweets from badass VC Dave McClure, the pitches you overhear at Philz and Sightglass—all are integral parts of the Valley atmosphere.

I've found myself unconsciously comparing the feeling here with my experiences in med school, and even more, in grad school. In many ways, my PhD experience (in biology at MIT) seemed culturally almost the polar opposite of what I've witnessed here. While MIT biology certainly featured its share of self-promotion, the dominant ethic was to emphasize the limitations of your work, and the enormity of the unanswered questions remaining. It would be unimaginable to tell your colleagues that you planned to change the face of biology—not only because it would be arrogant, but also because it would seem so ignorant. I also don't recall buoyant cheerleading (or even significant external encouragement) as a dominant feature of the MIT grad school experience.

Hype

On the other hand, most of my colleagues in grad school and I were drilling down on pretty fundamental problems, trying to work out the molecular mechanisms underlying cancer, cystic fibrosis, and Alzheimer's disease. I often think about this when I hear Valley VCs forever exhorting others to work on something important.

The idea that the Valley has become more than a little caught up in its own hype is gaining currency. San Francisco Chronicle columnist James Temple hit the nail on the head in a brilliant recent piece, "The Hypocrisy in Silicon Valley's Big Talk On Innovation," noting the contrast between grandiose ambitions and disappointing delivery. For all the talk about disruption, innovation, and aiming ridiculously high, most of Silicon Valley, "concerns itself primarily with getting people to click on ads or buy slightly better gadgets than the ones they got last year," Temple writes.

Many in the Valley share these concerns. In a now-classic post, "Why Facebook Is Killing Silicon Valley," serial Valley entrepreneur Steve Blank argued that the growth potential of social media has created a situation where the total available market is in the billions of users, and "the potential revenue and profits from these users (or advertisers who want to reach them) and the speed of scale of the winning companies can be breathtaking." He adds, "social media startups can return 100's of millions or even billions in less than 3 years." Technologist Dan Munro has argued along similar lines on Quora.

The tremendous upside opportunity can almost blind you to the fact that most startups fail, and only a small fraction—something like 1/700 (35 companies of the 25,000 financed between 2000 and 2010)—represent the billion-dollar exits we hear so much about.

(On perhaps a more positive notice, when Silicon Valley startups succeed, they tend to share the wealth with employees more broadly than most other corporations. According to Steven Johnson, citing "The Company of Owners," the top 100 tech companies granted 19% of their ownership to non-senior executive employees, versus just 2% for the rest of corporate America. As Johnson points out, "billionaire founders or CEOs are nothing new; but multi-millionaire middle managers—that's something else altogether.")

Health

From an investor point of view, healthcare turns out (perhaps surprisingly, as Bruce Booth points out) to have outperformed other venture sectors over the past decade; in fact, the two best subsectors in venture were reportedly healthcare services, followed by biopharma. The time required to achieve an exit in biopharma—again, surprisingly—turns out not to be longer than other sectors. The key difference seems to be the nature of the returns in healthcare—consistently solid, rather than occasionally spectacular. You get singles and doubles, not home runs. Consequently, and perhaps unfairly, life science funds are often regarded as "the ugly stepchild" of the venture business.

The lack of a dominant, brand-name venture firm in the healthcare space has created a gap several ambitious firms with roots on the technology side have tried to fill—VCs such as Google Ventures, Founders Fund, Khosla Ventures, and more recently, S+C. While these firms have each highlighted the importance of big innovative ideas, most have also invested in plenty of small-ball healthcare companies. Some of the more ambitious flyers they've taken (e.g. on life-extension) seem of questionable value, and often appear to be based more on the hope (and the narcissism) of the investors than the quality of the underlying science.

Moreover, it isn't clear that the most successful companies are necessarily those that begin with the most grandiose initial thesis; as Scott Berkun describes in his (must-read) "Myths of Innovation," many ultimately successful companies started out with far more limited ambitions.

Identifying future winners is notoriously difficult, as YC founder Paul Graham observed in his memorable "Black Swan Farming" essay:

"History tends to get rewritten by big successes, so that in retrospect it seems obvious they were going to make it big. For that reason one of my most valuable memories is how lame Facebook sounded to me when I first heard about it. A site for college students to waste time? It seemed the perfect bad idea: a site (1) for a niche market (2) with no money (3) to do something that didn't matter."

Graham adds, "One could have described Microsoft and Apple in exactly the same terms."

Notably, Epic—the electronic medical records powerhouse that everyone loves to hate—grew out of a focused effort to solve a specific problem (a research group in the psychiatry department at the University of Wisconsin needed help tracking patient data over time), and not out of a desire to fundamentally reshape the way U.S. hospitals manage medical information.

Nevertheless, I can't get away from the idea that having some kind of grand ambition is especially worthy. I admire companies trying to do something original and significant more than those trying to capitalize on the latest tweak—even as I acknowledge the value of such incremental innovation. When I read about biopharma R&D strategies that focus on formulation plays, or create drugs that are simply different rather than manifestly better—risk-mitigating strategies likely to remain a key part of pharma's future—I resonate with Peter Thiel's frustration with the quality of innovator ambition (though I recognize the new products may offer meaningful benefit to some patients).

My hope is that we're inspired by technologies and ambitions of Silicon valley to go beyond the creation of more efficient healthcare processes and more consistent service delivery—as important and difficult as these goals are—and learn how to develop profoundly improved therapies, that cure—or better yet, prevent—disease and disability. And while I share Khosla's belief in patient empowerment and consumer engagement, I also believe physicians offer patients—especially the chronically or acutely ill—far more than medical analytics, but also compassion, hope, insight, and comfort.

The game-changing technologies of the future will include those, like patient portals, that enhance the physician-doctor relationship—and those, like the polio vaccine, that obviate the need for one. – DS

After The Rapture: Life Science Copes With Tech Envy In The Valley

The challenges of bathing in the dazzling reflected glory of exalted technologists was front and center in D.C. when Congress invited Apple CEO Tim Cook to testify about the company's practice of "shielding billions of dollars overseas from U.S. taxes," as Politico phrased it.

Magnificently captured by the Daily Show, the anticipated inquisition turned into a love-fest, as lawmakers fell over each other to testify to their adoration of the Cupertino, CA-based computer company.

Cook even had the chutzpah to ground his suggestions for tax code improvement in Apple's ostensible commitment to simplicity—a principle that (as Jon Stewart observed) might come as news to anyone familiar with the iTunes TOS.

Safe to say, a pharma executive facing this committee would have had a very different experience.

It could well be that Cook's tax reform suggestions are good ones, and that all CEOs, including pharma leaders, deserve intense Congressional grilling. Even so, there's still a conspicuous differential between the way we think about (at least some) tech companies, and how we view everyone else.

Over at Fortune, Dan Primack raised similar questions in light of the disparity in coverage this week between the reporting of Actavis's $8.8B acquisition of Warner Chilcott, and Yahoo's purchase of Tumblr for $1.1B. Guess which takeout generated the most online stories (by a factor of nearly ten)?

Why, Primack asks, are "media folk so obsessed with the acquisition of a low-revenue blogging platform and so dismissive of an $11 billion combined revenue drugmaker?"

The answers, he suggests, are that tech companies are usually easier to understand, often have more telegenic CEOs, are covered by many more media sites, and are of greater interest to readers who scour web content and account for the majority of pageviews.

For healthcare folks, especially those in biopharma like me, interest in understanding tech buzz goes beyond mere device envy. As life science VC Bruce Booth elegantly summarized this week, investors appear to overestimate tech returns (and underestimate life-science returns), despite compelling evidence to the contrary. The big tech wins, though almost vanishingly rare (and necessarily absent from most funds) are so spectacular that they overwhelm logic, skewing investment dollars in a fashion that contributes to the struggles of early-stage life-science companies, and arguably supports an ever-increasing number of derivative tech startups and equally derivative venture investors.

My colleagues and I in the business of making medicines find ourselves wondering why businesses built around creating new therapies are often viewed with such contempt, while gadget makers are revered.

In part, as Primack suggests, this reflects the tech publications that monumentalize each brain fart and photo-sharing app generated by the wizards of Mid-Market.

He's also right that we feel closer to personal technologies like iPhone and Tumblr than we do to large pharma companies (or most enterprise tech companies, for that matter). I suspect most biopharmas have done a particularly poor job of establishing trusted relationships with consumers, in part due to regulatory barriers, but in part due to an increased focus on other stakeholders, such as doctors and especially payors. Because patients are often (but not always—e.g. DTC advertised products) viewed as having little input in prescribing decisions, they may be overlooked and ignored. Conversely, a distinguishing feature of some of the early, successful orphan drug companies—most notably Genzyme—was an incredibly deep-seated commitment to its patients, at an ultra-personal level.

However, I suspect that the most important reason we love the makers of amusing gadgets far more than the makers of serious medical products is precisely because gadgets *aren't* essential—we can choose to purchase an iPhone, or an iPad, and, like Cook's Congressional committee, we often find ourselves delighted with the results.

It's not the same with medicines, usually. Medicines are a negative good—we use them because we need to (or we feel like we need to), not because we want to. We resent our medications even as we use them. We're upset that we're sick, we're upset that we require a drug, and then we're upset if the drug only helps a little bit, rather than a lot. An imperfect tech gadget still leaves us better off, but a partially-effective drug can leave us still feeling sick—as well as upset and disappointed. Undoing a negative might be a greater hurdle than increasing a positive.

A win for a gadget is if you enjoy using it every day. The ultimate win for a drug would be only needing to take it once. Many digital health entrepreneurs seem to forget that most patients don't want their disease management to be fun, they want it to be minimized, and would prefer to lead their lives spending as little time as possible dwelling in Sontag's Kingdom of the Sick.

At some level, I think most people understand that creating new medicines is different—and I'd argue, generally more substantive—than making clever apps and elegant gadgets. Nobody studying cancer needs Mark Zuckerberg to assure them that their work is important—or to call attention to the value of curing cancer: we all get it.

The dream of digital health, of course, is to unite these worlds, and leverage the engagement of technology to motivate behaviors that prevent or mitigate disease, and capture data that might be used to fashion more effective treatments.

But until then—well, there's always iFart (TechCrunch coverage here, here, here, and here). – DS

Growth Junkies: The Neurobiology Of Startup Addiction

Silicon Valley is defined by startups. While more than half a million new companies are started each year in the United States, only a tiny minority have the potential to get really big really fast—i.e are "startups" in the Silicon Valley sense of the term. As Paul Graham, founder of the legendary seed accelerator Y Combinator succinctly summarized, "Startup = Growth."

If you define growth based on revenue increase over four years (the way Inc keeps score), or based on achieving revenues of $100M within several decades of founding (the metric used in this recent Kauffman Foundation report by Paul Kedrosky), then most "high-growth" companies are admittedly not the venture-backed, Silicon Valley IT companies that probably come to mind. In fact, most of the $100M revenue companies founded since 1980 are not in IT, and are not in California—the Southeast actually leads the nation here.

But the growth Graham describes is different, and reflects a very specific, characteristic phase in a (tech) startup's development, after it's been through an initial phase of "slow or no growth while the startup tries to figure out what it's doing" (Graham's words), and before a successful startup begins to reach either internal or external limits, and growth starts to slow.

There's an amazing period in between—"as the startup figures out how to make something lots of people want and how to reach those people"—where growth can be explosive; at Y Combinator, Graham looks for weekly (!) growth of 5-7% a week—corresponding to yearly growth rates of 12.6x-33.7x, according to Graham's figures.

To be sure, this period of growth may not last very long, if it's achieved at all. Bruce Booth of Atlas Venture and Bijan Salehizadeh of NaviMed Capital calculate that in the 2000s, 75% of IT firms generated returns of 1x or less. More generally, Booth observes that as a whole, tech investments have underperformed life science investments, and have taken about as long or longer to achieve exits.

Yet what tech startups may uniquely offer is their potential to deliver at least a burst of exceptional growth, which (on rare occasions) can lead to exceptional (100x) returns. You don't see this in life-sciences, for example.

As serial entrepreneur Steve Blank has pointed out, the internet provides a historic opportunity to scale. "Facebook has adroitly capitalized on market forces on a scale never seen in the history of commerce," he writes. "For the first time, startups can today think about a Total Available Market in the billions of users (smart phones, tablets, PC's, etc.) and aim for hundreds of millions of customers."

It turns out that this phenomenon of ultra-fast growth may have an interesting biological correlate—in the field of addiction. In particular, the addictiveness of drugs of abuse such as cocaine and methamphetamine seems to be driven by the rate at which the neurotransmitter dopamine increases.

As George Koob of The Scripps Research Institute and Nora Volkow of the National Institute on Drug Abuse write, "fast dopamine changes are associated with the subjective perception of reward, whereas slow and stable dopamine increases do not induce these subjective responses." Elsewhere, Vokow and co-authors observe that "the reinforcing effects of drugs of abuse in human beings are contingent not just on dopamine increases per se… but on the rate of dopamine increases. The faster the increases, the more intense the reinforcing effects."

While the time scales of startup growth and dopamine accumulation are clearly different (weeks vs seconds), it's tempting to speculate that our fascination with tech startups is in some way connected to this same neural circuitry. Yes, some tech startups (like Tumblr) may enjoy widespread name recognition, and yes, some—a rare few—generate extraordinary returns. But you have to wonder if what really captures our attention, what hooks so many entrepreneurs, venture capitalists, journalists, and wannabes is the explosive rise in value, an exponential increase that, once you experience it, may leave you desperate for more, and lead to a frantic scramble to find another hit.

Pando Daily has offered a cynical send-up of what so-called "startup junkies" are really drawn to—titles, conferences, freewheeling culture. There's probably some truth to this. But I'd suggest that what really attracts people to tech startups just may be the chance to experience the exhilaration of explosive growth—and, of course, the dopamine surges that accompany it. – DS

IV.

Doctors, Nurses, And Health Professionals

50% Of Doctors Are Worse Than Average

If you hired a lawyer who the world's nicest office and excellent coffee in the lobby, but who lost the case for you every time, what would you think of that lawyer? How about if you hired a hairdresser who was always on time and had some great gossip for you when you sat in their chair, but who made you look like a refugee from Flock of Seagulls every time you left the salon? I am guessing that your general view on these people would be negative, despite their incidental charms.

However, when people are asked to rate their doctors, it is precisely the incidental charms that count the most. The primary correlates to doctors receiving high patient satisfaction scores are: 1) whether they were made to wait for an excessive period of time in the waiting room; and 2) whether the doctor spent a long period of time with them in the exam room. In other words, patients value comfort and attention and that, in their minds, tends to equate to high quality care. Buyer beware.

A research team from the University of Michigan School of Public Health recently analyzed data from around 15,000 patients who used a patient satisfaction survey tool called DrScore.com. What they found is that, on average, patient satisfaction with their own physician ranks in the 90th percentile. The categories most highly correlated with satisfaction were, as previously noted, waiting time and amount of time spent with the patient. I don't know about you, but if I'm ranking my doctor, I'd be thinking about outcome and invasiveness of treatment as a big part of how I feel about them. And yet, the question of whether their illness was effectively cured or whether they suffered unanticipated side effects is not nearly as big a factor in patient satisfaction as is the courtesy of the office staff and the timeliness of appointments and follow-up.

If you look at the questions asked in the DrScore survey, which you can find HERE, you see that only 2 of the 20 non-demographic questions in the survey get directly at clinical outcome. The first is: On a scale of 1-10, how do you rank your treatment success? This question is actually number 11 of the survey of 20 questions. The second question is more indirect, asking "on a scale of 1-10, where 0 is the worst possible care and 10 is the best possible care, where do you rate your doctor?

So what? You might ask. Patient satisfaction has been measured this way forever. If people are happy with their doctors, then good for them.

True, but here's the rub. If you ask people if they are satisfied with the healthcare system and whether they think they get good value for dollars spent, they say "no." As many as 80% of Americans say they are dissatisfied with the U.S. healthcare system in typical surveys. If you ask people if they think money is wasted in excessive treatment they say "yes." If you ask 100 people if they have a friend or family member who got bad treatment and/or harmed by the medical care they received, you will get 100 yeses. And yet those same people who hate the medical system love their doctors. It's similar to how people separate their feelings about "Congress" from their feelings about their own Congressional representatives. When you poll voters, they tend report 70%-80% *dissatisfaction* with how Congress is doing its job and 60-70% average *satisfaction* with the efforts of their own congressional representative. No wonder you can never get rid of any of these people.

I have to believe this consumer schizophrenia is one of the reasons it is so hard to change the healthcare system for the better. Payers have tried for years to effectively reduce the size of their provider networks to reward physicians who demonstrate better outcomes and to exclude those of less clear quality (the basic idea around pay-for-performance). Yes, no doubt these things are hard to measure in the aggregate; everyone wants to bring in risk-adjustment and all that other stuff. But for one individual patient, it is pretty easy to measure these things. I go to my doctor; he/she makes me feel better or not. I feel more in control of my health or not. Etc. Yet whenever a payor tries to cut any provider out of its network, bedlam ensues as consumers fight the perceived reduction in choice. And this is because every provider has his/her fans, not because every provider is effective. I used to work for a doctor that used to always tell me, "by definition, 50% of doctors are worse than average." Hard to argue with that logic.

As health reform rolls along–and it will roll along in some form or another because the economic imperative is there regardless of the form the final law takes–it will become necessary to force more accountability into the system. A big part of that accountability will and should fall in the lap of consumers, who are, in the end, responsible for what happens to them and how their own money is spent. It will be interesting to see whether consumers will be willing to trade the provider of their choice (he has such great lollipops!) for the provider that costs less or delivers faster or better results when push comes to shove and their own cold hard cash is at stake. Certainly those would be the primary determinants in any other significant consumer purchase. No one buys a car because the dealer is highly attentive and has fresh minty breath or a piece of real estate because the realtor has such a nice car and is a good listener. People are able to rapidly overlook these things if they think they are not getting a good value.

Over the last several years many new businesses have formed that are focused entirely on delivering quality and cost results to consumers so they can make better provider choices. Virtually all of these are still pretty small enterprises with fairly light levels of consumer adoption. Yet as consumers are put in the driver's seat for the purchase of health insurance plans, as they will be through the health insurance exchanges that will likely soon be pervasive, will these businesses become as popular as Consumer Reports is for cars and appliances? Today the average person spends far more time interviewing contractors and financial advisors than they do physicians; will this change when consumers have a greater sense that it is their own money being used to pay physicians? Taken to its logical extreme, maybe the next big reality show will be the one where physicians compete for consumers' affections and get voted off the island by Paula Abdul when they fail to deliver in the charm department.

One of the questions on the DrScore.com is "to what extent does your doctor include you in decisions about your care and treatment?" This reminded me of that Seinfeld episode where Elaine's doctor decides she is "difficult" and writes secret notes in her file before blowing her off with a cursory treatment plan. When she goes to the next doctor, he has already received her records (what are the odds of that happening in real life?) and treats her with the same disdain, driving she and Kramer (posing as Dr. Van Nostrum) to try to steal her medical records. Thought I'd include the video clip of that scene, as it always cracks me up. I'm guessing these guys wouldn't have fared so well in the DrScore.com study. – LS

What Silicon Valley Doesn't Understand About Medicine

Where's Silicon Valley when we need it? The inexorable rise of healthcare costs has created not only a crisis waiting to happen, but also an urgent need for innovation—exactly the sort of thing for which Silicon Valley is justly famous. So where is it?

While entrepreneurs in the Valley and elsewhere have achieved remarkable success (at least historically) developing new drugs and devices , more fundamental innovation in healthcare delivery—particularly the sort designed to take costs out of the system—has proved far more elusive.

It's not for lack of trying. Almost every legendary Silicon Valley entrepreneur (see here; also here) has recognized the opportunity: our healthcare system is legendary for its inefficiencies, complexity, and opacity—all areas that seem utterly amenable to a technology-driven solution. Yet, to date, the results have been middling at best. Why hasn't there been a Google or a Facebook in the healthcare space?

One reason may be that existing stakeholders are more entrenched than generally appreciated; we may also be more reluctant to tinker with our health than we are to try out the latest app. It's also likely that at least until recently, entrepreneurs were more incentivized to create expensive solutions than to engineer cost-effective ones (as this McKinsey report suggests).

Yet I'd argue that the most significant disconnect I've found here in Silicon Valley is a failure to understand the nature of the problem to be solved. Most engineers and computers scientists with whom I've spoken conceptualize medicine as primarily a rational, evidence-based, problem-solving enterprise focused on well-defined conditions, rather than a discipline that in my experience owes more to scientism than science, is far more ambiguous than most engineers tend to recognize, and is founded on relationships, connectedness, trusted advice, reassurance, and frequently the off-loading of significant responsibilities from patient to doctor. Perhaps the physician's greatest responsibility is helping to compassionately mediate the patient's experience of illness.

Simply put, medicine is so much more than simply a diagnosis and treatment (although regrettably in today's world of rapid-fire outpatient medicine, it occasionally seems to be reduced to this cartoon), and patients—especially those with chronic illnesses—value more than just the rigid outcome measures traditional metrics tend to capture. A novel technology platform that overlooks the integrated needs of patients or underestimates or fails to account for the complexity and messiness of illness as it actually occurs and is experienced by patients (and those closest to them) will inevitably fall short.

Former Google CEO Eric Schmidt represents the pervasive Silicon Valley perspective in this dialog with surgeon and author Atul Gawande. Stanford Medical School professor (and author) Abraham Verghese presents a contrasting perspective in this NYT Op-Ed.

This disconnect between the reality of medicine and its Silicon Valley conceptualization is especially important because technological innovation—the sort of ideas the valley was founded upon—is urgently needed in medicine, and offers the potential to radically disrupt the way we think about health and disease, and can make it easier for us to stay healthy and understand what may be ailing us when we're sick. There's also an urgent need for improved communication between providers so that successful approaches can be shared, and less effective approaches identified and called-out (highlighted in this BCG white paper). There's also a growing need to adopt what might be called a network or systems view of medicine, and develop ways of integrating complex data over multiple domains to uncover new patterns and suggest new approaches to diagnosis or treatment.

An especially useful starting point for an aspiring healthcare company would be to think about ways to deliver a "positive good." Most contemporary medicine is generally regarded, economically, as a negative good—something we use or engage in because we have to, not because we especially want to. While this creates a ready market, it's also results in a tense and uncomfortable relationship between the "producers" of healthcare —who have often invested a significant amount of resources with the intention of making a profit—and consumers, who have little choice but to pay (or co-pay) for expensive care, and consequently tend to resent it.

Back when I was in the clinic, I remember feeling confused by patients who would complain about the cost of care while seeming to have few qualms about the going on pricey vacations or buying expensive gadgets. On reflection, however, I think the key difference is that patients at least felt they had a choice about buying a gadget, and liked selecting something they thought they might enjoy. The opportunity here for technologies companies is to develop an attractive and engaging platform that will warmly incentivize positive behaviors, and help patients nudge themselves in healthier directions. The business case hinges upon its voluntary adoption, rather than obligatory usage.

Consequently, I'd argue there's a significant opportunity for a platform focused relentlessly (think Jeff Bezos) on the patient, providing patients with significant value and benefits from engagement that are both immediate and accretive. Jamie Heywood's PatientsLikeMe has achieved much deserved recognition for the ALS patient community it has developed, and may be one model to consider; the question at this point is whether there's it's possible to achieve this level of community benefit and participation for less devastating diseases, especially considering that most patients want to live life, not spend their days fixated on their particular medical condition.

It will also be important to ensure that even as we recognize—and seek to capture, leverage, and ultimately monetize—the value associated with the collection of an ever-increasing amount of data, we also recognize that most people don't want to be perpetually monitored (at least not intrusively). While there's a much-discussed movement called quantified self, focused on capturing and sharing vast quantities of physiological data using sensors and other devices, this sort of excessive monitoring is almost certainly not something most of us want. One challenge will be figuring out how to capture useful physiological information in a way that offers benefit while also remaining unobtrusive and respecting privacy concerns.

Steve Jobs famously recruited Pepsi's John Sculley by asking him, "Do you want sell sugar water for the rest of your life or come with me and change the world?" Perhaps it's time for the next generation of technology entrepreneurs to revisit this challenge, and discover that there are some things in the world even more rewarding than the latest iPad—though I suspect my young kids would emphatically disagree. – DS

A Cautionary Prognosis For Algorithm-Based Care

A distinguishing feature of the U.S. healthcare system—let us suspend judgment, for the moment, on whether this is an asset or a liability—would seem to be its variability, the fact that two patients with a similar disease can receive very different care. This may have its historical routes in the development of medicine as a profession, where physicians traditionally functioned as independent agents, practitioners who could essentially put up a shingle and go to work, striving to provide what each doctor individually perceived as the best care to each patient. However, as extensive recent research has demonstrated, the practice patterns of physicians turn out to vary widely.

This variation is just the sort of thing modern business management (think Six Sigma) seeks to reduce in other industries, and replace with a standardized, optimized process that ensures efficient and effective production. Rather than have ten factories building cars in ten different ways, according to the whim of the local manager, standard operating procedures (SOPs) typically will be created based on perceived best practices, and then utilized in all ten locations.

In medicine, a much-discussed alternative to the current, expert-based system is an approach that relies on SOPs in the form of treatment guidelines or more explicitly, algorithms; the idea is that patients with particular diagnoses are placed on a pathway and treated in a relatively uniform fashion. These can vary in complexity, from some of the basic checklists advocated and implemented by Peter Pronovost and others, and described eloquently by Atul Gawande, to very sophisticated treatment algorithms explicitly incorporating a range of contingencies and variables.

The appeal of algorithms is simple: it guarantees a basic standard of care for all patients, and ensures that vitally important elements are not forgotten—making sure certain surgical patients receive medicine to prevent blood clots is a classic example; requiring providers to wash hands prior to examining a patient is another. The point is that these should be "automatics"—the kind of interventions that truly almost every patient should receive, minimal reflection required. One much-discussed tragedy of contemporary medicine is the recognition of just how many patients are not receiving these basic fundamentals of care, often due to reluctance of physicians to change how they've always done things, and their disinclination to be told by anyone else what to do. (A classic example from my training was a transplant surgeon who refused to administer the flu vaccine to his patients after his wife came down with the flu despite receiving the vaccine, leading him to conclude, erroneously, that the vaccine was universally ineffective.) The legendary difficulties experienced by Pronovost and others in trying to implement the most basic checklists speak to the very real, and very worrisome, reluctance of many physicians to modify their behavior, and least when this is presented as an externally imposed requirement.

Another appeal of algorithms is their scalability—you don't need experts to administer them, and in fact that's the point. Patients who satisfy basic criteria can be tracked, essentially put on autopilot (or at least aspects of their care go on autopilot), and a series of prescribed actions is performed. A great example of the success of this approach is the worldwide adoption of highly-active antiretroviral protocols, which has enabled millions of patients across the globe to benefit from current medications. Offloading the requirement to administer such care from experts to low-cost providers (as discussed in Clay Christensen's fascinating book, The Innovator's Prescription) also offers the potential to deliver care at a profoundly reduced cost. Not surprisingly, such offloading is also a source of profound tension, particularly among the highly-paid "experts."

There are many obvious and not-so-obvious concerns about algorithm-based care. Clearly, one worry is that such an approach often fails to acknowledge and account for individual differences between patients—it threatens to lump together patients who might benefit from more customized treatment—and who would almost certainly benefit from the perception of receiving personalized, tailored care. Patients with the same formal diagnosis are still different, and most seek and value a sense of connection and recognition for the unique way they are experiencing their illness (captured with particular eloquence here).

Algorithmic medicine can also represent a significant challenge to physicians, calling into question many of the central tenants of a physician's faith. For starters, most doctors have been taught from the first day of medical school to treat each patient as a unique individual who must be carefully understood and thoughtfully treated. Beyond that, many physicians feel threatened or challenged by the notion that a protocol administered by a non-physician could provide the same level of care; in this sense, algorithms can be perceived as a real double-whammy, potentially threatening not just a doctor's job, but also his or her privileged status (and authoritah).

Yet another worry relates to the quality of the algorithms. A frequently critique of US healthcare is the amount of care that doesn't follow standard treatment recommendations. The problem, however, is that all treatment recommendations are not created equal (see this controversial WSJ op-ed by Jerry Groopman and Pam Hartzband); while some are based on very rigorous science and thus can be considered robust and reliable, many others are not, and often represent simply a political consensus following a conversation among putative academic experts (many of whom have staked their professional careers on one particular therapeutic approach or another). While treatment recommendations (such as those listed in the National Guideline Clearinghouse, www.guidelines.gov) typically include a measure of the degree of confidence behind each suggestion, in practice, treatment recommendations necessarily tend to be presented and, more importantly, implemented in a summarized and simplified form, making it very difficult to discern which are truly reliable.

As discussed in a recent post, medicine is generally far more hazy and imprecise than popular perception might suggest (and than Silicon Valley engineers generally appreciate). In particular, for physicians and patients, figuring out the relationship between care provided and outcome is a difficult and often uncertain process, depending on many more factors than what the doctor may have recommended at a given visit. An apt analogy might be to the observation that only a fraction of most diseases are due to genetic causes, and external factors often account for a significant amount of the risk (for example, if one identical twin has type 1 diabetes, the chance of the other twin being afflicted is less than 50%). On top of this, the benefits of providing the right evidence-based care can be difficult if not impossible to see; many patients often need to be treated in order for a benefit (preventing heart attacks through use of statins, say) to be realized in one, and many patients receiving appropriate treatment (such as statins) will get sick (e.g. suffer a heart attack) nevertheless. The tenuous relationship between treatment and outcome for an individual patient interferes with the opportunity for conditioning (positive or aversive) of physicians, and can reduce their incentive to embrace new guidelines or constraints, especially those that are perceived to be of dubious intrinsic value. – DS

Why Is Medicine's Killer App An E-Textbook?

If you walk the floors the nation's leading hospitals, chances are you'll see a number of physicians hunched over computers, busily pecking away. Look closer, and you'll see that many are probably using an application called UpToDate, a for-profit platform that provides doctors timely (up-to-date—get it?), authoritative information on a wide range of medical conditions, written and edited by an expansive team of experienced clinicians, many associated with top-tier academic medical centers.

Fundamentally, UpToDate is an electronic textbook, incorporating a minimal amount of technology that enables rapid cross-referencing and frequent online updates. These two features, together with consistently high-quality content, have enabled UpToDate to render the classic medicine textbooks effectively obsolete; if you are a physician, and you want to look up a medical condition, odds are the first place you'll look is UpToDate. Many drug developers, investors, and industry analysts also subscribe. The company was founded in 1992 by Burton Rose, a Harvard nephrologist, and was acquired by Wolters Kluwer in 2008 for an undisclosed price. (FWIW, I have no relationship with UpToDate, other than as a paid subscriber.)

The popularity of UpToDate offers a window into how physicians currently view and value information. Most obviously, UpToDate suggests physicians prize authority; they want to know the latest thinking associated with a disease area, and are interested in a distillation of the latest published data and expert consensus. Significantly, UpToDate generally offers not just a summary of recommendations but also an explanation of the associated physiology and a review of relevant clinical studies. Thus, it provides doctors not so much a recipe for treatment, but a sense of knowledge, empowering them to make informed therapeutic decisions without explicitly telling them what to do.

While the idea of using a medical textbook to guide clinical decision making does not strike most physicians as a particularly radical idea, it's useful to consider alternative approaches that are not generally used. For instance, you might imagine an open source textbook, perhaps analogous to Wikipedia, that could have emerged as the reference of choice; or you could envision (as many have) an information system that told physicians how their peers were actually treating other patients in similar situations, or how other patients actually fared in response to different treatment approaches. You could also imagine the regular use of an online physician community to crowdsource information and leverage experience; while this sort of activity does occur today (mediated by companies such as SERMO) and seems to provide an occasionally useful source of orthogonal input, it certainly has not emerged as the go-to reference for most physicians.

There's one other important feature of UpToDate that I've discovered while working on the commercial side of things: it turns out that the guidelines offered by these learned authors frequently do not correlate with what the vast majority of practicing physicians are actually doing. Even as many physicians seek out the latest advice and information, they don't necessarily translate this into practice.

Consider, for example, sitagliptin, a DPP-IV inhibitor developed for the treatment of diabetes. Read UpToDate, and you might assume that the drug would be utilized only in highly specialized situations, and would consequently achieve marginal sales at best, essentially as a niche product. Yet drug usage and sales data tell a far different story—by these criteria, sitagliptin has achieved solid blockbuster status.

Industry critics will pounce on this contradiction as offering evidence of the unhealthy impact of pharma marketing, while proponents might highlight the benefit realized by patients and argue that most medical guidelines, including those articulated in UpToDate, are scripted by self-righteous academic elitists who reflexively shun both novelty and industry.

I'm not sure I'd endorse either of these perspectives, and would instead suggest that in general, what drives treatment decisions for individual patients can be so much more complex or obscure than most outsiders would suspect.

Here's a case in point from my days in management consulting: we were looking at a market where there were several very similar products, essentially indistinguishable clinically. Product A was about to go off-patent and become available as a generic, and we were trying to anticipate the effect this would have on sales of Product B, still on patent. I remember one conversation in particular—we asked a physician who tended to prescribe Product B whether he'd immediately transition his patients to the generic form of Product A. Probably not, he told us, explaining that if he did, his patients would want to know why they hadn't been put on Product A to begin with, and the time required to adequately explain this to his patients would chew up too much of the allotted fifteen minutes. Thus, until his office started to get "hassled" by pharmacists and payors to switch to generics, he planned to keep his patients on Product B. While this particular rationale for a therapeutic choice may be idiosyncratic, factors such as ease of explanation and likelihood of being hassled play a surprisingly large role in physician decision making, even if absent from traditional guidelines such as UpToDate.

In college, I remember that a particularly useful resource was an unofficial guide to classes produced anonymously by students, offering a colorful and highly opinionated companion to the infinitely more sober course catalogue; this guide purported to tell you how things "really were," and often but not always enhanced decision-making. While I'm sure there'd be a range of legal obstacles to overcome, it's intriguing to speculate whether physicians might benefit from a similar sort of guide, one that strived less for political correctness and more towards offering the sort of information that busy physicians in practice tend to value. Meaningfully optimizing patient outcomes would naturally remain a central focus, of course, but optimizing reimbursement would be discussed as well.

Such a guide (which I'd envision as a companion to, not a replacement for, UpToDate) might also provide patients, policymakers, and entrepreneurs with a useful view into how physicians actually think, and the range of considerations that matter to them (spoiler alert: therapies that reduce patient calls to the office nurse will be highly valued). I suspect most of us would be appalled, amazed, and ultimately enlightened by what such an approach would reveal about how medicine, in the trenches, is actually practiced. – DS

Priests Or Mechanics? The Tricky Case For Medical Exceptionalism

As a profession, medicine has taken its hits lately—a recent article suggests that since the 1970s, "medical doctors have evolved … from fee-for-service professionals totally in control of their own workplace to salaried body mechanics subject to the relentless cost-cutting mandate of a corporate employer. They've gone from being Marcus Welby—a living monument to public service through private practice—to being, as one comprehensive study put it, harried 'middle management.'"

More generally, there's a view—highly prevalent in the corporate world as well as in the entrepreneurial community—that medicine isn't so special, and at the end of the day, it's just a business like any other. Sure, some particulars may be different, but fundamentally, the right lens (as consultants like to say) is that of a traditional service business, which can be analyzed and optimized accordingly.

This perspective seems off to me, but I also can understand how it may have evolved. For years, physicians viewed themselves as a priesthood of sorts, a profession that was doing something so unique and special and different that the laity couldn't possibly understand, and therefore should best not interfere. This gave physicians remarkable power and exceptional secondary gain (something still savored by many of the profession's most self-righteous advocates).

At some point, however, critics from both within and outside the profession started examining medicine's fundamental assumptions, and began asking whether doctors always knew best, whether their years of required training in organic chemistry and anatomy lab had really led them to provide the best care and most optimal outcomes. The results of these inquiries revealed previously underappreciated limitations of medicine and medical practice: doctors may have been confidently laying on hands and administering medications, but they were doing this with exceptional variability, often related to an individual physician's idiosyncrasies or to the conventions of a particular hospital and region, and typically not related to what the best science—to the limited extent such data are generally available—might suggest.

It's not surprising that physicians decried the "corporatization" of medicine; how much more satisfying it is to be viewed as essentially omniscient and infallible than to be critically evaluated, reviewed, questioned, and second-guessed—even though arguably such a dialectic should be considered an integral component of any truly scientific discipline.

The problem now, however, is that the effort to remove medicine from its pedestal seems to have gone too far, and in particular, has managed to overlook aspects of medicine that really are unique and not like any other business of which I'm aware. I tried to capture some of this in a NYT op-ed about 18 years ago, and I stand by this original description.

The opportunity to participate so intimately and so significantly in something as important as a patient's health is a profound responsibility, with few true parallels in the business world (military leadership is presumably another example). The contrast between truly high stakes and the illusion of high stakes was perhaps most evident to me during my days as management consultant, when our teams would race to assemble powerpoint decks that could be distributed to a client by a particular deadline; the faux urgency of this contrasts profoundly with the sense you feel on the ward when you hear a patient's blood oxygen level is starting to go down, or you're trying to figure out whether a chemo patient's immune system will recover before an opportunistic infection settles in.

In the corporate world, there's considerable emphasis on capabilities, competencies, and leadership skills; yet I'm not sure most business colleagues have any sense of what most physicians go through—routinely—during their training. These experiences typically involve assuming personal responsibility for the care of many sick patients, and requires a mastering of the complex organization and social dynamics of a modern hospital ecosystem. Miss a corporate deadline and Bill Lumbergh calls you onto the carpet or suggests you catch up over the weekend; miss a critical lab value, and it could really cost someone their life.

In fact, as I think back to my internship and residency, and think about what the new interns who start this week are likely to experience, I suspect that they may be least prepared for the overwhelming emotional intensity of their ward experience. While most admitted patients are treated, do reasonably well, and are rapidly discharged, the sickest patients tend to stay for the longest time, and are the ones you get to know the best, and feel the greatest sense of attachment; unfortunately, many of these are also the patients you are least able to help, at least in terms of their disease. It's true that you choose to become a physician because you want to help those who are sick, but the training experience also tends to significantly enrich for the patients who are the very sickest. The absolute amount of death and dying physicians encounter during their training is something I think few are truly prepared for (I certainly wasn't).

I was also struck by how little my medical school training—extremely rich in biomedical insight—actually prepared me for the exigencies of the wards. It was often remarked that the doctors who attended the least fancy schools (i.e. those that emphasized practice over theory) actually arrived on the wards the most prepared to take care of patients, while those who benefited from what was presumably an enlightened and intellectually enriched curriculum often stumbled initially when they had to take care of an actual person. While there may be an element of truth to this, I think the greater reality here is that as a med student, even when you are on the wards, you are never responsible the way you are as an intern, and there's nothing that focuses the mind like genuine responsibility (a lesson I think translates extremely well into the business world, incidentally). I suspect that I learned—and retained—more my first night on call than I did during all my years in medical school

Surprisingly, the most helpful aspect of my training was arguably the limited experience we had in a medical simulator—similar to a flight simulator, but involving a simulated patient on a hospital floor instead of a mock-up airplane cockpit. It's artificial responsibility, to be sure, but it demands and engenders type of thinking and responsiveness you need on the wards. It's a quirk of medicine that such simulation is the exception rather than the rule, and again, probably reflects the atavistic desire of physicians to be priests rather than mechanics. But the truth is that if you are able to learn the mechanics, and develop the ability to respond rapidly, comfortably, and instinctively to the urgent but often predictable crises that unexpectedly develop on the wards, you are then able to devote much greater attention to the needs and fears of the patient you are treating.

More generally, I suspect that if physicians were able to move away from the false choice —mechanic or priest—and recognize that optimally, a doctor's role involves a unique blend of both, then perhaps they might be able to provide patients what they most need, and regain in the process at least a small measure of their former glory. They deserve it.
– DS

Are Doctors Becoming Obsolete?

The challenge for medicine is not only to utilize patient-focused technologies, but also to recognize the unquantifiable benefit that comes from a reassuring nod, a hand on the shoulder

The idea that physicians are going to be far less important in the medicine of the future seems to be a central assumption of many next-generation health companies, an assertion that, like undergraduate Shakespeare productions set in the present day, may once have felt daring and original, but now seems merely tedious.

The logic goes something like is: Patients are accustomed to seeking insight from their doctors but doctors are far less good at providing this advice than most patients realize. As more consumer-based tools for managing health become available, patients will recognize that they now have the means and the motivation to take care of their health better than their physicians, and medical care will move directly into their hands.

Arguably, a form of this already happens today, as patients make extensive use of non-prescription products (e.g. the Vitamin Shoppe reported net sales of $750 million in fiscal year 2010), non-traditional practitioners (e.g. total revenue received by chiropractors is estimated by Hoovers to be about $10 billion), and seek medical advice from friends on Facebook (which may have directly saved at least one life).

What these data don't convey, however, is something I've had the privilege to experience first-hand: Doctors enjoy an exceptionally durable bond with patients—especially those patients with chronic illnesses. The level of trust reported by patients for their physicians is remarkable, and the role of physician as trusted adviser is difficult to overstate. It's a huge burden to manage disease on one's own, and it's generally reassuring to know your physician is with you at every step—something I believe still happens, by the way, although obviously not in every case.

The problem is, while patients may feel better by believing their physicians are delivering excellent care, this confidence may not always be warranted: The reality is that the care provided by doctors is uneven and inconsistent. While the importance of "discrepancies from standard of care" (a common performance metric) has probably been overstated (the evidence base for many guidelines can be pretty thin), it's also likely that a lot of patients would enjoy improved health if their doctors were simply better; look no further than the difficult time Peter Pronovost and colleagues have had getting physicians to do things as basic as washing hands and following simple checklists (see Better, by Atul Gawande, as well). And every medical resident knows about "gome docs," physicians who seem to provide unusually poor care, and yet are beloved by their patients. Some physicians are clearly much better than others, a phenomenon discussed with characteristic eloquence by Gawande in this wonderful essay focused on the care of children with cystic fibrosis.

So perhaps there are really two questions here: First, will doctors become obsolete? I doubt it, and suspect that reports of their demise have been greatly exaggerated. Second —and arguably more interestingly: Should (most) doctors become obsolete—or less provocatively, does the practice of medicine need to change? Here, the answer must be yes. We urgently need to track and review outcomes that can already be measured, and we must dramatically improve our ability to measure patient health and real-world effectiveness, so that physicians can get better, and patient care can improve.

This is a distinctly non-trivial undertaking. Medicine is a profoundly conservative discipline. Change comes slowly, and with great resistance. There's also a tremendous stake in maintaining a form of the status quo; I've also heard my share of stories about the risks of keeping score—I've heard of hospitals trying to maintain their favorable mortality statistics by transferring sick patients before they die, and I know of the pressures on physicians to give patients the suboptimal medicines they demand or risk a scathing patient review; and I appreciate as much as anyone how metrics can deceive, how algorithms can stultify (see also here and here), and I know how difficult it can be to capture some of the most vitally important aspects of patient care.

I am reminded of the famous quotation by management guru W. Edwards Deming—a quote often rendered, incorrectly, as "you can't manage what you don't measure." In fact, he wrote, "the most important figures that one needs for management are unknown or unknowable, but successful management must nevertheless take account of them."

Similarly, the challenge for medicine is not only to utilize patient-focused technologies to measure more precisely and more meaningfully the quality of care our patients receive, and the quality of life they are able to enjoy, but also to ensure that we recognize the inevitable limitations of measurement, and the unquantifiable benefit that can come from a reassuring nod, from a hand on the shoulder, from an empathetic doctor. "The good physician treats the disease," Sir William Osler said. "The great physician treats the patient who has the disease."

My hope is that, informed by metrics but driven by heart, the doctor of the future will be uniquely empowered to treat both. – DS

The Real Danger Of Medical Referrals: Physician Overconfidence + Lack Of Quality Assessment

Of the many factors that make improving the health system difficult, few challenges are greater than the misty-eyed recollection—often from genuinely distinguished practitioners—of how great things used to be. Doctors were highly regarded authority figures, pure and beloved, while patients were meek and grateful in the presence of such brilliance and expertise.

Of course, this caricature has been thoroughly debunked—perhaps to an excessive degree (I've actually argued that many of those jumping on the desperately hip "disrupt medicine" bandwagon may be missing or at least undervaluing important elements of the "traditional" doctor-patient relationship).

Nevertheless, it's still surprising how frequently we reference, and pine for, the supposedly good old days of medicine, a misinformed comparison that tends only to muddy the waters and prevent us from focusing in on the real problems to be solved.

A representative case in point is an article today from Smart Money describing the emerging business of specialist referrals. The basic idea is that if you see your primary care doctor, and need expert evaluation in a particular area (such as surgery or endocrinology), you get referred to an appropriate specialist. The article makes the point that while patients believe these referrals are on basis of their doctor's opinion of the expert's quality, in fact they may be based on the aggressive marketing of a dedicated consultant who the expert hired to increase business.

Unfortunately, rather than arguing *both* of these approaches are misguided, the author fondly invokes "a now-retired Nobel Prize winning cardiologist who practiced for more than five decades in the Boston area who says the emphasis [in the old days] was usually on someone's medical bona fides—where they trained, what they published and what they've accomplished as a healer. The bottom line, he says: 'They looked for patient outcomes.'"

Say what? If there's one thing abundantly clear about the practice of medicine (and look no further than this op-ed in the NYT, and this HBR contribution by same authors), it's the nearly total lack of visibility into actual outcomes, and beyond that, to physician quality.

It's true: we may have a sense of how knowledgeable other doctors may seem in conversation, we know where they trained and who they trained with, and we can figure out pretty quickly if their patients tend to like them or not; but do we know the quality of the care they ultimately are providing? Generally, the answer is no—and to believe otherwise suggests profound physician overconfidence, of exactly the sort described by Kahneman in so many other domains.

The key take-away from the medical referral story shouldn't be: let's go back to the old days when doctors cared enough to refer patients to the best specialists—or at least the specialists they knew best.

Instead, let's use this opportunity to think a bit more carefully about how to measure the quality of care (non-trivial), and particularly the ability of doctors to achieve improved patient outcomes. Such an approach could not only help primary care physicians give the best advice to their patients, but could also help the specialists themselves improve the care they provide, and elevate the overall quality of our medical system. – DS

Want To Revolutionize Health Care? Enable Physicians, Don't Replace Them

The reality of today's funding environment for digital health entrepreneurs is that it's traditional tech investors who have the lion's share of the money, while most long-time healthcare investors are on the ropes, contending with fleeing LPs and at least the perception of disappointing returns.

While it's great news that some tech funds seem interested in dipping their toes into the healthcare space, it's concerning that the investors with the most resources are not necessarily the ones who understand health care the best.

Tech investors, in general, are not always comfortable with physicians, and seem much more at home with engineers and developers. These investors also tend to gravitate to businesses selling directly to consumers rather than dealing with the sordid complexities of our current healthcare system.

Many tech investors are also—understandably—drawn to the power of data, and the possibility of analytics, a sensible affinity but one that at times can translate into an excessively reductive view of medicine that fails to capture the maddening but very real ambiguity of medical science, and especially of clinical practice.

While almost everyone contemplating the problems of the current healthcare system acknowledges that often stubborn, intransigent doctors can be part of the problem, it's arresting how many technologists don't also view doctors as a key element of the solution; instead, there seems to be a common, techno-utopian vision in which medicine has been profoundly disrupted, and the role of physicians largely replaced by computers —see here (a particularly vivid example), as well as here.

In the words of digital health investor and doctor Bijan Salehizadeh, "IT rooted VCs don't know how to relate to or speak the language of physicians. They bow at the altar of revolutionary disruption. That works in non-regulated consumer markets. Not in highly regulated hierarchical fragmented spaces like HCIT."

The more technology investors I speak with, the more I worry there's something elemental about medicine that many don't seem to understand—and worse, they don't always know what they don't know.

Doctors have a unique perspective

The experience of being a doctor provides unique insight into the meaning and significance of health.

For starters, as a physician, you develop a profound, overwhelming appreciation of how serious health is, and you experience and help patients and their families in dealing with every phase of illness. When I listen to a young entrepreneur extol his or her new approach to saving large files or sharing music as an example of changing the world, I appreciate and love their enthusiasm and passion—how can you not? At the same time, I also find myself reflecting upon other talks I've heard—Judah Folkman discussing his discovery of angiogenesis, or Bruce Walker discussing advances in HIV therapy—and I think: now this—*this* is changing the world.

Second, for all the emphasis placed in medicine on arriving at a diagnosis and suggesting a treatment, the truth is that medicine is just so much less precise than anyone could possibly imagine. Diseases, diagnoses, best practices: all are so much grayer and less-well demarcated than most appreciate, and patients are far more complex. For all the advances in molecular diagnostics and high-tech imaging, medicine remains far more scientism than science.

Third, once you've had the experience of caring for patients, had the privilege of developing relationships with patients over time, it's impossible not to be moved by the power, complexity, and importance of the doctor/patient connection. Twenty-something Palo Alto engineers may struggle to understand why anyone would waste time with human care providers, but I suspect the many patients with serious concerns or chronic conditions who are fortunate enough to receive regular care would likely offer a very different perspective on the value of this unique relationship.

At the same time, while physicians may genuinely aspire to deliver the best care possible, they demonstrably struggle achieving this; many rely on vague recollections rather than current data, and are notoriously reluctant to discard bad habits (such as not washing hands), and embracing new recommendations (such as utilizing a basic checklist), despite the demonstrated evidence for both.

The real opportunity in medicine, then, is not to replace physicians, but to enable them, and enable patients. This will entail recognizing the foundational value of the close, longitudinal relationship between doctor and patient, and then building off of this by creating tools for both patients and physicians that will enhance this therapeutic connection. To develop such tools, a company will need to combine deep healthcare knowledge with technological sophistication, and create solutions that deliver not just clicks, but durable improvements in patient health.

Areas of opportunity and challenge

One category of opportunity here is turning mHealth into mMedicine (to borrow two terms from Dr. David Albert, founder of AliveCor). Right now, there's an overwhelming number of consumer-focused wellness apps and fitness gadgets, products like the Eatery and Fitbit which may be pleasant to use, and could potentially support health. The real opportunity is robustifying these sorts of measurement technologies and approaches, so that they not only provide casual entertainment, but could also be used to drive and monitor real medical benefit—see here and here for a discussion on the importance of these sorts of measurements in medicine.

A second opportunity is behavior modification—a staggering amount of illness results from the many poor choices each of us make everyday, habits that are notoriously difficult to change. The degree of user engagement engendered by many gaming and social apps is remarkable, and could be harnessed to drive measurement improvements in health. Early versions of this have been used for employee wellness programs, but I suspect there are real opportunities for platforms that can maintain patient interest over time (a huge problem right now), and which can nudge the patient towards improved behaviors and better health.

A third category: care delivery/health system improvement. It's difficult to identify an individual aspect of the current care system—from hospital admissions to managing illness at home—that doesn't appear to be a historical relic, and which seems thoughtfully designed with the patient in mind. There are so many opportunities to rethink aspects of this, and ask how could this process be better constructed—ideally incorporating key aspects of design thinking. Traditionally, healthcare innovation has focused on new drugs and devices, but there's an increasing recognition of the need to improve systems as well—a key focus of leading-edge initiatives such as Dr. Arnold Milstein's Clinical Excellence Research Center at Stanford, aimed at improving healthcare services.

A fourth category: Chunking big data. While the idea of chasing big data in health is certainly not new, figuring out how to actually acquire the relevant data remains non-trivial, and turning this information into actionable insight remains an abiding challenge—with the key word being actionable, i.e. usable by physicians, or patients, in as frictionless—and ideally delightful—a fashion as possible. Success will require far more than robust analytics. Combining clinical and payor data, meanwhile could be used to support value-based healthcare, highlighting the best way to allocate limited resources. This information could used to improve the quality and efficiency of care, and also could be provided to other financial stakeholders (which will likely increasingly include patients themselves) to support informed decision making, a la Castlight.

A key challenge that all entrepreneurs face, and which seems especially pronounced in the healthcare space, is finding not only an important problem to solve, but a way to get paid for solving it. The perverse incentives in the current healthcare system mean that in many cases, physicians and hospitals are actually rewarded for not being better—they often make money on the extra charges that suboptimal care can generate.

This may explain better than anything else why tech investors like consumer plays—investors understand them, and know how to assess the value, how to monitor, and when to pivot. They've also made a lot of money on at least some of these companies, and understand the business model.

In contrast—and unfortunately—the business case for improving care can be surprisingly difficult to make; it's likely that entrepreneurs may need to carefully identify a specific situation (a concierge practice? A private oncology clinic?) where their proposed improvements can demonstrate the most compelling impact. It's also why some forward-thinking healthcare entrepreneurs such as Avado's Dave Chase have focused so much of their efforts on the need for incentives better aligned with patients' interests.

Partnerships **for the Future**

While there's not going to be a magic formula for digital health companies, a leadership team combining healthcare and technology experiences seems a common pattern.

"Homogenous teams all coming from outside of healthcare have the deck stacked against them," digital health investor Salehizadeh asserts. "The best teams couple doctors with savvy business people or technical founders."

These sorts of partnership are exactly what Halle Tecco of digital health incubator Rock Health, say she's seeing among many of the young companies Rock Health supports.

According to Tecco, "Any startup that excludes the MD perspective puts themselves at a disadvantage… just like any doctor-founded company that overlooks design or business model puts themselves at a disadvantage. Most startups in the space need it all! An understanding of the system, an insight for disruptive business models, an eye for design, and a back-end engineering ninja to help the product scale." She adds, "This is an exciting time for cross-collaboration."

While it's far too early to say whether these collaborations are going to yield transformative digital health companies, it's hard to argue with the approach. Moreover, given the urgent need for innovative healthcare solutions, we should all hope that these broad-based partnerships involving physicians and technologists represent the beginning of a wonderful, productive, and healthy relationship. – DS

Do You Believe Doctors Are Systems, My Friends?

In *The New Yorker*, surgeon Atul Gawande provocatively suggests that medicine needs to become more like The Cheesecake Factory—more standardized, better quality control, with a touch of room for slight customization and innovation.

The basic premise, of course, isn't new, and seems closely aligned with what I've heard articulated from a range of policy experts (such as Arnold Milstein) and management experts (such as Clayton Christensen, specifically in his book The Innovator's Prescription).

The core of the argument is this: the traditional idea that your doctor is an expert who knows what's best for you is likely wrong, and is both dangerous and costly. Instead, for most conditions, there are a clear set of guidelines, perhaps even algorithms, that should guide care, and by not following these pathways, patients are subjected to what amounts to arbitrary, whimsical care that in many cases is unnecessary and sometimes even harmful—and often with the best of intentions.

According to this view, the goal of medicine should be to standardize where possible, to the point where something like 90% of all care can be managed by algorithms—ideally, according to many, not requiring a physician's involvement at all (most care would be administered by lower-cost providers). A small number of physicians still would be required for the difficult cases—and to develop new algorithms.

A variant of this view, discussed by technologists such as Vinod Khosla, and commentators such as John Goodman, imagines that one day even the low-cost providers can be cut out of the loop, and patients (consumers) can do most of the work with their computer and perhaps a few gadgets.

Doctors, as you might expect, tend to reject this vision of standardization, as it ruthlessly undercuts the view that physicians are particularly wise, special, insightful—and worthy of autonomy—and instead seems to assert that medicine should be run like an assembly line, with limited opportunity for customization.

The patient perspective may be more complicated: on the one hand, it's absolutely true that the current system generally fails even the most basic standards of customer service. There's virtually nothing in the current system that appears to be designed around patients; Gawande shares an example about the care a patient received in the emergency room that could have been told, with few modifications, by virtually everyone I know, and holds true whether you're talking about a small community hospital or one of the nation's leading teaching centers.

In other words, learning a bit about customer service from The Cheesecake Factory—or a number of other industry-leaders—would do medicine a world of good.

On the other hand, I worry that a lot of medicine really isn't quite as reducible, as standardizable, as many of the advocates and management gurus would like to believe, and by doing the classic economics trick of "assuming a can opener"—assuming medicine is standardizable because, gosh, wouldn't it be nice if it were—these experts may not be helping as much as they'd like to imagine.

Patients deserve and increasingly demand far better "customer service" than they currently receive; at the same time, at least the patients who are fortunate enough to have physicians tend to give them surprisingly high marks. Critics contend this is how the system is harmful to patients—patients can be suckered by good bedside manner, and not realize how poor the care actually is.

Yet, I'd argue that given the incredibly limited amount of solid evidence for most things in medicine, the individual relationship between physician and patient can be of remarkable therapeutic value (although perhaps less so in surgery than in internal medicine).

Thus, while Gawande claims that "Patients just won't look for the best specialist anymore, they'll look for the best system," I wonder whether this is generally true and realistic. While Romney was roundly criticized for suggesting that "corporations are people," I wonder if Gawande is overreaching in making the reverse claim: essentially, that "doctors are systems," and that patients should, and will, reach for the best system, not the best person.

I certainly appreciate where Gawande's coming from here, but I also worry that we might lose something important by accepting this premise—something vital and distinctive about the patient-doctor relationship that is unlikely to be captured with the same depth and nuance if it's instead between a patient and a system.

As I've previously discussed, it's a challenge to balance consistency and innovation, and it's difficult to know how best to remove the "bad" variability in care delivery while still supporting the customization of care so central to medicine, and to healing. We might want our $15 dinners to look the same, but I doubt most of us want our medical care delivered in as rote a fashion.

The question is whether there's a way to improve care and preserve individualization, and avoid imposing what is effectively centralized control and a litany of standardized processes.

Doctors may be running out of time to figure this out. The writing is on wall (and, it seems, everywhere else as well). If doctors don't want to wind up as commoditized participants in a Taylorized vision of medicine they will need to recognize their limitations and seriously up their game.

I've too much respect for the practice of medicine and too much concern for the care of patients to believe that the Cheesecake Factory really defines how we want American medicine to be served. – DS

Humanism In Digital Health: Do We Have To Sacrifice Personal Connections As We Improve Efficiency?

The human connection is threatened by medicine's increasingly reductive focus on data collection, algorithms, and information transaction.

If you follow digital health, Rachel King's recent *Wall Street Journal* piece on Stanford physician Abraham Verghese should be required reading, as it succinctly captures the way compassionate, informed physicians wrestle with emerging technologies—especially the electronic medical record.

For starters, Verghese understands its appeal: "The electronic medical record is a wonderful thing, in general, a huge improvement on finding paper charts and finding the old records and trying to put them all together."

At the same, he accurately captures the problem: "The downside is that we're spending too much time on the electronic medical record and not enough at the bedside."

This tension is not unique to digital health, and reflects a more general struggle between technologists who emphasize the efficient communication of discrete data, and others (humanists? Luddites?) who worry that in the reduction of complexity to data, something vital may be lost.

Technologists, it seems, tend to view activities like reading and medicine as fundamentally data transactions. So it makes sense to receive reading information electronically on your Kindle—what could be more efficient?

At the same time, it's hard not to resonate with humorist Joe Queenen, when he movingly writes, "People who need to possess the physical copy of a book, not merely an electronic version, believe that the objects themselves are sacred."

He adds, "Certain things are perfect the way they are. The sky, the Pacific Ocean, procreation and the Goldberg Variations all fit this bill, and so do books. Books are sublimely visceral, emotionally evocative objects that constitute a perfect delivery system."

I read this, and on many levels, agree. While I appreciate the convenience and immediacy of a Kindle, it doesn't compare with reading a real book to my kids before bed. At the same time, however, I'm sure that when the automobile first arrived, many swore never to forsake their trusted horse and buggy.

Is there something deep and emotional about books that Vulcan-like engineers are missing, or are they better able to embrace the future, while others resist change and cling atavistically to the past?

The issues in medicine, of course, seem strikingly similar: Technologists (and others) tend to see medicine as fundamentally a data exercise, where you seek to collect information and make a rational decision.

This perspective was evident in a notable dialog between Google's Eric Schmidt and the New Yorker's Atul Gawande, and was also an important feature of VC Vinod Khosla's vision of an algorithm-dominated health care future (here,here), a viewpoint that generated a significant response (here , here, and here).

The electronic medical record has been a particular nidus of tension, as it seems to perfectly capture the transformation of medicine from a day when it was—choose your descriptor—[more personal/less robust] to a future when it will be [less human/more effective].

While, like Verghese, I intend to conclude that both technology and humanism are vital, I want to argue for something stronger than a Solomonic, "split the difference" compromise.

My sense is that most physicians, like Verghese, are all too aware that traditional record-keeping is terrible, and that vital patient information can be difficult to track down, much less share in a timely fashion with other providers. They would love a better approach, and would welcome intuitive technology—although most would emphatically not place the majority of current electronic medical record options in this category.

I'm far less sanguine about the ability of engineers to recognize, appreciate, or value the "soft-side" of medicine, and fear most regard the patient-doctor relationship as an inefficient and antiquated tradition whose time has passed.

Indeed, many technologists view doctors themselves as an outdated profession—like carriage drivers, or librarians (apparently the exemplar of choice among technologists). In Silicon Valley, there seems to be a palpable (though certainly not universal) disdain for physicians, who seem to be regarded as healthcare's fundamental problem rather than potentially part of an emerging solution.

For his part, Verghese embraces new technology, or at least, tries to. King writes, "Just as he's found ways to bring technology to the bedside and integrate it with patient care, he would like to find a way to integrate inputting data into electronic medical records more seamlessly with the actual exam."

"We have to find ways to not separate the two processes so much, and I'm not sure what the answer is," Verghese says, capturing digital health's greatest challenge and most significant opportunity.

I deeply believe medicine's value far transcends data collection and evidence-based decision making; there is a vital human connection that is threatened because it's so difficult to reduce to zeros and ones.

The danger is that if we don't find a way to recognize, express, and capture the value of the human connection in medicine, we are unlikely to preserve it, and it will become engineered out of healthcare – at least until an entrepreneurial, humanistic developer appreciates just how important and valued such connection can be. – DS

Workflow Is The New Plastics. Open EMRs Should Show, Not Tell

A few quick thoughts on two digital health topics—workflow and EMRs—dominating (at least my) conversations at a recent JP Morgan conference and elsewhere.

Workflow. There's not a term that emerges more frequently in my conversation with stakeholders, as everyone seems to agree that workflow, as currently structured, is horrible. Not only is this true on the clinical care side, but it permeates almost every area of healthcare administration as well. While many other industries seem to have figured workflow out, healthcare, manifestly has not.

Consequently, this represents both an important consideration and a tremendous opportunity for anyone thinking about entering the space: it's difficult but essential for new products either to integrate seamlessly into existing workflows (and hence not make anyone's job even worse) or, ideally, to find an implementable way to streamline existing workflow and get the system into a better place.

EMRs. The shocking statistic to emerge from the most recent Rock Health digital health investment report was the relatively small amount of new dollars that went into venture-backed EMR companies in 2012, suggesting a reluctance to compete with established players, notably Epic.

There seem to be two schools of thought around Epic: one (recently discussed here by Bessemer VCs Kraus and Bhattacharyya) suggests essentially that the battle may be over, Epic seems to have won, and the smart money should go to companies that position themselves under, around, or on top of the Epic platform—or (on the service side) who consult on Epic-related issues.

Others, however—including CEOs of cloud-based EMRs (see this priceless recent interview with Athenaheath's Jonathan Bush), and (especially) their investors, argue that it's absurd to concede to what they view as a benighted company that employs such a closed and outdated approach—and which seems to be universally despised by virtually all who use it.

Both groups are right—sort of: short-term, investing in Epic adjacencies makes a lot of sense. It's also true that even many institutions who use Epic have likely held their nose while making the decision, and would thrill to a better choice down the road. But for the moment, Epic solves problems for health systems in a comprehensive way that many other EMRs do not.

And while competitors endlessly tout the value of the cloud, and of open architecture, they must take the next step and show why this matters—they must demonstrate to users, for example, that the increased access to innovation enabled by an open system translates, in compelling fashion, into an improved user experience. This is precisely what Athenahealth seeks to do with their "MDP" (More Disruption, Please) concept; the proof will be in the pudding. – DS

Recipe For Relevance: Blend Digital Health Developers And Clinical Providers

I wanted to capture a few quick top-of-mind reactions to a much-needed, well-executed event I recently attended, a "Meeting of the Minds," co-sponsored by the digital health incubator Rock Health and the UCSF Clinical and Translational Science Institute (CTSI). The goal: bring together health care providers who have specific pain points with technologists eager to develop solutions.

This event happened to showcase several of my favorite themes: the importance of "field discovery" (i.e. innovation driven by practitioners, as described by MIT Professor Eric von Hippel), the need to create more useful digital health companies (vs more trivial apps); and the need to crowdsource problems not just solutions.

The organizers—particularly UCSF surgeon Aenor Sawyer—clearly put a lot of effort into selecting the handful of healthcare speakers, and in guiding them to succinctly describe their key problems.

The result was a captivating, diverse series of presentations highlighting key challenges with which various folks at UCSF were actively struggling:

Ralph Gonzales, an internist and epidemiologist with an interest in health systems, discussed the increasing use of specialists, and the associated impact on healthcare costs; his specific question was whether alternative approaches (perhaps technology-enabled) could reduce the need for follow-up visits with specialists.

Christine Ritchie, a geriatrician, discussed the increasing use of potentially dangerous opioids to manage chronic pain in the elderly, and asked whether there were approaches that could permit the more comprehensive monitoring of such patients between visits.

Kate Possin, a researcher in UCSF's Center for Memory and Aging, discussed the rising incidence of dementia, and emphasized the need for improved assessment tools for early cognitive impairment, tools both sensitive and efficient.

Kirby Lee, a faculty member of UCSF's School of Pharmacy, provided an overview of the remarkably complex challenges of medication adherence; he highlighted some of the solutions already available, and emphasized that an effective solution might bring together existing tools in a creative way.

Christine Kennedy, a researcher and pediatric nurse, discussed the need for health applications that are relevant in the community, where the degree of "health literacy" may be appreciably lower than most developers appreciate. In particular, she highlighted the need for greater use of images and videos, and tools that help "regular" people (i.e. not QS fitness freaks [my phrase not hers]) increase activity in their daily lives.

Michael Turken, a thoughtful fourth year med student at UCSF, reviewed the existing process of medical training, and pointed out a number of specific areas where technology-enabled approaches might be helpful.

Is this forum going to lead to the next (some wags would say first) great digital health company? Who knows. But I was delighted and heartened by the approach, which in many cases surfaced opportunities that those outside of healthcare might never have known about, or conceptualized correctly.

I was also pleased by the range of topics; while perhaps a bit heavy on the operational improvement side, you could also see how some solutions (e.g. to the improved assessment of early cognitive impairment) might lead to profound basic scientific insights as well.

If some of the presentations were flawed, it was in their vision of their problem, a perspective that (understandably) tended towards the immediate and pragmatic. For example, during the discussion of how technology might be used to help med students memorize anatomy, metabolic pathways, and differential diagnoses, all I could think (not for the first time) was how pointless—especially given our access to technology—so much of this rote memorization is. As Clay Christensen might say, we might want to take a more careful look in some of these areas at the underlying problem that truly needs to be solved.

Given the size, energy, and motivation of the developer community, and the number of challenges healthcare providers contend with every day, I can imagine that it might make sense for Rock Health and UCSF's CTSI program to consider repeating this event, virtually —bringing together geographically dispersed developers to address discrete pain points described succinctly by similarly dispersed providers and researchers.

True, provider/technologist meetups—whether live or virtual—are unlikely to provide a panacea for our nation's healthcare challenges; however, they could easily spark ideas and establish connections, and lead to new approaches to medically-relevant questions. – DS

Four Reasons Doctors Worry About Social Media—#GetOverIt

I'm fortunate enough to spend a lot of time interacting with physicians, entrepreneurs, and investors on the bleeding edge of digital health—and it's a consistently thrilling experience.

At the same time, the continuous exposure to the imaginative and the extraordinary can also be a bit deceptive. Self-associating groups, as Sunstein has discussed, tend to adopt relatively extreme views, and it's easy to envision this happening in Silicon Valley in general, and to digital health innovators in particular.

Consequently, it was probably healthy, and certainly arresting, to attend a breakout session on social media at recent a medical conference; the audience members were mostly practicing physicians, seemed passionate about patient care, and were explicitly interested in learning about social media. Yet, most of the clinicians were not prepared to embrace it, and many were poignantly struggling to come to terms with a phenomenon they recognized as important, yet which viscerally troubled them.

Their concerns seem to fall into four categories, two involving patients, and two involving physicians.

1. Patients Receiving "Bad" Information

Many physicians described the challenges of dealing with patients who had retrieved wrong or incomplete information from the internet. This turns out to be a remarkably common problem; doctors reported spending a lot of time undoing bad information.

The challenge was highlighted by the observation that 25% of Google searches for headache reportedly discuss brain tumors, even though such a diagnosis would be exceptionally uncommon. The thought was that while physicians have learned during their training to appropriately weigh pre-test probabilities, patients have not, and are likely to fixate on extreme diagnoses rather than those that are most likely.

It seemed to me that "Dr. Google" upset many doctors not only because it complicated office visits, but also because it fundamentally altered the traditional doctor/patient relationship; as one physician said—verbatim—"I've lost my authority." It's hard not to see this as a profound shift in perspective many experienced physicians understandably struggle to manage.

2. Patients Transmitting "Bad" Information

Many doctors in the audience were also visibly troubled by the ease with which patients could share "misleading" information, whether about medicine or the doctors themselves.

Despite the clear repudiation of a link between vaccines and autism, for instance, many patients continue to worry, a concern reportedly spurred on by an active internet anti-vaccine community.

Doctors were also fretting about the ease with which disgruntled patients could use the internet to besmirch reputations—one physician complained that when he Googled himself, the first links that came up were bad reviews he said represented a small number of extremely vocal patients.

3. Physicians Receiving Information Badly

While some senior physicians worried that young doctors might start to rely on tweets rather than peer-reviewed articles, it seemed that the most significant concern raised was the impact that the "internet culture" was having on the practice of medicine. "We need to teach students that traditional values are still important," one audience member said (again, verbatim), suggesting that students have become progressively less reflective.

The use of mobile devices—what consultants call "phone hygiene"—emerged as a particular source of physician aggravation. Rounding residents would routinely look at the cell phones rather than pay attention to either the patients or the senior doctors, leading at least one doctor to prohibit the use of mobile devices on rounds—except for a 5' phone break he built into the schedule, to accommodate what he described as the young doctors' obvious addiction.

Another senior doctor, in a complaint evocative of this recent, much-discussed NYT article, noted that residents would routinely update her by text, rather than by phone. She suggested this reflected a more general trend of young physician disengagement, evidently preferring to interact with devices rather than with other people.

4. Physicians Transmitting Information Badly

The ability afforded by social media to share information rapidly and broadly was another source of concern. Many senior physicians worried young doctors might use social media in unprofessional ways—sharing things they shouldn't, saying things they shouldn't—potentially placing themselves and their institutions at risk.

In some cases, even seemingly innocent activities might be deemed inappropriate. One young physician offered as an example a (medically-related) internet survey research project he wanted to do. He said that while he could do this very easily, nearly instantly, and essentially for nothing using Google, he learned from his department this would violate institutional policy, and to conduct the research with the required protections in place would cost at least $25,000; naturally, the research has not progressed.

Moving Forward

Predictably, medicine seems to be reacting to change the way it often does—by publishing (see Figure below) an ever-increasing number of journal articles (such as—not kidding—"Twitter for Neurosurgeons"), and by issuing well-intentioned (albeit largely unreadable) guidelines; this just-published position statement, from the American College of Physicians and the Federation of State Medical Boards, represents the genre well.

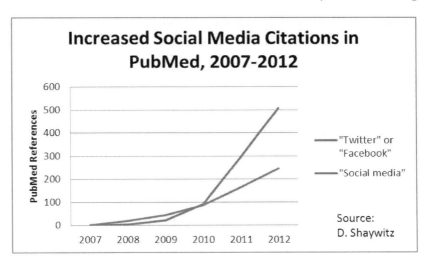

It could be that doctors have to go through familiar, well-established processes as a way of coping with things that seem so new. At the same time, it's hard not to get the feeling that organized medicine is effectively solemnizing the vitality out of social media. From reading all of the dry documentation discussing social media, you'd struggle to come away with any real sense of why it's so exciting and engaging.

To be sure, many of the critiques offered by senior physicians who offer the wisdom of their experience are spot on. They're right about the hazards of online diagnosis, and right to worry about the potential harm that can be associated with the disproportional amplification of voice the internet can offer. They're also right to urge young doctors to remember the value of professional behavior, and to celebrate reflection as a virtue.

But I also suspect many senior physicians are struggling—not always successfully—to envision a world that operates in a very different way, at a very different speed, and in a very different style than that to which they've grown accustomed.

I reject the view that the internet and social media are somehow degrading the culture of medicine, or causing it to change for the worse. Instead, I see emerging modalities as offering the profession an urgently needed chance to radically update its approach, and interact with patients, data, and each other in important new ways. Care can evolve from episodic to continuous, and physicians, increasingly accountable, will appreciate the opportunity to partner with patients who are informed, empowered, and engaged.

Rather than isolating doctors, the new technology promises to be fundamentally enabling, allowing doctors to redefine and strengthen their relationships—with patients and with colleagues. The result: a new sense of connection and meaning.

Medicine could be fun again. – DS

V.

Pharma, Biotech, Device Companies

Open Innovation—An Emerging Hope For Biopharma?

This is a time of profound negativity and concern within the biopharma industry, as old products face patent expiration and new products have not been developed to replace them. Much of the blame has been attributed to a failure of the pharmaceutical industry to innovate, which has, in true academic fashion, led to a slew of publications and presentations on "The end of innovation."

It's a little silly, and perhaps just a shade too tidy and convenient, to lay the blame for this at the feet of industry alone—my sense (as I've previously argued) is that if scientists from both universities and industry had been able to better characterize and more deeply understanding the fundamental basis of most dreadful diseases, then more effective drugs would certainly have been forthcoming. The difference is that while you can be a successful academic researcher by publishing papers, a biopharma company must generally drive the science into actual application in order to be rewarded, and while the standards for drug approval seems to be continuously climbing, the proliferation of journal articles (generally in the absence of meaningful clinical progress) suggests that academic research may not be similarly burdened by escalating expectations. Moreover —as I've also argued previously—I think this makes sense, it's great to have more data available for discussion—but let's not confuse this heat with genuine light. (More on the fragility of academic research here [my take] and here [great posting by Bruce Booth].)

In the midst of this miasma, however, there is also some emerging hope, in the form of the Sage Commons Congress focused on open innovation in medical science (terrific article on Sage by Xconomy's Luke Timmerman here). Disclosure: I was a founding advisor to Sage, which was founded by Stephen Friend—who leads the non-profit—and Eric Schadt—the wunderkind geneticist here profiled in Esquire.

The theme emerging from an earlier meeting was that biomedical innovation is impeded by, among other things, constrained communication and interaction between scientists; knowledge turns (to use the much-cited phrase former Intel CEO Andy Grove discussed in this JAMA article [abstract only, unfortunately]) need to be accelerated, and scientists in different labs need to share data and information as if working side-by-side. The most compelling presentation by far was an exceptional moving talk by Josh Sommer, who (together with his mother) established the Chordoma foundation after he was diagnosed with the disease in 2006, while a freshman at Duke University (you can watch the talk here). Josh's goal—obviously shared by so many others with so many different conditions —is to accelerate the development of a cure, and he poignantly describes his often frustrating effort to get academic scientists to collaborate, work together, and share information. Both the need for such collaboration and the tremendous power of open innovation is what I think has attracted so much interest—and particularly so much passion—to Sage and other open innovation initiatives.

The need for open innovation in drug discovery is increasingly recognized, and at least discussed, by many industry experts, including former Lilly strategist, and recent founder of "Innothink" Bernard Munos, in the latest issue of In Vivo (again, only small excerpt available—here). As a colleague and I discussed in the Boston Globe, open innovation could help identify new uses for existing medications, emphasizing the value of "inquisitive physicians" (to borrow the late Judah Folkman's phrase—unfortunately a posting of his legendary Soma Weiss address on this topic isn't available, but should be) and the potential downstream harms of an overly restrictive regulatory process (as discussed recently in greater detail by the AEI's Scott Gottlieb in his chapter of this collection).

I was recently introduced to a fascinating article from 2006 that provides data supporting the value of open innovation—termed "field discovery"—in figuring out new places to uses an existing drug. The research—by Harold DeMonaco of MGH, Ayfer Ali of the Harvard School of Public Health, and Eric von Hippel from MIT-Sloan—looks into the origins of new indications for new molecular entities approved by the FDA in 1998. The remarkable finding is that the majority of new indications were "discovered by practicing clinicians through field discovery." These clinician-innovators (a subset of whom were subsequently contacted by the authors), came up with their ideas on their own in order to solve a pressing clinical problem they had encountered; no industry sponsorship or direction was noted or discerned.

I draw two conclusions from these data: first, the research highlights the value of open innovation, of permitting those with the best understanding of "the problem to be solved" to actually solve the problem. Second, it also highlights the role of the inquisitive physician, and emphasizes (as Flowers and Melmon Argued in Nature Medicine in 1997) the impact an impassioned physician (or, I'd argue, care provider, patient, or invested loved one) can have in the development of new medical therapies.

Margaret Mead famously advised, "Never doubt that a small group of thoughtful, committed citizens can change the world. Indeed, it is the only thing that ever has." Open innovation communities provide a mechanism to capture, amplify, and leverage the focused input of such thoughtful citizens; our challenge now is to change the world. – DS

The Next Killer App

New drugs are subject to exhaustive critical scrutiny, yet there has never been a corresponding effort to collect reports of drugs delivering unexpected benefits. If open innovation can lead to the creation of the world's most complete encyclopedia, a top-selling cleaning duster, and the game Angry Birds, it's time to ask whether this approach might be used to capture the exceptional untapped value associated with existing drugs, and to power the discovery of important new medicines.

Half a century ago, astute clinicians noticed that patients receiving the new anti-tuberculosis drug iproniazid experienced an enhanced sense of wellbeing, a chance observation that led directly to the development of antidepressants and the birth of psychopharmacology. More recently, an unexpected side effect reported by patients in a clinical trial of a drug for chest pain led to the development of Viagra.

These stories of medical discovery may not be so unusual. The idea of using a leukemia drug for stomach cancer, an anti-seizure drug for nerve pain, a cancer drug for gout—all were impactful suggestions proposed by physicians or researchers outside the company developing the drug.

In the age of Facebook and Google, it seems there should be a better, more systematic way of harnessing this communal wisdom and cultivating this sort of medical discovery. Enter open innovation.

Open innovation describes a range of approaches for sourcing ideas externally. These approaches share an appreciation for the richness of ideas and experiences in the world as a whole.

The remarkable power of the open innovation approach and mindset is obvious to anyone who has used Wikipedia, shopped for an iPad app, or used a Swiffer duster—a product developed through Procter & Gamble's "Connect and Develop" open initiative.

A thoughtfully constructed open innovation platform built around existing medications could offer enormous value in the development of new therapeutics. Consider a community where patients and physicians share their experiences with a specific drug, contributing their expertise for the same reasons that lead so many people to offer

Amazon reviews, Wikipedia revisions, and Twitter tweets.

A critical mass of participants could identify the unexpected benefits of a medication, and elicit suggestions for new uses. Some of these individual insights might lead to exploratory research studies, generating data that could be deposited in open-source fashion so that others could leverage and learn from it. If these early studies seem promising, rigorous company-sponsored clinical trials could then be conducted to appropriately validate the proposed new indication.

Many of the required components currently exist separately in some form—physicians discuss cases on the websites Sermo and Ozmosis; patients discuss their experiences on PatientsLikeMe and on many disease-oriented websites; while open-access data repositories are offered by both governmental organizations, such as the NIH, and non-profit groups, such as Sage Bionetworks. Yet, there remains a need for a common forum, a community where patients and physicians can interact and iterate, motivated by a desire for understanding, and grounded in a common set of accessible data.

Why aren't drug development companies trying to set up such open innovation communities to explore potential new applications for their products? The short answer is: they're not allowed. As useful as it might be to introduce an open innovation platform, any attempt to explore potentially unexpected benefits of a product would almost certainly be critiqued by regulators and industry scolds as "off-label promotion," subjecting the offending company to significant fines and its officers to profound legal consequences.

Companies are also hesitant about seeking any additional knowledge beyond the bare minimum needed to garner approval and fulfill safety obligations, for fear of attracting too much attention from overeager regulators, hammers in search of nails, a phenomenon research analyst Jack Scannell refers to as the "Narrow Clinical Search Problem."

To foster the discovery of important new medicines, regulators will need to re-envision themselves as vital enablers of intelligent drug development, and consider the many benefits—both established and unrecognized—of new medications, as well as the real harms of suppressing innovation.

The very quantity and visibility of information generated by an open innovation platform might paradoxically provide the greatest hope, as the sheer abundance of information will emphasize the need not to overweigh any individual data point, while the transparency of data will ensure statistically suspect analyses are appropriately challenged.

Ultimately, of course, the success of an open platform will rest with the community of users themselves. If patients and physicians volunteer experiences in an open and honest fashion, and engage in interactive conversation, the result could be a remarkable opportunity to learn from existing drugs in an unprecedented fashion, accelerating the discovery of powerful new therapies.

A killer app? No, but potentially, a life-saving one. – DS + Mathai Mammen

The Golden Mean: Balancing Innovation And Execution In Biopharma

As the biopharmaceutical industry looks to revitalize itself through innovation, a lot of companies have started to think deeply about what it means to be more innovative. In the WSJ, I review an interesting new book by Peter Sims called Little Bets that discusses the importance of deliberate experimentation in innovation and highlights the role of thoughtful improvisation in driving progress.

The difficulty, as I see it, isn't that most people fail to appreciate the value of trying new things, and more generally, pursuing a portfolio of options. Rather, it's that almost everyone wants to be the one doing the diversifying, and often wants the entities within their portfolio (companies, programs, people) to execute in a lean and focused fashion.

For example, growth investors generally want their companies to relentlessly pursue a specific thesis, often high risk/high reward; for these investors, each company in their portfolio is a small bet. But most companies prefer to diversify and hedge their risk—statistically safer for them, but not necessarily what their investors had in mind. The pattern extends down through project teams even to the level of an individual employee, who must balance pursuit of promised objectives with the ability to pivot if something changes. In each of these situations, everyone understands the value of small bets—the issue is that each person wants to be the one holding the cards.

From a management perspective, the dilemma is that in the short term, investing in game-changing "disruptive" innovations are a drag on the balance sheet. Organizations are always seeking ways to cut costs; this is especially true these days for pharma companies, as they anticipate patent expiries. Without a serious long-term commitment, and mandate, from senior management, pursuit of such so-called "non-core" activities face serious, even prohibitive, challenges. (See this thoughtful HBR piece by Clay Christensen and colleagues for an excellent discussion of how the financial value of disruptive innovation is systematically underestimated.)

It's also critical to recognize the very real limitations of constant experimentation—the success of any innovation requires not just a promising idea, but also focused and determined execution. I imagine someone could write a parallel volume to "Little Bets" (and probably several exist already) arguing that it's all about execution, and that in practice, the actual limitations on innovative success are the fortitude to stay with a difficult idea, grinding through the sweat and tears to ensure it becomes a reality.

Such perseverance is as vitally important in academia as it is in business—I can think of many graduate students who were brimming with potentially interesting ideas, but were never able to muster the focus needed to shepherd any individual idea through the necessary period of unglamorous, gritty exploration, and would instead constantly jump to something new.

By contrast, the most successful academics I know are relentless about following up promising ideas, ensuring they are adequately developed and successfully published. (I suspect there are actually far more academics whose career success results from the dogged pursuit of mediocre ideas than from the tepid pursuit of great thoughts.)

The obvious answer, of course, is that it's all about balance—both exploration and execution are essential, and you need to know when to do each. But therein lies the rub. Consider this disturbing thought: perhaps it's not really possible for anyone to know, for any particular situation, just what the right balance is. Arguably, "the right balance" is largely dependent upon randomness, externalities that are impossible to foresee despite one's best guesses, and potentially out of one's control.

Nevertheless, the success stories will be captured in business books, case studies,and on the "analog" slides so popular among consultants and bankers; the wins will be attributed to brilliant thinking (and implicitly, to great advice), while the failures (though frequently the result of similar advice and a similar strategy) will quickly be forgotten. (See The Halo Effect by Phil Rosenzweig, or Fooled by Randomness by Nassim Taleb for a more complete discussion of these issues. Additional books recs can also be found here.)

I continue to believe—strongly—that good management matters; while you may not always be able to make good decisions, you can certainly avoid making some very bad ones. In biopharma, specifically, I deeply believe in the value of—and absolute requirement for—effective execution, but I remain passionate about the primacy of good new ideas, the value of R&D, and the importance of innovation. I've witnessed the "innovation dissipation" that can occur in large corporate structures that kill new ideas not by fiat but through stultifying bureaucracy, onerous processes, and falsely precise spreadsheets and modeling, as previously discussed here.

It's not surprising that some of the most innovative leaders carefully protect nascent ideas from institutional antibodies, especially those associated with productivity metrics. Sims writes that at Amazon, "when trying something new, Jeff Bezos and his senior team (known as the S Team) don't try to develop elaborate financial projections or return on investment calculations. 'You can't put into a spreadsheet how people are going to behave around a new project,' Bezos will say."

Similarly, Mark Fishman, head of R&D at Novartis, has reportedly banished the use of sales forecasts from early research, and (in a stimulating 2008 HBR article by Amabile and Khaire) has derided Six Sigma as "one device that has destroyed more innovation than any other," adding that efficiency-minded management "has no place in the discovery phase."

Steve Jobs's dictum, "People don't know what they want if they haven't seen it" seems especially relevant for drug development, as huge resources are spent trying to figure out what patients and physicians want, yet the ability of such market research to anticipate the value of a novel product is notoriously poor, as discussed in this JCI article by former pharma VP Jose Cuatrecasas. (I've yet to meet a senior pharma commercial executive who will acknowledge this limitation.)

Overconfidence in forecasting turns out to be a more general problem, as concisely summarized by noted University of Chicago behavioral economist Richard Thaler in this NYT piece.

Innovation continues to matter for Big Pharma. But, as Anthony Nicholls notes, simply restructuring themselves in the image of biotechs may not be the magic answer. It's worth noting there's little evidence that biotechs are any more productive than big pharma. It's just that they often evaporate when they fail, and their losses tend to be invisible, rather than accounted for on a balance sheet, as HBS professor Gary Pisano discusses in his book Science Business.

I've seen so many people within big pharma who were attracted by the opportunity to make important new medicines, and who still, despite everything (including the formidable internal challenges as well as the relentless attacks of the pharmascolds), maintain this worthy ambition.

The challenge for top pharma leaders—a challenge that I'm not sure most big pharma execs either fully appreciate or deeply believe—is to recognize this potential, engage these aspirations, and support and enable these latent innovators, before it is too late. – DS

Biopharma + Digital Health

Biopharma—especially big pharma—gets all sorts of grief for being large, stodgy, and unable to innovate (or evolve); this Corey Goodman interview represents the perspective well.

Before writing off these companies entirely, however (an ignorant reaction in any case), it's important to consider how much experience they have in doing two very difficult, very important things: (a) documenting the medical value of their products through a rigorous series of clinical studies conducted in a highly regulated environment; and (b) navigating their way through a complex maze of stakeholders in order to successfully market their products.

Much of the difficulties facing the industry these days stem not from their lack of regulatory experience or marketing skill, but rather from the intrinsic value proposition of the products they offer; simply put, making an impactful new drug is extremely hard and quite expensive, as this Matt Herper's piece makes clear.

My sense is that the view from the digital health/start-up side is in many ways the mirror-image of this: the space seems to be brimming with promising nascent ideas; yet, as I've discussed before, the measurable health impact of these technologies is usually unclear (at best).

Some emerging digital health companies don't worry about this—they are deliberately seeking to circumvent the regulatory process by aiming directly at consumers, and avoiding explicit health claims. Others seem to be leaning pretty heavily on the concept of being so disruptive that, in effect, the world will change for them.

I'd suggest that there still is a huge opportunity for digital companies that are keen to robustly demonstrate health benefits, at the high level of rigor that is standard in the medical products industry.

Looked at from this perspective, it seems there should be an opportunity for convergence here, a way to combine big pharma's experience in demonstrating clinical significance and value to stakeholders with digital health's likely (if unproven) ability to develop novel products that might make a difference. Perhaps digital health startups are creating the impactful health products that pharma so desperately seeks—but just not in a form pharma is prepared to see and able to handle.

And yes, there's the money thing: pharma is able to charge a lot for drugs that eventually make it on the market—but again, this is proving to be the vanishingly rare exception. It's hard to see how you couldn't make a business out of a digital health innovation whose worth you are able to robustly demonstrate—and demonstrate at a cost likely to be much less than that of developing a new drug, probably at much lower risk, and also with the opportunity to adapt and refine your approach along the way, in a fashion not really possible with a traditional drug.

One final thought here: not only do I believe this convergence is coming, but I'm going to go out on a limb and predict that the early adopters here will be generics companies like Teva (I've no relationship with this company), both because they've historically been more inventive, and because they are in a good position to readily apply some of these digital technologies to their existing products, a logical intermediate step in the evolution that may occur.

Right now, generic companies are competing primarily on cost, yet one can imagine that by bundling the appropriate companion technologies to their products (e.g. technologies that improve and document adherence), they might conceivably be in a position to make more aggressive efficacy claims, to demonstrate to stakeholders that they are delivering greater value, and ultimately command somewhat higher pricing, yet still below the cost of new, branded products.

If history is any guide, most biopharmas will embrace digital health "as a meme and a marketing term," to borrow Steve Lohr's wonderful turn of phrase (see here), but will proceed extremely cautiously. I suspect that the intrepid biopharmas that truly see the opportunity (and threat) here, and realize they need to figure this out, will be rewarded—assuming they are able to brave the learning curve, and embrace and learn from their inevitable mistakes. I imagine their new-found start-up colleagues could probably give them a little useful advice about getting to Plan B. – DS

Drugs Vs Mobile: Two Ways To Create $1B In Value

We've recently observed an interesting contrast—two radically different approaches to creating $1B in value.

Not long ago, the acquisition of mobile app Instagram by Facebook was announced, shocking some while awing others. Jon Stewart probably captured the zeitgeist best: "A billion dollars… of money?" For a smart summary of the deal, see this New York Magazine story (h/t Ruth Coxeter).

In the same week, URL Pharma was acquired by Takeda for nearly the same amount— $800M. The story here in brief is that for hundreds of years, colchicine was used for the treatment of gout and other conditions; it was an effective drug but had to be used carefully. In 2006, the FDA launched the "Unapproved Drug Initiative" offering a period of exclusivity for companies willing to take existing drugs that had never been rigorously validated through an extensive clinical study and FDA approval process.

URL invested in the formulation development and clinical studies required for colchicine, and ultimately received FDA approval, and associated exclusivity, in 2009. As a result— patients finally had a "trustworthy" (i.e. FDA-validated) version of colchicine to take, but at a steep price—about 50x what it used to cost. This has resulted in significant revenue for URL, ultimately leading to the eventual take-out.

URL and Instagram present two very different approaches to innovation and value; Instagram has created value by coming up with something either imaginative/cool/delightful or utterly trivial, depending on your point of view, while URL has created value by delivering either a reliable important medicine or by focusing on process and working the system, again depending on your point of view.

My own take: rather than debate the relative merits of a delightful technology or a reliable drug, imagine the exceptional potential to be found at the intersection of these worlds. Right now, there's a lot of energy at the intersection of mobile and health; the great challenge, and opportunity, will be figuring out how to turn this heat into light. – DS

Pills Still matter; So Does Biology— Managing Expectations About Digital Health

Reviewing "The Myth of The Paperless Office" for the New Yorker in 2002, Malcolm Gladwell argued that if the computer had come first, and paper didn't exist, someone would have had to invent it. Paper, it turns out, is a lot more useful than we typically appreciate.

It occurred to me that perhaps the same might be said of another product we seem to take for granted in the digital age—medicines. (Disclosure: I work at a company that makes them.)

Medicines—you know, those little white pills that everyone loves to critique—are in many cases remarkably effective solutions to very difficult problems; it's actually kind of amazing how useful some of these products can be. What an incredibly powerful idea— addressing a difficult and complex health problem with a simple pill you can pop before breakfast.

I read a tweet recently asserting that physicians may soon prescribe health apps as an alternative to medications; my initial reaction: good luck with that one. It's certainly easy enough to envision how magical thinking about the power of health apps will soon be replaced by disappointment as app developers realize something drug makers have known for years: it's hard to improve health, and it can be very difficult to get patients to stick with a treatment long enough to make a difference.

At the same time, it's clear there are profound opportunities in digital health; I imagine the most effective applications will find a way to complement and enhance traditional therapeutics, rather than position themselves as "alt apps"—the alternative medicines of the digital age (you can just see the eBook now: "Health Apps 'They' Don't Want You To Know About").

There are at least two major areas where digital medicine might be expected to play a significant role. The first opportunity is in helping to motivate behavior change by spurring patient engagement, whether in something as basic as completing a full course of antibiotics (I could easily imagine a motivational app being useful here) to a task as monumental as achieving sustained weight loss (a goal of many apps, of course, though it's not clear any have proved to be broadly game-changing).

The second key area is in measurement, a topic I've discussed extensively (see here, here, and here), and around which I've co-founded a new academic initiative, the Center for Assessment Technology and Continuous Health (CATCH), together with MGH Chief of Medicine Dennis Ausiello and several Boston-area colleagues. The basic idea is that improved phenotypic measurement—measurement of relevant parameters in a fashion more comprehensive and more continuous than typical patient data—could immediately improve care while also advancing future science.

An interesting underlying challenge associated with both of these areas that we must confront is the need to figure out how to do more than preach to the choir—see this characteristically eloquent discussion of the phenomenon by Duke University's Mark DeLong.

The specific issue for digital health is that the costs and burdens of healthcare are not evenly distributed, and a relatively small number of people drive most of the costs and also bear most of the suffering. I'm not sure these patients are always the ones who are eagerly sampling the new health apps or at the leading edge of the quantified self movement (although the participants in PatientsLikeMe and similar communities may represent important exceptions). Finding a way to bridge this gap will be important to demonstrate a meaningful impact on health—and also to provide a sustainable business model in this cost-focused era.

The flip side is that the need for improved measurement of real people is so pronounced that if you embarked on a serious effort here—as CATCH plans to initiate—and could achieve more comprehensive measurements in a broader selection of people and patients, there's a good chance it could generate results that might improve health delivery almost immediately. The key hurdles will be the logistical obstacles associated with actually collecting these data, as highlighted in Chapter Two of this recent Kauffman Foundation report, and discussed extensively at the recent Sage Commons Congress. But if acquired, these data are likely to render healthcare more efficient and effective, and can help us ensure we do a better job of understanding current practices and getting a better sense of what works best—acknowledging, importantly, that there's usually not going to be a single best approach that should be applied reflexively to every patient, as discussed here and here.

Less certain, however, is how these digital approaches can help us improve care in a revolutionary, not just evolutionary, way (as I've previously discussed in context of Steve Jobs). It's terrific to understand what sorts of approaches to antibiotics and physical therapy work best for cystic fibrosis patients (see here), but how much better would it be for patients to have a new medicine that fixes the underlying problem completely and permanently?

To put it crudely, the development of an effective vaccine did a lot more for the treatment of polio than applying the best design thinking to the construction of an iron lung ever could. I worry a bit that in our fascination with technology and design—which matter a lot for patients in the here and now—we're neglecting the need figure out some way to get at the difficult biological questions that remain at the root of disease. I really don't believe a clever app is going to cure cancer—though one might improve and help optimize the experience of patients now suffering from the disease.

What I can imagine, however, is that the focus on patient measurement will highlight the importance of understanding disease in the context of a person, rather than in a petri dish or a model organism, and beyond that, will lead to the development of technologies that make the study of human physiology, and pathophysiogy, increasingly robust. Perhaps the ability to characterize cancer cells more precisely in a living patient could help identify more effective treatments, for example.

The good news is that there seems to be a lot of interest now in balancing classic reductionism with a more physiologic perspective; this includes a renewed emphasis on phenotypic screening (see here and here), and an interest more generally in understanding diseases though patients rather than model organisms. For example, a scientist responding to a previous piece noted that the development of the recently-approved Vertex drug for a variant of CF reflected a more patient-based approach than was typical for industry.

A final point to contemplate is how big pharma should view the nascent efforts in digital health; I think Avado's Dave Chase (who certainly gets my vote as contributing the most consistently insightful writing about the evolving digital health landscape) nails it in this piece, in which he describes the pharmaceutical industry as essentially watching with bemused interest and applauding politely from the sidelines. On the one hand, they've more than a sneaking suspicion they need to change their business model, but on the other hand, they're sitting on a ton of cash, and seemed inured by this point to the endless invocations of a burning platform—it's almost as if they've decided this is more of a PR problem than a core business issue.

The thing is, biopharma companies may be positioned better than almost anyone to take advantage of the opportunities in digital health; as I've suggested, they have a unique understanding of the complexities of the healthcare system, and have a deeper familiarity with the many stakeholders. They also would be operating in a space where many potential competitors fear to tread.

Bottom line:

1. Digital health is not a magic answer but an important part of an integrated solution

2. Key opportunities for digital health are behavior modification (patient engagement) and phenotypic measurement, and both activities must involve more than just self-selected early adopters

3. We still need to focus on understanding the biological basis of dreadful diseases; hopefully, improved patient-focused technologies will help.

4. Big pharmas could evolve to become leading players in digital health, but are likely to continue to observe from the sidelines—in their luxury boxes—at least for the foreseeable future – DS

Does Big Pharma Need Entrepreneurial Leadership?

In a post I wrote for Atlantic.com ("America's healthy infatuation with entrepreneurs"), I discussed the appeal of the entrepreneur ideal, and contrasted the persona of the representative entrepreneur (exuberant, brash, emotional, excitable) with that of the typical Fortune 500 CEO (measured, dispassionate, methodical), a difference that presumably reflects the very different needs of the two types of businesses (startup vs multinational).

In response, several readers raised a point that's been on my mind as well, highlighting examples of well-known CEOs who seemed to run large companies while maintaining their youthful energy and unbridled enthusiasm—obviously Steve Jobs, but also leaders such as Virgin Group CEO Richard Branson. In this context, I particularly enjoyed this NYT interview with Ruckus Wireless CEO Selina Lo, a leader who has clearly maintained her distinctive individuality, albeit in the context of a relatively small (350 person) operation.

I suspect the reason we are so familiar with these leaders is precisely because their behavior is not representative of top CEOs. While it strikes me as profoundly inspiring that each of these executives has managed to run companies while maintaining their visceral passion, it's also true that these leaders each founded the companies they run (or ran), or joined at a very early stage. The relevant question is whether someone like Branson or Jobs could ever rise through the ranks of a typical large corporation, or whether their distinctive personalities would have thwarted their ascension. The image of Jobs or Branson participating in a typical HR team building event or communications training activity is admittedly difficult to envision.

On the other hand, if the way to rise to the top is to suppress one's intrinsic distinctiveness, the question is whether this is ever likely to re-emerge—if Branson or Jobs had been forced to toe the typical corporate line for a decade or more, and work his way up the ladder in the usual fashion, would either of them have been able, with equal facility, to re-access his distinctive qualities once he emerged as CEO at the end? I suspect the experience might have made each a more effective manager, but a less inspirational and effective leader.

The pharma industry seems clearly to have moved in the other direction—we've long ago decided that making medicines is far too important to be left to either the doctors or the scientists, and as a consequence, large companies are now run, for the most part, by seasoned business executives who seem a world removed from founder scientists. At first blush, this makes sense: running a multinational corporation is a distinctly non-trivial undertaking, and you can understand why it's comforting to have this role in the hands of an experienced business expert. On the other hand, without the passion and drive of an entrepreneur, I suspect something vital gets lost.

The continued acquisition of small young companies by mature pharma behemoths is almost certainly the future of the industry; yet, one imagines how exciting it would be if a promising young company, led by its founders, could grow to the point of being an industry leader. Following the acquisition of Genentech by Roche, it's difficult to think of a company that seems ready to step into this role.

Pity. A bit of passion and a dash of brashness could be just what our industry requires. – DS

Time For Biopharma To Jump On The 'Big Data' Train?

In a piece posted at TheAtlantic.com, I discuss what I see as the next great quest in applied science: the assembly of a unified health database, a "big data" project that would collect in one searchable repository all the parameters that measure or could conceivably reflect human well-being.

I don't expect the insights gained from these data will obsolete physicians, but rather empower them (as well as patients and other stakeholders) and make them better, informing their clinical judgment without supplanting their empathy.

I also discuss how many companies and academic researchers are focusing their efforts on defined subsets of the information challenge, generally at the intersection of data domains. I observe that one notable exception seems to be big pharma, as many large drug companies seem to have decided that hefty big data analytics is a service to be outsourced, rather than a core competency to be built. I then ask whether this is savvy judgment or a profound miscalculation, and suggest that if you were going to create the health solutions provider of the future, arguably your first move would be to recruit a cutting-edge analytics team.

The question of core competencies is more than just semantics—it is perhaps the most important strategic question facing biopharma companies as they peer into a frightening and uncertain future.

In my experience, a company's view of its core competencies translates directly into how it prosecutes its mission, as well as in the quality of talent it's able to recruit and retain. An enterprise that sees itself as defined by world-class sales and marketing would be expected to look very different, and emphasize different things, than a company that specializes in making novel biologics, for example, or a company that's focused on clinical development. Companies are usually built around what they do well, and can underestimate the complexity of other areas, especially those selected for outsourcing. You don't know what you don't know.

In the case of big data analytics, this means that unless a pharma company is deliberately built around this capability—or this function is developed and nurtured in a fenced-off, skunkworks fashion—it's unlikely to get adequate traction, and will be vulnerable to the usual corporate antibodies, especially when budget time comes around.

Conversely, I suspect that a biopharma company built entirely around analytics would suffer from a problem similar to that experienced by many academic researchers who seek to drive their laboratory discoveries into real-world application: it's far more difficult to successfully develop, manufacture, receive approval for, and market a new medical product than most outside the business appreciate.

(Perhaps a stretch, but you might also argue health portals such as GoogleHealth and Microsoft HealthVault failed in part because sponsors were so focused on the data and analytic opportunities that they lost sight of essential real-world considerations, and didn't have a sufficiently granular sense of what's required to be a successful business in the always-difficult health space.)

Presumably, once big data analytics firmly establishes itself as an essential capability, serious biopharma players will have no choice but to consider this function vital and integral—and I suspect most eventually will. Thus, the real question for big pharmas is when to jump on board the big data train; they've been burned in the past by premature investments in overhyped technologies, so you can certainly appreciate their reluctance.

At the same time, given both the overwhelming amount of available data and the fact that traditional pharma approaches to innovation seem to have largely run out of steam, you'd think that a bet on big data analytics might make a lot of sense now. Given the headwinds facing the industry, it's a bold play you've got to believe someone will be wise enough, brave enough, or desperate enough to make. – DS

Want To Industrialize Healthcare? Ask How Well It Has Worked For Pharma R&D

If you enjoyed the recent discussion around whether medicine should emulate the Cheesecake Factory, be sure to have a look at this interview in *Fortune With* Ralph de la Torre, former surgeon at the BIDMC and now CEO of the private equity-owned Steward Health Care System (h/t Ellen Licking).

The key quote:

"You have to look back at America and the trends in industries that have gone from being art to science, to being commodities. Health care is becoming a commodity. The car industry started off as an art, people hand-shaping the bodies, hand-building the engines. As it became a commodity and was all about making cars accessible to everybody, it became more about standardization. It's not different from the banking industry and other industries as they've matured. Health care is finally maturing as an industry, and part of that maturation process is consolidation. It's getting economies of scale and in many ways making it a commodity."

There, in a nutshell, is the basic argument: industrialization of medicine is not just inevitable but also desirable; this process will improve average quality and make healthcare more broadly affordable.

I hope two other experts I associate with the BIDMC will weigh in on this: former BIDMC CEO Paul Levy, who just published this savage critique of private-equity-backed for-profit healthcare systems, and Drs. Groopman and Hartzband, who have written so thoughtfully about the false charms of best practice guidelines.

I also wonder whether the experience of big pharma is relevant here; a decade or so ago, flush with the excitement of the genome project, big pharma was certain that they knew enough to effectively industrialize R&D, to discover new treatments essentially at scale.

Like medicine, drug discovery was described as something that used to be an art but now was a science, and thus amenable to industrialization, and well-positioned to reap the associated benefits: economies of scale, benefits of standardization, robust metrics, etc.

Of course, biology turned out to be far more complicated than most had appreciated, and discovery remains something that we've now recognized isn't ideally performed in an industrialized fashion—indeed, most big pharmas are now trying, in many ways, to "deindustrialize" their discovery process, and break it down into smaller and more individualized teams, with less central control and direction.

The point here isn't to argue by analogy—obviously pharma R&D isn't delivery of healthcare—but rather to question the progress vector implicit (and often explicit) in the argument of many advocates of healthcare standardization. Progress doesn't always equal a move towards standardization, and there are clearly instances where the harms of such industrialization far outweigh the benefits, however appealing (and measurable, and attainable) they might be. In some cases, to paraphrase Nassim Taleb, it's better to be generally correct than to be precisely wrong, and turning the nuance of medicine into rigidly defined processes strikes me as more likely to offer false precision than true insight.

The essential issue here is whether attempts at industrializing medical care will result in the broad improvements the Taylorists seem to envision, or whether the result will be the evisceration of a system that, while imperfect, has a great many extraordinary strengths, and once destroyed, will be difficult or impossible to re-establish.

My strong preference would be to retain the individuality I view as essential to the practice of medicine, and to incorporate—aggressively—the use of evidence where it's available, but not to impose standardization simply for its own sake, metrics for the sake of metrics.

Patients—in all their blessed complexity—deserve better. – DS

Pharma's Digital Health Strategy: Four Options

As pharma companies confront the digital health wave and contemplate their digital health strategy, I see four high-level options:

(1) **Opportunistic adjacency**: Leverage healthcare knowledge and regulatory expertise to develop technology in a related but distinct area, ultimately anticipating it evolves into a discrete business unit, analogous to animal health (e.g. Lilly's Elanco), generics (Novartis subsidiary Sandoz), nutrition, and consumer health.

Given the challenge of finding workable business models here, it's difficult right now to justify this logic; some winning strategies for stand-alone businesses may emerge in digital health, but is a pharma company especially likely to discover and develop them? For the moment, most pharmas—correctly, I'd say—agree the answer is "no."

 (2) **Follow with interest**: Determine that digital health, while promising, is still in its earliest days. Just as some pharmas may be relieved they resisted investing in the first round of stem cell technologies, for instance, they might be similarly inclined to adopt a watchful waiting posture, and give the field some time to settle out. Functional areas could utilize specific digital health solutions when they evolve to the point they are available from vendors, similar to the way other solutions are utilized by the industry.

While this fundamentally conservative approach avoids risky investment, it arguably comes with a significant opportunity cost (a key lesson of the 2012 Presidential campaign): a missed chance to take advantage of technologies already available and to gain expertise in navigating this important, emerging space.

Nevertheless, most pharmas seem content to remain here for now, though they might resource several small, exploratory/pilot efforts just to test the waters.

 (3) **Elevate**: Set up a dedicated "digital health" division envisioned not as a standalone business unit, but tightly integrated and explicitly intended to support the main pharma business, similar to the way many companies have dedicated "biomarker" divisions, for example. This group could be responsible for monitoring external developments and

internalizing and operationalizing the most promising technologies.

The main advantage of this approach is that it might help an otherwise traditional and somewhat hide-bound corporation better understand the emerging opportunities, and aggressively move up the adoption curve.

The key concern I'd have is that at the end of the day, I'm not sure it makes sense to view "digital health" as its own discipline, but rather as a diverse group of technologies that ultimately will be used (in the context of pharma) to help deliver solutions to already existing functional areas, from basic research (to the extent this still occurs in pharma) to biostatistics to clinical development to marketing.

 (4) **Planned obsolescence**: My personal choice, this approach would set up a dedicated "digital health" group, as in (3), but with the stated mission of catalyzing technology adoption, and with the explicit expectation that it would wind down within a set time (say five years). If successful, awareness of the relevant digital health opportunities and expertise in their appropriate utilization would by that point be located in the individual functional areas.

What I like most about this approach is that it recognizes digital health offers enabling technologies that provide improved approaches to solving fundamental problems that exist in many, if not all, functional areas.

One important pragmatic concern here is that a division with an expiration date may face political challenges within a large and fiercely competitive organization, and may struggle to gain adequate traction; functional areas might feel they can pick up what they need to on their own, and don't require the additional "help," potentially marginalizing the nascent digital health group.

On the other hand, precisely because of its limited mission, a digital health group might be less threatening to other functions, and more likely to be embraced—provided it clearly adds value, rather than just creating extra work (unfortunately but not always inaccurately, the way many biomarker groups, for example, are now perceived by the rest of the organization).

Bottom line: I am tremendously excited by the potential synergies between digital health and medical product development; capturing this value, however, will require a sophisticated understanding—not only of the technologies, but also of the specific functional needs and tacit local politics of the organization that hopes to deploy them. – DS

Strategy: Why Big Pharmas Do What They Do—And How Silicon Valley Might Help Them Think Differently

AstraZeneca's revitalization strategy, announced recently, follows the same well-worn playbook used by so many in the industry, employing approaches vividly familiar from my consulting days: cut headcount, externalize R&D, focus on select therapeutic areas, push biologics, and explore an interesting flyer (in this case, technology from Moderna, a Cambridge, MA-based company developing novel mRNA therapeutics—see Luke Timmerman's recent Xconomy post).

While not offering profound solutions, these restructuring activities, through cost cutting and distraction, are likely to buy AZ at least a little bit of breathing room from the increasingly critical analysts that have massed at the company's gates.

I'd like to review what may be driving these changes in the industry, and conclude with several alternative strategies big pharma might consider.

Pharma's Underlying Challenge

The fundamental problem the industry is wrestling with is this: car companies know how to make a car, soft drink companies know how to make soda, yet drug companies really have no reliable way of knowing where their next products are going to come from, and in a sense, have to start from scratch each time—at least if they want to make radically new, "first-in-class" products that offer unprecedented, dramatically better benefits to patients.

The problem is, these products are incredibly difficult to come by. Disease Remains very complicated, and it's exceptionally hard to devise a new molecule that durably interferes with a pathological process yet leaves the rest of the body alone; the technical risk, as it's called, is ridiculously high.

Not surprisingly, strategies that involve tweaking existing products, or reformulating them in a new way (e.g. liquid Ritalin, as Bruce Booth has discussed), remain popular because they at least reduce the technical risk, and may offer an incrementally—and often meaningfully—better option for patients (see here). However, an increasingly difficult payor environment is likely to make this approach ever more challenging, materially elevating the commercial risk. Proving an incrementally better product enhances value can be expensive (because it takes many patients to demonstrate a small difference in an active comparator trial), and of course, risky as well.

Not only is R&D uncertain and expensive, but no one seems to have demonstrated a consistent aptitude for this, at least in the context of new mechanisms. Data suggest neither big pharmas nor small biotechs have been especially productive, although (as Gary Pisano has shown) pharmas appear to have worse statistics because they have to eat the cost of failures, while small companies tend to disappear, and thus their costs are often not included in productivity calculations. While it's always possible to force-rank companies (a favorite technique of consultants), it's far less certain whether the R&D shops that seem to be performing the best at any given moment are actually good (as the consultants would have it) versus just lucky (as simple statistics might suggest). I agree it's possible to be especially bad at novel drug discovery, but I think it's quite difficult to be reliably good (or consistently successful) at discovering and successfully developing drugs that utilize unprecedented mechanisms.

To improve the odds and the economics, many pharmas are now embracing what some are calling a "pick the winners" approach, which (as a consultant explained to me) is better described as "kill the losers." The basic idea is that the astronomically high cost of drug development is driven by the high failure rate, and especially by the staggering cost of late failures—failures in Phase 2 and especially in Phase 3. Ruthlessly kill bad programs early, the logic goes, and you'll save money. The problem, of course, is how to do this.

There are two basic impediments to early kills: scientific (figuring out what should be killed) and organizational (actually doing the killing). I've discussed the organizational challenges previously—please see here and here; see also this Drug Baron post, and references therein. To address the scientific challenges, some companies have looked to genetics and biomarkers to increase their probability of success or conversely, let them know when they're failing. Typically, these are motivated by a conspicuous success, a development program that was driven by the strength of beautiful molecular data, and the canonical example these days is PCSK9, a target which seems to feature an almost unprecedented alignment of human genetics, biomarker, and animal model data. Clearly, Amgen (one of two companies leading the PCSK9 pursuit) hopes that through the acquisition of DeCode Genetics, additional high-probability targets will be revealed; other companies have gone down this route without conspicuous success, and it will be interesting to see whether (as my colleague Matt Herper has argued) this time will be different. I hope he's right, of course, but I'm somewhat less sanguine.

The challenges of R&D have led many large drug companies to ask whether it makes more sense to let the early-stage innovation happen outside of big pharma, and then in-license or acquire the rare development programs that seem adequately promising. Rather than drop research entirely (as the sharp industry analyst Andrew Baum provocatively proposed in 2010), most big pharmas are managing their exodus from basic research by initiating a series of high-profile alliances with academic centers at the same time they reduce R&D headcount. Depending on your degree of cynicism, this approach represents either the embrace of open innovation or covering fire used to obscure a massive intellectual retreat.

Given the sad state of early-stage life science financing (for pretty much the same reasons—almost everything fails, and investors have now figured this out), it's unclear whether there will always be enough promising companies and products for the big companies to pick off, at least at reasonable valuations. To this end, many pharmas are using in-house venture groups to support early-stage companies, and as Atlas VC Bruce Booth reports, life-science financing these days (especially early-stage) increasingly involves at least one corporate VC. While such funding is unquestionably useful, it's hardly enough to support a vibrant range of early-stage activities.

Pharmas are also continuing their strategic embrace of biologics, a move driven by two key considerations. First, most biologics target serious conditions, for which a high level of reimbursement is expected. Second, biologics are really difficult to copy, and thus even after the patents expire, knock-off biologics (biosimilars) are far less a threat than knock-off small molecules (generics). This makes sense: biologics are notoriously tricky to manufacture, and both their safety and efficacy depends not only on the specific protein sequence of the molecule, but on the highly specific culture conditions used to manufacture it. With a few exceptions, I would readily prescribe, use, and recommend a generic drug, but I imagine I'd be reluctant to consider a biosimilar in place of a required biologic.

So long as they have enough cash to purchase and complete the development of promising products—especially biologics—most big pharmas can (and likely will) use the strategies discussed above to stay in the game. That said, the megatrends remain concerning; while drug costs represent only a small fraction of the overall healthcare equation, they are likely to remain (like other health care costs) under intense pressure, and it will be increasing important to demonstrate that the benefits of innovative new products justify their high costs.

Two prominent threats facing big pharmas are: (1) payors may figure out more effective ways to reign in the cost of specialty drugs, particularly those offering only modest incremental benefit; (2) the early-stage innovation ecosystem may sputter to the point where there aren't enough products to purchase, and those available command prohibitively high valuations.

I suspect a more likely outcome is that the industry will continue to slowly consolidate and shrink its footprint, and that we'll see a few more mega-mergers in the years ahead.

Three Alternative Approaches

The far more interesting question is whether there are alternative, creative options pharma companies can consider as they look to an increasingly uncertain future. Three considerations are: analytics; phenotype; and risk.

Analytics: While most pharmas employ talented biostatisticians, the companies' analytics capabilities tend not to be exceptional; drug companies are more likely to be consumers of analytics services than they are to be developers of powerful new platforms (i.e. they are approaching data like Romney's campaign rather than Obama's). I'm intrigued (as I've noted before) by the possibility of a pharma company that decides to differentiate by focusing on brilliant analytics, analytics that would be the envy of the industry—and of others. Imagine if you had a team comprised of the sort of people who now work at Google, Facebook, Palantir, and turned them loose on all the different sorts of data pharma companies deal with, from basic science to marketing. It's hard not to envision this would be radically transformative.

Phenotype: The explosion of sensors and mobile technologies, and of digital health more generally, has dramatically increased our ability to understand a patient's experience of disease, providing the opportunity for continuous versus episodic assessment, and understand phenotype at a far more granular level. Beyond the obvious immediate challenges—figuring out what to measure, figuring out how to measure as passively and unobtrusively as possible, figuring out how to capture and incorporate the data in the patient's record—there's the even more difficult task of making sense of it all, and (as Recon Strategy's Tory Wolff and I have discussed), turning this data into insight, and the insight into value. There are at least two reasons for pharma companies to jump into this space: (1) as reimbursement barriers get higher, being able to demonstrate your new drug meaningfully impacts patients will be increasingly important; a far more detailed understanding of the manifestation of disease in the patients you're trying to help should enable better demonstrations of efficacy and value; (2) longer term, the ability to combine phenotypic and genomic data may reveal different subgroups, that respond distinctly to therapies, or that reflect a common biology that could be understood and perhaps targeted.

Risk*: As the healthcare system increasingly focuses on delivering outcomes, it might make sense for some medical products companies to own part of this risk. This could be done in collaboration with providers: either you could jointly assume risk (for example, splitting risk 50/50) or apportion out different risks to each other depending on who can most impact outcomes. Alternatively, and perhaps more boldly, it might be done directly —for example, by owning the surgical centers, contracting the care of hip repair patients, and making money by managing the entire process well and delivering the best results. Or you could run diabetes clinics and make your money by contracting the care of diabetic patients, incentivizing the delivery of quality outcomes rather the prescription of expensive drugs. While the margins would be lower, the business model might be more durable, and better aligned with the needs of patients. This would also be expected to drive further value-oriented innovation. (*Hat-tip to Tory Wolff for useful discussions.)

Bottom Line: Medicines, in many cases, represent remarkably effective solutions to vitally important problems. Unfortunately, they're also incredibly difficult to devise, validate, and economically justify. The aggressive application of emerging analytic and digital health technologies, while currently viewed as "nice to have" at best, are likely to emerge as table stakes in a world focused on the more precise identification and delineation of value. Medical product companies that figure out how to embrace and most effectively apply these emerging technologies, and think creatively about new risk-sharing business models, will be best positioned to deliver impactful medicines to patients, durable health to populations, and long-term returns to stockholders. – DS

VI.

Patients And Consumers

Online Diagnosers Exceed Number Of Words With Friends Players

We all like to think we are one-of-a-kind, but the truth is, not so much. In the past month I have found myself among the (estimated) <5% of women who attended the JP Morgan conference, the <10% of women who are partners in private equity firms, and, apparently, one of the 100% of working people who play Scrabble-related games during working hours, but today I find myself one of the 35%. According to a recent a Pew Research Center survey of about 3,000 people, about 35% of Americans are "online diagnosers," meaning people who consult the Internet to self-diagnose a medical condition.

Not looking for sympathy, seriously, I am feeling sorry enough for myself to cover all of us; but I found myself, after weeks of media hysteria and the most congested head on earth, reading this article entitled How to Tell If You Have the Flu. I read this as I helped the Kimberly Clark Corporation have a record quarter due to extreme Kleenex consumption. Here is a tip: go out and buy Kimberly Clark stock as I think this may last a while. Incidentally, according to Kimberly Clark, I am thus one of the 25% of people worldwide who use their products every day. I guess I am in good company.

I think the idea that 35% of Americans are attempting to self-diagnose in order to determine if they should go to the doctor is very interesting. Of course it is free to do this–doesn't cost the patient anything–so why not? And the Pew study found that 53% of those who sought Internet self-diagnoses went to a clinician for follow-up; incidentally, 41% of these had their self-diagnosis confirmed by said clinician, so the online-diagnosers are doing well below average.

The quest for home diagnostics has been a long and fruitful one for the medical industry (and venture industry) and has become the sine qua non of the mobile health movement. As I have written in the past, Qualcomm has sponsored a whole Tricorder XPrize ($10mm prize) based on this premise and there are at least 719,578 companies who have come through my office promising to use cell phones to diagnose everything from diabetes to cancer to sexually transmitted diseases (not mine). My trip to Russia, previously reported in great detail, was focused very much on this topic, as that country has the kind of lack of consistent access to healthcare that we Americans only fear we could have, so taking care of yourself at home isn't just convenient, it's essential.

But as I look at the Pew data I wonder: is it true that 47% of office or ER visits were avoided by those 35% of people who self-diagnosed due to information on the Internet? Or that the right visits were avoided? Very hard to say. Is there money to be saved as a result of this information being available to patients and how will we ever know?

Deloitte recently published a report stating that "Mobile technology will transform the healthcare industry with increased productivity gains saving $305 billion over the next 10 years." Now 66% of this savings was associated with tele-monitoring/telemedicine technologies, not self-diagnostics (in fact the opposite of self-diagnostics), but theoretically some portion of the rest comes from some form of patient empowerment/engagement that takes cost out of the system, at least in theory.

This is a very nice idea and I sincerely hope it to be true, but access to self-diagnostic tools could just as easily drive up costs as reduce them. In the medical device diagnostics world we have seen exactly this correlation: make it easier and cheaper for diagnostics to be used and you get a lot more patients getting screened for whatever illness du jour, real or imagined. Always the question must be asked, "Who Pays?"

Some of my fellow healthcare venture capitalists (no surprise I am referring to Vinod Khosla) have posited that 80% of doctors will be all but obsolete in the next few years, going the way of the rotary phone and the brontosaurus as machines take over. On the other hand, others of my colleagues (you know who you are and many of you are the potential brontosauri) have said they will believe that when Mr. Khosla is doing his own home colonoscopy. I have to tell you, I'm a big doctor's office fan when it comes to colonoscopies—I just don't have a convenient home location to perform one.

As usual, somewhere in the middle lies the truth and we are going to need real studies of outcome and efficacy before we should believe savings estimates thrown around by so many. The level of economic data that accompanies most pitches about mobile health products is akin to the level of leafy green vegetables one consumes at Wendy's, home of the Triple Baconator, so we are going to need to do better to justify pouring diagnostics into the home. If we don't we risk seeing the same hockey stick line that accompanied the widespread use of ultrasound, MRI and other diagnostic imaging modalities, not to mention all of the other diagnostic tests done at a patient's insistence, even when the doctor knows it to be unnecessary. – LS

A Tale Of Two Doctor Visits

"It was the best of times, it was the worst of times, it was the age of wisdom, it was the age of foolishness." –Charles Dickens, A Tale of Two Cities

We all talk about how wonderful patient engagement in the healthcare system is, but in today's flawed health care system there is almost nothing worse than to be a healthcare savvy person using it. We know too much. We know what injustices to look out for and what can go wrong. We know when we are being over treated and poorly treated. We know the doctors generally wish we would shut up and stop asking questions.

In the past month I have had occasion to visit a doctor twice. In the first instance I had a pain in my mouth that made me understand where the expression "I thought my head would explode" came from. It was mind-numbing, blackout-inducing pain the likes of which I haven't felt since childbirth. I had to invent whole new swear words to even describe it. Turns out I needed an emergency root canal due to a broken tooth.

In the other recent encounter I had with the medical system, I voluntarily paid a visit to a cosmetic surgeon to inquire how much money and what kind of promises I would have to make to God to look 25 again. Turns out that there is no promise big enough to make good on that bill–God already has everything and the Devil was on vacation–even if I could afford to pay the monetary part of the tab.

Nevertheless, the experiences of those two doctor visits were so widely different from each other that I felt it warranted writing about, even if I have to admit in writing that I am older than 25. I know, I'm sorry I lied.

A few weeks back I wrote a post called Give Em That Old Razzle Dazzle which touched on the kind of marketing and customer service that spas use to separate people willingly from their money. I contrasted this to how reluctant those same consumers are to part with their cash even for life-saving products and services, when the services fall under the "should be covered by insurance" umbrella. This post offers another flavor of that same dish, but in this case one that reflects on provider behavior when faced with an insured patient vs one who would be footing the bill personally (were either God or the Devil in a negotiating mood).

One would like to think that the source of payment wouldn't matter and that every patient would be treated like a valued customer, but my own personal experience belies the truth: when you're viewed as the INSURED MEMBER you are in coach; when you're viewed as the CUSTOMER, you're in first class. It's a bit like the difference between staying at Motel 6 as compared to the Four Seasons. At Motel 6 you're lucky to get a bar of soap and a towel big enough to dry your hands. At the Four Seasons they put flowers in your room, use your actual name when talking to you and and let you know that someone can be sent to personally towel you off if you just call the concierge. The difference becomes berry meaningful as we have started to make the slow march towards a healthcare system where patients are being moved into the position employers and the government have long occupied–the one between the wallet and the doctor.

The Tooth Ache

I am one of those lucky people who grew up with fluoridated water and thus have had only one cavity in my entire life. I am not one of those people who is afraid of dentists because, for the most part, nothing bad ever happened to me there. So when I showed up unannounced on a Monday morning after a night of hell I was very appreciative that the dentist agreed to see me right away. Granted, I latched myself to his office door and refused to leave, but he didn't put up a fight. He took one look at me, asked me three questions, looked in my mouth for less than 10 seconds and declared, "You need a root canal on tooth number 31.". I said, "How do you know?" and he said, "I've been doing this for 35 years.". He followed that with, "But I need to do an X-ray to verify it." Fine, I figured. Better for me if we know he's right. I wouldn't want an unnecessary procedure. This is what I'm thinking as they light me up.

While waiting for the X-ray to process, he calls his pal, the local endodontist, and arranges for me to go right over there to get said root canal, which I do appreciate. Then his assistant hands me the X-ray, which has not been looked at by the dentist, and she tells me to bring it to the endodontist. I say, "Aren't you going to look at it to be sure you're diagnosis is right?" He says, " I know."

So now I'm thinking why the heck did we do this X-ray if I didn't need it? My immediate cynical thought was to assume because he gets paid to do it, assumes my insurance will cover it, and that's that. I try to check my cynicism at the door since I appreciate his getting me seen quickly. I remind myself that the endodontist will need it to know where to do his thing so the X-ray was probably necessary after all.

Fast forward half an hour and I'm now filling out, by hand, form after form of repetitive information at the endodontist's office. I literally write my name and address on four different forms. Same goes for my medical info. Clearly the whole EMR tsunami has not made it to these shores. I point out that they have asked me to sign a form agreeing to whatever procedures they are going to do when they have yet to tell me what they are going to do One of the guys in scrubs hanging out in the lobby, says, "Yeah, good point. Just sign it and we'll work it out." I refuse to sign it until I know what's happening. He shrugs. By the way, i later find out this guy is the endodontist because later, when I lay in the chair, he is the one with the tools. At that point I say, "Oh, so you are the doctor?" He confirms.

Meanwhile, back in the waiting room, I ask what this whole fun fest is going to cost and what will be covered by my insurance and what will not. They give me a rundown but not a guarantee of costs. In fact, I will find out later when the bill comes that I owe twice as much as I was told it was likely to cost. Not cute.

After a brief wait (I have to say, they were fast to see me and didn't make me sit around) I sat down in the dental chair of doom and hand the doctor the X-ray, still virginal in its jacket having been unviewed by anyone. The doctor says, thanks, puts it aside and says he will be doing new X-rays. I say, "What the hell? What's wrong with the X-ray you just dropped into the circular file," and he says, "Oh no, mine is a digital X-ray and we have to do it here because we use it to guide the treatment." I have a small fit.

"What was the point of the first X-ray then?," I ask, "Why are you guys double-treating me? I don't want the extra radiation to my head, for one thing–I can kill my brain cells all on my own thank you." Now my cynicism comes roaring back. I tell the doctor that I think he is suggesting an unnecessary procedure. He, smiling, says to me, I won't treat you without the X-rays." He knows that I can't continue in pain like this and in fact I have a flight to the East Coast scheduled to depart in 6 hours. "It's your choice," says the doctor." Checkmate. I am furious but despite what he said I feel I have no choice. I feel very annoyed and they haven't even started drilling yet. In case you were wondering, the drilling did, in fact, amplify my annoyance.

I am told after it's all over–5 more X-rays later–that I am done and that is that. I am given no information about how to take care of myself except "Keep it clean and don't bite on that side until the anaesthetic wears off." I am told I will also need to go back to the regular dentist for a crown within no more than 3 weeks. An appointment is set for 4 weeks hence because I am told that is the first available time. On top of that, the dental assistant calls me to reschedule the appointment no less than three separate times, further pushing out the timeline. I say that i thought i needed to be seen within 3 weeks. They tell me not to worry. I am worried.

Yes, after all this, my tooth is fixed and the pain is gone, but the entire experience left me very cold. There was little regard for my interests here and I felt like a victim, not a consumer. I know dentistry is supposed to be unpleasant, but when you add in the lack of transparency, inaccuracy around costs and the feeling like my X-rays were paying for a couple of dentists' Porsche payments, unpleasant was an understatement.

The Age Defier

Meanwhile, back at the ranch, I have decided I am curious about all these minimally invasive plastic surgery procedures that all my VC friends are funding and making a bundle from. Of course when I ask them about this stuff they tell me it is great, but I decide I want to find out for myself. I ask around and through my research come across a guy in San Francisco who is supposed to be both good and honest and highly experienced. While I am suspicious that this combination can occur in nature, I call to set up a consultation. I brace myself for the pain of visiting a new doctor.

My suspicions are amplified when they try to set the appointment around my schedule, not caring that I am suggesting evenings and other strange times when physicians rarely work. They tell me this is no problem and that they will make it work at my convenience, which they actually do. They send me both an email and text confirmation of the time selected. They also send me an email link to their EMR so I can input my relevant personal and medical history. Once.

When I show up for my appointment, the assistant introduces herself, shakes my hand and thanks me for coming. I am offered a cold beverage and a nice cushy seat in which I wait approximately one minute before being shown to the back. I again wait for about a minute before the doctor comes in, shakes my hand and introduces himself. He tells me a bit about his background and qualifications. He asks me why I am there. I give him my story. He offers to explain in great detail the technology and clinical information relevant to all of the products about which I enquire. He is patient and detailed and says, "I love it when people ask me lots of questions-it means they care about their health." he goes and gets props and photos to explain. He proactively describes how he minimizes unnecessary procedures and visits.

When we are through, his assistant, who is beautiful, of course, and has a soothing accent, goes through costs, risks, process, everything you can imagine in extraordinary detail. The pricing document has a guarantee about virtually all costs so you cannot be readily surprised. There is an extensive package of take home patient education information. After the appointment I receive a thank you email. Seriously. It's like I went to a wedding shower, not a doctor's appointment. I email back one lingering question I had. I receive a response within the hour. I have not decided whether I am going to do anything service-wise yet, but I want to go back to the office just because it was so pleasant.

"We had everything before us, we had nothing before us, we were all going direct to Heaven, we were all going direct the other way. . . ." –Charles Dickens, *A Tale of Two Cities*

I found the contrast between these two experiences very interesting in light of the thinking I have been doing about what happens in a "reformed" U.S. healthcare system where people directly choose their insurance products through exchanges. These decisions will be based largely on benefits offered and cost, but if history is any judge, they will also be based in large part on the doctor network they will be assigned. In this brave new world, consumers will be able to fire their health plan and switch doctors when they are unsatisfied with the services received. This is in stark contrast to how things work today. It is nearly impossible to switch health plans unless your employer does it for you and changing doctors is a hassle extraordinaire. In a world where data is portable and consumers can vote with their feet and wallets, customer service is really going to matter in a way it does not today.

I have seen a proliferation of programs for doctors to teach them more about technology and finance for the new world healthcare system, but I have seen little to suggest they are being trained to live in a Nordstrom-style world. This is probably a great opportunity for healthcare consultants that used to teach doctors how to "code" aka overbill. Perhaps we will see medical schools open up their curriculum to include a little foray into hospitality services and how to remember that the customer is always right, even when they are a pain in the neck. That plus a little charm school would go a long way toward ensuring the brand loyalty that providers will need to prosper in a more complex world where the financial transaction has been simplified from a three-way (provider-payer-patient) to a two-party relationship between provider and patient.

And in case you're wondering, all those extra X-rays have given me a special iridescent glow and previously absent super powers. If they need a female Hulk for the Avengers sequel, I am ready to go. – LS

Give Them That Old Razzle Dazzle

I frequently am in a position to tell young companies that our firm is not ready to invest in them because their business model is, at least in the current world, overly dependent on consumers paying for the product or service being offered. While there are a few examples of successful consumer-pay healthcare companies, they are so far exactly that: few and far between. While there is much in flux in the U.S. healthcare system that will likely change this dynamic greatly over the next 5-20 years, it is an almost-certainty today that consumers will open their wallets to pay for healthcare services only at gunpoint.

Health Care, by which I mean doctor and hospital visits, diagnostic tests, medicines, preventive care services, you name it, is "supposed to be" paid for by insurance or the government or anyone except the individual, according to most individuals. People will shell out $5-10 for a pack of cigarettes or a triple grande caramel frappuccino with a muffin without a second thought, but balk at paying similarly-sized copayments for necessary prescriptions or office visits that could significantly improve their health. This is not an irony limited to people of lesser means, by the way. The phenomenon of not thinking one should pay for ones own "insurable" healthcare services is shared by rich and poor alike, just as is foregoing essential healthcare services because one doesn't want to pay for them.

The above set of thoughts came roaring back at me while I was fortunate enough to be spending part of last week in Sedona, AZ at the Enchantment Resort. This place is pretty plush and one of its key attributes, amid the Vortexes and crystal power trips and Native American mystical traditions, is its spa, called Mii Amo (which is probably Native American for "welcome one percenters"). I spent one of my days in the spa, where I was hanging around soaking up the mystical power of not working, and I started to take a good look at the spa's marketing materials, because I am a nerd who does things like that. What jumped out at me was how much time and space the spa spends marketing not just feel-good stuff, but what they tout as honest-to-God health and wellness services, FDA approval be damned. In fact, the spa brochure specifically says, that at Mii Amo "whether you are in good health or have nutritional challenges, learn tools to establish or maintain a healthy lifestyle."

So why did this strike me so vividly? Well, here's why: in a brochure replete with services that are more of the pampering or tree-hugging variety (flower essence bath or vision board creation anyone?), there are an abundance of services for which consumers drive a billion miles through the Arizona desert and pay handsomely, specifically to improve their health and prevent chronic illness, pain, and other medical miseries. These services include weight management counseling, exercise physiology, sleep therapy, nutritional therapy and associated healthy foods, menopause therapies, even one treatment, called Abhyanga Shirodhara, which purports to "stimulate the pituitary gland, help balance the endocrine system, and relax the nervous system." In case you are wondering, this last one works by pouring oil on your head and draining all the money out of your wallet–$370 for 90 minutes and not a doctor in sight.

What I noticed was that the listing of the many health and wellness services that are offered at Mii Amo and many similar places around the world could just as easily been lifted from an Aetna or United Health or Blue Cross Blue Shield or Kaiser member booklet of covered services as from a spa's marketing materials. And yet, when they are in the realm of health insurance, the carriers often have to beg and bribe to get people to use programs like these for the benefit of their own health. Not only are covered members unwilling to pay for most health and wellness services in the context of the medical system, but they typically must be paid to use them, sometimes at a rate higher than they would actually cost. In contrast, I had to jockey for position in the Mii Amo spa waiting room because people were lining up to pay $150-$400 an hour for this stuff; it was so crowded they had stopped adding people to the waiting list.

The irony was amplified for me during the actual facial I received (yes, it was good but they would not take my insurance card, go figure). The funniest moment was when the aesthetician told me she was going to put iPads on my face, to which I responded, "wow, getting pretty high tech here at the spa.....I didn't know there was a facial app." She told me that eye pads were aromatherapy-infused cotton pads (implying I was an idiot, which is accurate) that go over the eyes. Um, duh.

Anyway, the actually ironic thing was the description of the skin products she was using as they were applied to my face. If you have ever had a facial, you know they give kind of a running commentary about the amazing qualities of the products as they apply them. Just like movie theaters make their real money from concessions, spas make the big bucks when you purchase for home use the products they use on you (note: average spa line skin care regimen could easily set you back $1000 retail). So in the dulcet tones of marketing set to Yanni-like spa music, I was regaled about the aesthetic and medicinal qualities of the Lucrece Physicians Aesthetic Research brand of products, which relies heavily on the use of nano-peptides and stem cells for its efficacy. Granted, they are apple and lilac and grape stem cells, not fetal ones, but it was a huge part of the story.

I am in possession of the Lucrece Physicians catalog (tagline: Inspired by Nature, Realized by Science) and let me tell you, Pfizer and Merck wish they could produce materials this appealing and medically informative that would result in such big ticket purchases. If there were a medical clinic somewhere in the US that so blithely offered stem cell therapy, you know there would be protestors standing outside holding pictures on placards that we would not want our children to see. Because this stuff is packaged for the world of anti-aging and beauty, and because the apples and grapes have a hard time organizing a political rally, there is no controversy here, just a lot of credit card usage.

In fact, this particular product line is also distributed through physician offices, primarily dermatologists, that would get to bill insurance for the consultation on acne or rosacea that some of the Lucrece line is targeted to treat. I bet you that if a patient bought these products through their doctor they would no sooner pay for the doctor visit than they would pay to have their fingernails pulled out. And yet my facial and most of the other skin care services offered at Mii Amo were $150-300, plus tip. I wonder if there is a dermatologist out there who ever got a tip other than, "it would be better if you waived my copay."

After my facial I was handed a "Personalized Rx Form" torn from a Lucrece Physicians "prescription pad" which provided me a handy dandy list of products I should buy if I wanted to keep the stem cells and peptides going. If I had purchased all of them it would have cost about $500 (a bargain!) but I couldn't get my Medco card to cover it. And therefore I was a non-compliant patient and didn't fill my prescription.

Anyway, the whole experience made me think about how the healthcare system needs to rethink the way it markets to and communicates with consumers. As I have written several times before, we are entering an age where consumers will be expected to pay for and be more accountable for, more and more of their healthcare decisions. This will occur concomitantly with the requirement that health insurers learn how to sell directly to consumers to survive in a world where a majority of individuals will likely be purchasing their health benefit policies directly through health insurance exchanges. (see HERE for more on that topic).

By catering to the side of us that wants to be nurtured and pampered, spas have figured out how to separate people from their money in the name of health and wellness. If health insurers and physicians can tap into that vein, the system may have a chance of fostering the preventive health models it so desperately needs to proliferate for the good of our nation's health and the health of our national economy. Actuarial science and newly engineered payment structures and modern-day operational models will undoubtedly be key to the solvent healthcare system of the future, but old-fashioned advertising and marketing acumen may well be the secret sauce that makes it work. If you can get someone in Sedona to pay $480 to "Explore the energetic realm beyond the physical...by tuning into the helping energy of your natural intuition," there's got to be a way to increase grandma's desire to pay $4 to fill her Lipitor prescription.

Author Peter Nivio Zarlenga has been attributed with saying, "In our factory, we make lipstick. In our advertising, we sell hope." We are going to need a little bit of that orientation in healthcare to move to the next level of consumer engagement. Or as they say in the musical Chicago, "Razzle dazzle 'em and they'll beg you for more!" – LS

Let's Get Personal

A recent article in the Wall Street Journal described a disappointing development in the field called "Personalized Medicine." For those who aren't familiar with this term of art, it is generally used to mean the use of a patient's specific genetic or other biologic information to match them with specific drugs that are more likely to be effective as a result of the person's individual genetic/biologic makeup. Many are familiar with the work that has been done to genetically test breast cancer patients to determine whether Herceptin will be effective in tumor control or not, for instance. In fact, the research described in the WSJ article noted that a tumor's genetic makeup can vary significantly even within the same tumor sample, rendering the application of Personalized Medicine questionable at best. The article states, "The findings don't diminish enthusiasm for the idea that genetic knowledge about tumors can transform cancer care, the researchers said. But it could make personalized treatment more complex—and more costly."

I find it very interesting that the concept of Personalized Medicine has been almost entirely limited to discussions about the combination of genetics and medication. In a world where consumer engagement in the healthcare system necessitates true personalization of the entire healthcare experience, I think it is time for the term to be applied far more broadly and without capital letters.

The goals behind the classic meaning of Personalized Medicine were and are to engage patients in an individualized process that fosters faster, better screening & diagnosis; enables effective matching of illness to treatment to maximize efficacy; and thus reduces the use of unnecessary resources (e.g., lowers cost) by avoiding treatments that would prove ineffective. In fact, these are precisely the goals of a vast array of activities that are more typically in the purview of the fields of healthcare services and healthcare information technology. We are seeing data-driven personalization happening in delivery systems, care management programs, value-based insurance programs, mobile health and consumer engagement platforms, among others. The marriage of wearable sensors with electronic medical records and other enterprise data is feeding "big data" analytics systems that drive significant personalization of consumers' healthcare experiences. Bottom line: personalized medicine is not just for genetics fans anymore.

The health plans of the not-too-distant, kinda-already-here future will (do) rely heavily on personalization to meet the demands of a market characterized by consumer direct purchasing and engagement (as a result of health insurance exchanges) and the essential economic and societal need to get the costs of chronic illness under control. Such health plans, which are likely to feature integrated payer and provider systems tied up in a high technology wrapper, will:

- Allow for multiple points of access to the healthcare system based on specific consumer preference (clinic, home, office, hospital, assisted living, mobile phone-based telemedicine, you name it)

- Enable tracking/monitoring of exactly the clinical indicators desired and use predictive analytics to predict trends/risks of treatment or it's absence

- Use those analytic findings to develop and execute personalized treatment plans that are highly tunable based on continuous loop feedback

- Identify people with common symptomatology and conditions and foster community around target diseases and behavior

- Rely on a feedback loop from patients and providers to create a fuller and more customized user experience

As an example, the value-based health plan offered by SeeChange Health is already well on its way to providing many of these features (self interest alert: SeeChange is a Psilos portfolio company). SeeChange's health plan encourages prevention and a more individualized health care experience by providing a comprehensive health risk analysis of the client population; identifying people with high risk chronic conditions (pre-diabetes, diabetes, asthma, etc.) and matching them with condition-specific and customized Health Action plans; dynamically incorporating highly individualized incentive and engagement programs; and providing an online portal that informs and motivates. In other words, it is a health plan that looks at individual members, figures out what programs and treatment interventions are best suited to keep each of them healthy, and delivers a personalized experience that results in earlier disease identification and optimized use of clinical resources. This is not one-size-fits-all health insurance and if it's not personalized medicine, I don't know what is.

There are similar efforts underway among healthcare companies that focus on personalizing the nutrition/food shopping experience (e.g. Zipongo), the care management/care coordination experience (e.g., Click4Care) and the delivery system access experience (e.g., Walgreens). Personalization is coming to healthcare and it is about time.

Personalization is a trend that will touch every part of healthcare as the system continues to evolve towards one where consumers are engaged clinically and financially. Healthcare information technology and healthcare services are primary tools in fostering this kind of personalized medicine...and we don't have to wait for any scientific discovery to utilize it. Just as with the promise of Personalized Medicine (old school style) , this broader view of personalized medicine affords a significant opportunity to positively impact medical cost and effectiveness. Even better, the market potential is not limited to a subset of the population, but applies to all Americans who engage with the our healthcare system.

Every industry in America is striving towards greater and greater personalization. You see it in the automobile industry, the clothing industry, the food industry, everywhere. Thank goodness it is finally coming to an industry where personalization can make a meaningful difference in our lives. And by that, of course, I mean the couture footwear industry. No, seriously, it is only by personalizing the healthcare experience that we will begin to effectively engage people in living a life built around health and not around healthcare. – LS

Enter The Consumer

Not long ago I was in Newport Beach chair IBF's Consumer Health and Wellness Innovation Summit. It was a very interesting event with about 100 people from many different segments of the health and wellness industry—a very eclectic crowd. There were people there from healthy food purveyors (Nestle, Kelloggs), provider organizations (MDVIP), health insurance firms (United Health Group, SeeChange Health) and even the U.S. Department of Health and Human Services. There were also a plethora of entrepreneurs representing a variety of emerging wellness and preventive health companies and, of course, the venture firms that they love and hate. 10 years ago you could not fill a room with people to talk about consumer health; now it is becoming a mainstream topic.

The consumer, aka the patient, has been largely absent from the healthcare discussion for far too long. Yet recently, a harmonic convergence of events has put the consumer center stage in the healthcare discussion. Those events include:

- The **devastating human and financial toll of chronic illness**. CDC estimates that 50% of Americans over 18 have one or more chronic illness. At the event I had the wonderful opportunity to do a fireside chat interview with Dr. Richard Migliori, EVP and Chief Healthcare Officer of United Health Group. I asked him why payers had so recently decided that they should, in fact, begin to pay for preventive health/wellness programs and he said, "everyone finally woke up."

- **The crash of the national economy** has made it impossible for payers of all types as well as consumers to ignore the cost of health insurance as well as the cost of poor health. One statistic: while the employers' cost to provide family health insurance has risen an average of 113% over the last 10 years, the cost to consumers has risen by 131%. A disproportionate share of the burden is cascading down to consumers' pockets. James Carville once said, "It's the economy, stupid." In this case it's the stupid economy.

- **Healthcare reform,** driven by the first two on the list, is next. Someone finally drew a line in the sand and it has catalyzed a major paradigm shift. Whether you love it or hate it, a key feature of the Patient Protection and Affordable Care Act (PPACA) is increasing attention to consumers' personal and financial accountability for their own health, as well as ensuring that consumers can access preventive care without barriers. The advent of health insurance exchanges will only magnify this impact as consumers move to purchase their own policies without their employers as intermediaries.

- **Technology**–the widespread availability of sensors and smart phones, augmented by the profound impact of social media, has made it feasible to efficiently engage consumers and to engage in true mass customization. True, we may be creating a whole race of activity monkeys who measure every bodily output including how many times they measure it, but we have a long way to go. Some consumers' idea of prevention is still ordering the DIET Coke with their Wendy's Triple Baconator.

It's a sign of the changing times when large insurance carriers are dedicating serious resources to preventing illnesses that may befall those they no longer insure, and the Hostess Corp, makers of Twinkies, have filed bankruptcy in part due to the trend towards healthy eating. At the conference there was a panel featuring representatives of the food industry, including Nestle, Kellogg (Kashi), Ralph's (retired executive), Immaculate Baking Company and The Hartman Group. James Richardson from The Hartman Group made the point that between meal healthy snacks are THE growth engine for the grocery industry these days. He cited a statistic that snacking accounts for 52% of all adult eating and that in the current U.S. food purchasing environment, 62% of snack choices are about people trying to achieve specific health goals. It's a good time to be an almond grower and a bad time to be a Twinkie.

On the other hand, Richardson also talked about how people are now more relaxed about body image than they once were. He said that "people have moved from the Jane Fonda orientation of pain and punishment" to achieve body perfection and now are "ok with a little chub." Well thank God for that, as most of the people I know are going to choose chub over punishment any day of the week. I am just hoping that no one comes up with a new market for things that are both punishing and chub-inducing. That would just be cruel. Ironically, the word "patient" is derived from an ancient term meaning "to tolerate or suffer" according to Mark Murrison from MDVIP, so perhaps punishment is simply unavoidable.

In response to the above-described market drivers, there is a nascent but rapidly growing set of ideas and business models blooming around consumer health and wellness. The consumerization of healthcare is and will take many forms depending on people's health status, age, technical literacy, and personal and financial motivation. Furthermore, this consumerization trend is forcing companies traditionally not thought of as consumer branding organizations to learn quickly about how to reach this powerful and lucrative emerging sector. There was a lengthy discussion at the conference about how traditional brands such as Kellogg and Nestle do not have any cache in the healthy food market so the companies go to some lengths to hide those names on the healthy food brands they own (such as Kashi).

Consumer branding is going to be an interesting exercise among the big insurance companies over the next several years. These entities will be forced to re-focus a sizeable portion of their marketing efforts toward the individual and away from the large employers as Health Insurance Exchanges (HIX) shift the purchasing dynamic downstream. Depending on whom you ask, between 30 and 100 million people will be directly purchasing their health insurance from a HIX within the next several years. No one knows better than payers how to follow the money, except maybe Deep Throat (the one from All the President's Men, not the one with Linda Lovelace). But on the other hand, this segment of the healthcare market has not been in the business of direct-to-consumer advertising like the folks in the drug industry have been. Will their brands carry weight with consumers or will they be viewed as punishment and be better hidden from view? By and large consumers are not especially in love with their health insurance providers these days so it will be a serious exercise in marketing genius to bridge this divide.

In closing, I must add that while not a primary focus of the conference, there was an odd tendency for it to drift towards the pet marketplace repeatedly throughout the day. Tom Blair, a Nestle/Purina executive, talked about how consumers who may sacrifice their own health will never do so when it comes to their pets. He cited a WalMart study that said in times of economic stress, consumers will cut back on every category of food purchasing except infant food and pet food and he described how pet foods are now becoming more and more organic, gluten free, and otherwise Whole Foods like. As I and my table-mate, a well-known medical device investor, watched a presentation about FitBits and other devices for tracking fitness, he leaned over to me and said, "Now I bet there's a pet market for that too," suggesting that people would fork over plenty of cash to put a step tracker on Rover's collar. Since every discussion about consumer health eventually turns to social media, there were also numerous remarks about the connection between social media and people's pets. Maybe there is an as-yet-untapped market for healthy between meal cat snacks to fortify them when they are resting between YouTube video shoots. Now there's a focus group. Marketing geniuses, start your engines. – LS

What Do Patients Really Want From Health Care?

A central theme of my writing has been the urgent need to understand medicine—and to design healthcare innovation (including biopharmaceuticals and health services)—from the patient's perspective, something many key stakeholders (and would-be stakeholders, such as entrepreneurs—see here) fail to do—at their peril.

So what do patients really want from health care, anyway? In JAMA, Dr. Allan Detsky, an internist and health policy expert at the University of Toronto tackled this question, based on his years of clinical and research experience. It's a terrific, and sobering, piece, as highlighted below.

Highest priority:

- Restoring health when ill—"the majority of patients focus on relieving illness and symptoms rather than disease prevention"

- Timeliness—care is wanted "immediately"

- Kindness—"in the days before health insurance, patients paid for care that consisted primarily of kindness"

- Hope and certainty—even in dire situations, patients "want to have hope and be offered options that might help"

- Continuity, choice, coordination—care from "same person or team" important

- Private room—including "their own bathroom and no roommate"

- No out-of-pocket costs—"patients want to pay as little as possible" themselves and to know that "insurance or third-party coverage is always available to them"

- The best medicine—patients want to know their doctors are "highly qualified" but do not want this information "to be statistical. They prefer testimonials from other patients or clinicians they trust"

- Medications and surgery—treatments that patients "perceive will require little effort" are strongly preferred, as are "medications and surgical procedures" compared to "clinical strategies that involve behavior changes."

Lower priority:

- Efficiency—patients only modestly interested in care that delivers "the most value with the least resources"

- Aggregate-level statistics—far less important to patients than treatments are likely to work "in their specific case." Also, as before, "testimonials trump scientific evidence."

- Equity—patients are more concerned with whether "they are receiving adequate health care services" than whether "all members of society should have a right to it, regardless of income"

- Conflicts of interest—patients are less concerned about motivation of provider in prescribing particular treatments "as long as the service helps make them better without increasing the costs they have to bear"

Lowest priority:

- Real costs—"individual patients have virtually no interest in costs they do not bear"

- Percent GNP devoted to healthcare—"just a number and has absolutely no relevance for individual patients"

Implications:

Detsky comments, "Some might say that the consumers' preferences described in this article are irrational and unrealistic; that may be true…. However, the lack of rationality does not render these preferences irrelevant." (I wonder if a seasonal reference to Steve Martin's "Holiday Wish" might be apropos here.)

He adds that these patient preferences do not "render efficiency, evidence, and rational thinking in health care unimportant," though they suggest that "policy makers need to truly understand and appreciate what the public really wants when they undertake efforts to reform health care." – DS

As Therapeutics Become Personal, Patient Social Networks May Become More Essential

An interesting WSJ article discusses how patients with an exceptionally rare disease—in this case, spontaneous coronary artery dissection (SCAD)—used social networks to find each other, to organize, and ultimately to drive research efforts into this otherwise obscure condition.

This story highlights the value of social networks to link individual patients into a community (PatientsLikeMe remains the canonical example) that has much greater voice, and also emphasizes the use of patient networks to provide not just peer support but also to drive progress both by (a) lobbying as a collective for more research; (b) catalyzing research by offering a ready-made cohort of patients, a potentially attractive proposition for both academic researchers (in this case, the Mayo Clinic) and industry investigators (see here for PatientsLikeMe example, here for broader discussion).

The second point is especially important. It's likely that patient communities will rapidly evolve from "nice to have" to "must have," especially as pharmaceutical companies focus increasingly on opportunities in the rare disease space (e.g. Ultragenyx, raising a $45M A-round this summer), and as diseases previously viewed as single entities are reconceptualized as collections of many, genetically-defined entities, each with its own patient population and potentially unique therapeutic (e.g. Xalkori, Pfizer's just-approved drug for patients with lung cancer associated with a particular genetic abnormality).

For university researchers, and particularly for drug companies, figuring out which of these rare disease to focus on depends on many factors, including the inherent tractability of the underlying disorder; yet, patients have a tremendous opportunity to drive the development of therapeutics by self-organizing and in essence making it as easy as possible to study their condition. Unfortunately, it's also possible that patients who don't organize in this fashion may ultimately miss out on the chance to help themselves—as if they don't already have enough to worry about. – DS

Getting Better: Online Communities Elevate Voice Of The Patient

I've previously discussed the need for a better way of connecting the discrete healthcare-related problems identified by patients and physicians with solvers who might be able to develop a solution—perhaps an immediate fix, perhaps a longer-term effort.

I'm grateful for the volume of feedback received about this idea, which has included specific suggestions from patients; an introduction by several CEOs to a range relatively-new efforts designed to tackle different key elements of this idea; and a few frustrated entrepreneurs who poignantly describe their struggles trying to change a fairly intransigent system.

A few observations about some of the online patient communities that I've encountered: First, there appear to be a number of patient-support (peer-to-peer) communities, both disease specific and more general. Several in the general category (e.g. MDJunction, Inspire, HealingWell) seem at least superficially similar; presumably the user experience depends upon the level of participation within a particular patient community.

Other models seem obviously distinctive: for example, AskaPatient provides fairly detailed patient-submitted reviews of various medications; the prose tends to be a bit less dry than the typical drug label—for example, a recent user of one neuropsychiatric medication reported that "Having an orgasm is like smashing a pimple. I am not sure if I want to continue taking this drug." Yes, think that one over.

HealtheTreatment, a website that explicitly aspires to be the Trip Advisor or Yelp of chronic diseases, solicits and concisely presents patient experiences and ratings, so that you can immediately see, for a particular condition, what therapies other patients have received and how they felt the various treatment options worked for them. Of course, as Eric Topol emphasizes in his topical book, "The Creative Destruction of Medicine," the real challenge is personalizing therapy so you are treating a specific patient, not a population; understanding the breadth of potential responses to a drug doesn't necessarily provide insight into how you, individually, will respond.

As I've discussed in a number of recent pieces (e.g. here, also this NRDD article with Eric Schadt and Stephen Friend), it would be extremely powerful to link the sort of detailed phenotypic measurements captured by HealtheTreatments with whole genome sequencing and gene expression measures, and then interrogate this coherent dataset with a robust analytic platform; these sorts of efforts are just starting to take off now, and are likely to become table stakes for serious drug discovery in the not-too-distant future.

HealthTap is a website that enables patients to ask questions of physicians, who can earn status points by providing answers with which other physicians agree. It has received a lot of attention recently, including this recent NYT article by Randall Stross. (One quick aside: I'm a big fan of Stross—eBoys is a Silicon Valley classic—but I didn't agree with his critique of HealthTap for not including physician certification. In general, the certification of healthcare providers [and, I'd suggest, certification more generally] tends to be poorly validated—if validated at all—and rarely associated in any robust or credible way with improved patient outcomes; it also a significant [and underappreciated] source of revenue for the societies and agencies responsible for administration. It's understandable that we all want our providers to be well-trained, but it's unfortunate that we've selected, and in many cases, really bought into a metric that may be more likely to offer false reassurance than meaningful guidance. See this piece I wrote about our "metrics fetish," and links therein.)

The Experience Project remains my most unexpected finding—it's essentially a collection of stories, individual narratives, that in some cases are health related, in other cases are not. It evidently grew out of a support community for multiple sclerosis patients created by a Stanford graduate, and evolved over time into a forum for people to tell their stories —sort of like Robert Coles' "Literature of Social Reflection" course (or his "The Call of Stories"book) meets Web 2.0. It's a fascinating site, which I suspect might offer newly-diagnosed patients an impressionistic overview of a particular condition, though perhaps not an engaged, interactive community of patient-solvers.

For that, you'd have to go to PatientsLikeMe, one of the earliest patient communities, and still one of the most innovative and forward thinking, as I've frequently discussed in this space (e.g. here, here, here, here and here). It's focused explicitly on the concept of patient empowerment, and has grown from a site focused specifically on Lou Gehrig's disease (ALS) into a broader community attracting a greater variety of patients. The big question has always been whether the PatientsLikeMe model would work for conditions that were serious but not as devastating as ALS; I'm not sure the verdict is in yet, but I tend to root for them, as I feel that founder James Heywood is an ambitious and disruptive thinker who has always kept the voice of the patient at the front of his mind and at the center of his efforts.

Interestingly, one fairly large swatch of white space is the uncaptured input from the millions of patients who contend with illness to the extent they think about it when they are sick or symptomatic, but otherwise aren't inclined to join patient communities, and are disinclined to define themselves (even in part) through their condition. We need to find a better way to hear the voices of these patients as well.

If you google "online patient communities," the first link you get is to this article written by KevinMD ("Social media's leading physician voice," according to his website) entitled, "How online patient communities may make money from patient data." The gist of the article is that some online communities—including, transparently, PatientsLikeMe—are supported, at least in part, by selling information they collect to industry. "Patients have to guard against being exploited for profit," KevinMD advises.

I'd look at this situation somewhat differently (though I absolutely agree on the need for complete transparency): patients may look for many things from an online community—support, understanding, advice. But for many, I suspect they might also want someone to pay attention to their most important problems, and to focus efforts and resources on solving these. In other words, if you have a difficult condition, you arguably *should* hope—fervently—that industry is trying to listen to your voice, trying to understand your problems, and yes, trying to use this information to make an effective product they can sell for a profit.

All too often, industry seems to be viewed as the villain, yet industry is ultimately responsible for bringing to the market almost all new medical solutions; as Tom Stossel and I have discussed in the WSJ, forward-thinking patient groups dedicated to medical progress get this, and partner with industry in a highly productive fashion, a collaborative relationship that could serve as a model for effective translation in online patient communities as well. – DS

The Star Thrower—Or How Healthcare Looks To Consumers

It is always interesting how events find ways of connecting themselves together even when they seem so unrelated.

I was at my sister Alexis' graduation from law school where I had gone directly from leaving a several day event organized by Health Evolution Partners. At the event I had occasion to meet with Dr. Charlotte Yeh, Chief Medical Officer of AARP. Charlotte and I had been talking about the substance of a future consumer-focused panel we would be doing together and I was telling her that what I want most to come from it is the true voice of the consumer. I told her that I go to too many conferences where we all talk about consumers but no one actually speaks from that point of view. That is why I wanted her, John Santa from Consumer Reports and consumer advocate and Director of the Institute for Sexual Medicine, Kim Whittemore, to be there to represent. "Can you imagine?" I said, "Actual consumers talking about consumers at a consumer health conference? Go figure. It will be a nice refreshing change from everyone else in the healthcare system talking about how consumers feel about changes in the healthcare system."

So the next day when I was sitting at the graduation ceremony, having left the healthcare world behind for a day, or so I thought, I was pulled right back to the consumer health topic by one of the graduation speaker's allegories. He told a story adapted from the essay called "The Star Thrower" (or "starfish story") written by Loren Eiseley. As I sat there listening, the story gave me a total epiphany about how to describe the difference in views between how the healthcare "system" talks about consumers (aka patients), and how consumers themselves actually feel when trying to get taken care of within the healthcare system. Here is a somewhat updated version of the excerpt from "The Star Thrower" that reflects the story told at the graduation (the original version has two men in it and is somewhat less hopeful, but this version has become the "go to" storytellers' friend):

An old man had a habit of early morning walks on the beach. One day, after a storm, he saw a human figure in the distance moving like a dancer. As he came closer he saw that it was a young woman and she was not dancing but was reaching down to the sand, picking up a starfish and very gently throwing them into the ocean.

"Young lady," he asked, "Why are you throwing starfish into the ocean?"

"The sun is up, and the tide is going out, and if I do not throw them in they will die."

"But young lady, do you not realize that there are miles and miles of beach and starfish all along it? You cannot possibly make a difference."

The young woman listened politely, paused and then bent down, picked up another starfish and threw it into the sea, past the breaking waves, saying, "It made a difference for that one."

Wow, that says it all, right? We healthcare people talk in categories and trends. We talk about how all consumers should be treated and how we will deliver products and services for the masses. We design systems that are supposed to work for all, or at least most, and we talk about the few for whom those systems won't work as the exceptions. But in reality, consumers (and I know this because at times I am one, just as we all are) don't think of engagement with the healthcare system at all. Consumers are there to get their own singular needs met and could not really care less about whether they are the masses or the exception, only that they get good care and have their voice heard and feel better after the experience.

I think the main reason these two stories—"The Star Thrower" and the consumer experience—connected for me was because of the stories that Charlotte and I were sharing as we sat on the cliff overlooking the beach at Laguna Niguel (rough duty...not). We were sharing stories of "one off" consumer experiences that defied the "norms" but which clearly typified my point above.

I told Charlotte a story that had been relayed to me years ago by Dr. Rick Chung, who used to be the Chief Medical Officer at the behavioral health company I worked at before Psilos. In that true story, a seriously mentally ill patient who lived at home kept calling into our clinical office acting erratic because he thought there were bugs crawling all over his house. "Yeah," said the clinicians in our office thinking as health systems people, "Poor guy is schizophrenic and must be off his meds. Let's counsel him on compliance and the importance of a regular schedule." And so it went for a few weeks, patient freaking out, care managers trying to remotely advise, costs of engagement rising, until finally someone from the office said they would go see him in person and determine if he needed to be hospitalized to be stabilized.

And you know what they found? Someone who happened to be schizophrenic but whose house was actually crawling with bugs. The poor guy didn't need a psychiatric admission, he needed a damn exterminator. And once the bugs were gone he was pretty much just fine; still schizophrenic, sure, but stable and doing his normal thing and not needing any expensive services.

Charlotte responded in kind by telling me a story of a 93-year-old woman she had heard about recently who lived in an apartment where much construction was going on next door. While old and frail, the woman was mentally quite stable but suddenly started having terrible paranoia at night and started forgetting where she was. Despite having 24-hour attendants at home, her situation was such that she was hospitalized, medicated and the sundowning (a syndrome of confusion that dementia patients often experience in the evening hours) actually got worse; many resources were expended trying to figure out what was wrong.

Charlotte was explaining that one of the most important things for patients like this is having familiar, unchanging surroundings. It took a non-medical person to figure out that the reason the whole episode started wasn't because dementia was increasing, but because someone had removed the photos that had graced her bedroom walls for years such that they wouldn't fall down as a result of the construction hammering going on next door. When she was going to bed she was getting confused about her surroundings and thus exhibiting the dementia-like symptoms that had previously not been present. When the pictures were returned to the wall, the patient was well again, as if nothing ever happened.

It is very true that setting up healthcare systems of any kind requires a certain amount of standardization. The manner in which medical personnel screen patients and the system receives them has to have some regimentation or there would be chaos and even higher costs, and, for the most part, it works pretty well much of the time. But like the starfish in Eiseley's story, looking at the healthcare system from a population-based approach isn't really good enough for the individual patient consumer. We have to figure out ways to balance resource management to serve the maximum number of people well with individual attention so we don't miss an individual starfish we could have saved.

As our U.S. healthcare system now takes a sharp right turn towards consumer-engagement and the purveyors of products and services figure out that the patients are now their customers (not just the doctors, the hospital administrators, the employer benefit managers, etc), this balance is going to be a hard one to achieve, particularly at the beginning. For instance, to set up a health insurance exchange for individuals to purchase insurance directly, we must establish basic processes and products that fit the most people and serve the lowest common denominator. I fear for the wave of patient horror stories that will emerge early from this process because expediency is often the enemy of personalization, and yet we need both.

As our healthcare system goes through massive transformation from the insurance system to the delivery system to the system of shared accountability with consumers that is emerging, it is going to be an incredible challenge to establish systems that don't let the starfish slip through the cracks. There will be an even greater need for a cadre of consumer ombudsmen who will look for those who need to be picked up off the beach for special attention when the population-based rules don't apply. I am sure it will be an iterative process.

It is worth noting that, according to the all-knowing, all-seeing Wikipedia, Eiseley's Starfish story has been edited and revised many times as people have used it to tell their organizations' stories. In 2003 it was adapted by an African children's AIDS organization to tell a more hopeful story; their new ending goes like this:

The old man looked at the young woman inquisitively and thought about what she had done. Inspired, he joined her in throwing starfish back into the sea. Soon others joined, and all the starfish were saved. - LS

VII.

Employers, Insurers, Regulators

Employers & Health Innovation: Go Long Or Advance One Yard At A Time

Not long ago I had the honor of being asked to moderate a panel on cardiology innovations at the first Innovation Day meeting of the Pacific Business Group on Health (PBGH). For those of you who don't know PBGH, they are a San Francisco-based organization founded in 1989 that has 60 member companies comprised of large employers providing health care coverage to over 10 million Americans. This is not your mom and pop crowd; companies involved in PBGH are those like Bechtel, Safeway, CalPERS, PG&E, WalMart, Exxon, Cisco, Twitter, Facebook, Intel, GE, McKesson...the everyday names everyone knows. PBGH helps them think about healthcare policy and how to implement logical health benefit strategies that meet their corporate objectives.

The idea for the meeting, designed by Amanda Goltz, Senior Manager Director of New Initiatives for PBGH, and Aaron Apodaca, a San Francisco-based consultant who works with investors, foundations, and health and technology companies, was to engage large employers and the payers with whom they work to engage directly with entrepreneurs/innovators and venture capitalists in a discussion about new approaches to tackling employee benefit issues such as diabetes, cardiology, and other health problems that lead to high costs and absenteeism. 10 young innovative companies* with solutions in these areas presented to the crowd of about 60 employer representatives; Chief Medical Officers and other senior executives from 5 of the nation's largest health insurance companies were on hand to comment on the companies' ideas and to engage in a discussion among the innovators, the employer representatives, and the hangers on there from the VC investor world. It was an interesting mix of people–one that rarely sits in the same room at the same time.

In fact, it is very unusual for young medical device and diagnostic companies to interact with the employee benefit people who actually sign the checks to buy what these companies sell. Under normal circumstances, the money these the medical device companies receive first travels through the hands of the employer, payer, and provider organization before it hits their bank account. Rarely do medical device companies communicate directly with those who actually speak for the consumer of their products. Even stranger, one rarely gets to observe the repartee that occurs between payer and entrepreneur and employer all at the same time–it's like looking behind the curtain at Wizard of Oz central. Having worked in the healthcare field for nearly 25 years, I have never seen quite this discussion. I was happy to get to be a fly on the wall (and for a brief while on the podium).

David Lansky, PBGH's CEO, said they had created this event because, "Employers want more disruptive ways of achieving health care cost goals." He also added that PBGH and its employer members' hopes that health plans would fix their problems have faded and thus they have to take matters into their own hands. He stated that employers' key issues are:

- concern about the effectiveness and sustainability of today's health care system; frustrated that cost of care is unrelated to quality

- belief that current tools—consumer-directed health plans, pay-for-performance, quality measurement—are having little impact

- a sense that most delivery systems and health plans are slow and timid in seeking efficiencies and improving quality; and,

- a recognition that health reform is unlikely to slow cost increases

Added Larry Leisure, an Operating Partner at Kleiner Perkins who has worked in around the health benefits field even longer than I have, added, "Employers should be the catalyst for innovation turned into action to achieve the Triple Aim."

But what became evident to me as I listened throughout the day is that there is still a pretty good-sized gap between what employers may ideally want to do and whether they really want to step up and own the job of catalyst. In particular, I was struck by how prophetic a comment Dr. Arnie Milstein, Stanford professor, health benefits expert and PBGH Medical Director, made during the introductions, saying that despite the need to manage costs, "Employers have limited bandwidth to take on too many innovation at any one time." While PBGH's members have an overall strategic goal of reducing health benefit inflation to CPI+1% by 2015, by the end of the day it was pretty obvious that they can and will bite off only so much.

The employers in the room made it clear that diabetes, cardiology and spine costs are the 3 horsemen of the health benefits apocalypse and that everything else was pretty much beyond their ability to think about. Remember that old poster of the U.S. as seen through the eyes of a New Yorker, where NY is huge in the foreground and everything else was either New Jersey or the Pacific Ocean? A good metaphor for their mindset.

Innovative medical device, diagnostic and wellness companies present at PBGH Innovation Day to pitch ideas about sinusitis, sleep apnea, fertility, asthma, wellness games, etc. were interesting and all, but seemed to barely rise to the level of attention when compared to the varsity league. The vendors there to discuss new screening and interventional tools or wellness apps to help weed out the unnecessary diabetes and cardiology treatments got some attention, but anything that was discussed under the category of "managing absenteeism" or around other medical conditions got far less mind share. Good thing there wasn't a company in the room promoting hearing loss interventions, as it would have fallen on deaf ears.

One employer said, "It is a real uphill battle for 2nd tier medical issues to get attention." Another said, "We can't measure absenteeism or how much bad sleep costs us so we don't spend too much time on it." Another added that Facebook probably led to more time lost in the workplace than did healthcare-related absenteeism—a provocative thought (it didn't come from the Facebook representative, natch).

Employers also made it clear that they expected their payer colleagues to screen innovations and figure out what was worth adopting—that the employers themselves don't want to be stuck worrying about product evaluations they feel ill-equipped to evaluate and that are, as far as they are concerned, basically not their table. They voiced frustration about the speed and efficiency with which this process has occurred on the payer side.

The payers (represented at this meeting by Aetna, United Health, Wellpoint, HealthNet and Cigna) clearly want to pay for innovations that may save money only after the innovators themselves have paid for independent proof that their new products and services could deliver improved quality at reduced cost. While payers were willing to try a pilot here and there, they were much more interested in adopting a sure thing, thus raising the bar for adopting new innovations higher than the gates of Troy. And this made it seem like the times, they are never gonna be changin', that innovators would be talking to the hand, as it were, and that this would deflect these innovation vendors back to employers as they seek an audience for their new wares.

This bounce-back strategy, however, is not likely to meet success, the employers said, because they are tired of interacting with a hodgepodge of narrowly-focused vendors and want the carriers to stitch these programs into a ready-made quilt for them. "Is it really an employer's job to buy all these apps for employees? Why don't we just give them an allowance and let employees deal with it? Let's give them an allowance and an exchange where innovators can sell to them directly." Innovators: welcome to your ping-pong game. You are the ball.

The bottom line according to the employers? "We only want to pay directly for things when the health benefit cost return on investment (ROI) is very tangible; intervening in lifestyle issues is not an employer issue." And by tangible they meant not just real, but timely. One employer described how a $700 incentive paid to employees to encourage them to stop smoking had a 7-10 year payback and questioned whether it was really worth it, particularly since that employee was unlikely to still work there 7-10 years later. In case you are wondering what employer expectations are when it comes to new innovations, Dr. Milstein laid it out for the audience. Innovations worth adopting should have:

- A low implementation burden (time and cost) relative to plausible advantage gain;

- Independent impact evaluations, funded by the innovator, to justify adoption and continued use;

- Results-based pricing, including zero pricing when an innovation is ineffective; and,

- An overall result of fewer treatments per person, fewer services or product inputs per person and/or less cost per person.

Furthermore, the employer audience noted that physicians are the ones that have to be engaged in this discussion since they are the real gatekeepers between the employees and what medical products really get used. 'We can say we will or won't pay for things but we've been doing that and strong-arming through the payer side for years without success." The conclusion from this discussion was that payment reform was key to reducing health benefit costs. Without true alignment of financial interests, change is out there grazing among the unicorns.

This orientation has led certain proactive employers to cut out the payer middleman (at least in part) and go straight to the heart of the delivery system to fix their health benefit cost woes. WalMart, a company that has the conveniently appropriate tag line of "Save Money, Live Better," is clearly intent on making sure its health benefit activities live up to this slogan, and have just announced an innovative Centers of Excellence program in which they will direct all heart, spine and transplant surgeries to 6 selected providers (unless patients are too ill to travel). If and when WalMart's 1.3 million U.S.

associates go to these providers for such services, WalMart will cover 100% of costs and associates will bear $0 in expenses. Go elsewhere and buyer beware. This is WalMart's way of saying they are tired of suboptimal outcomes but are willing to pay well for good performance, selecting the Cleveland Clinic, Geisinger, Mayo, Mercy Springfield, Scott & White Memorial and Virginia Mason for its small network.

This is an interesting deviation from past approaches that have favored consumer choice. If PBGH's participants are any indication (and I think they are since they represent over 10 million covered lives), they appear to care more these days about value for their healthcare dollar than consumer convenience and choice. And who can blame them? They also voiced a feeling that employers themselves are better at wielding leverage with the delivery system and that payers have lost this fight in their battle to please too many constituencies. On the other hand, employers also recognized how hard it is and will continue to be to positively communicate to their employees about this tightening down of the network—that employees are as suspicious of their employers as they are of the payers. Said one, "We are seen as the rule-makers and the take-awayers."

The challenge for employers is fairly profound, as it was noted that employees spend an average of less than one hour selecting their health benefit plan options and that most people select their doctors and hospitals based on proximity to home or referrals from a friend, not quality, cost or anything else the employers perceive as essential to better ROI. Employees are as resistant to "yet another app" as are their employers, and employees' ability to be part of the solution instead of part of the problem lies in their perceived sense of personal accountability outweighing their sense of entitlement, according to a benefits consultant present at the meeting.

What seemed clear to me at the end of the day is that more collaboration between the players in the room is essential if real change is going to happen. Payers, employers, innovators and providers need to figure out how to work collaboratively if we are going to advance the ball more than one yard at a time (I'm moving from baseball to football analogies in honor of Fall). Staying in a world where payers want to keep the castle gates closed as long as possible, employers want to stay out of the fray, providers don't want to be told to perform and employees don't want to be accountable is not a prescription for change.

As someone who works most closely with the innovators/entrepreneurs, particularly those in the medical device and diagnostic space, it is time to get to know the real payers, the employers. Don't approach them to sell your wares, but to learn how they think about the problem you are solving, whether they think about the problem you are solving, and how you might jointly approach payers with mutually beneficial opportunities to collaborate (mostly on your dime). You are going to have to come into the light, where economic studies reign supreme and where you can't get away with the bare minimum of clinical evidence to get attention. You think the FDA is tough? They aren't paying. The employers are and they are running out of cash and patience. But what they want is clear: simple to implement innovations that result in healthier employees and lower cost per employee when they pay the benefits bill. Seems reasonable to me. – LS

Doing The Right Thing: Priceless

An article entitled "Wal-Mart Cuts Some Health Care Benefits," details Wal-Mart's decision to eliminate coverage for new part-time workers who work less than 24 hours/week and to increase costs, including deductibles and premiums, for virtually all other workers. This is a pretty common story right now—you can read it any day of the week in any local paper where large and small business are the primary advertisers in that publication as the economy is driving employers to the brink. With unemployment at a record high and consumer spending driving downward, employers don't need to offer high benefits to attract workers and can't afford to spend such a large proportion of their income on them anyway. Yeah, yeah, we've heard it all before. Cue violins and angry union workers. People spend their time blaming the PPACA health reform law for wrecking the healthcare benefit system but that ire is misdirected: it's the economy, stupid, as they say in politics.

Anyway, it wasn't the overall punch line of the story that caught my attention, it was one particular section, to wit:

Wal-Mart's new health offerings will require many employees who smoke to pay a significant penalty. They will be required to pay an extra $10 to $90 each pay period— $260 to $2,340 a year—if they want health coverage. Several other large employers have begun charging higher premiums to employees who smoke, according to Mercer, a benefits consulting firm. Among the largest employers, about 28 percent vary their premiums based on tobacco use.

Mr. Rossiter defended the penalty for smokers, saying, "Tobacco users generally consume about 25 percent more health care services than nontobacco users."

In its health care brochures, Wal-Mart told its employees that diseases caused by tobacco result in $96 billion in extra health care costs nationwide. And it noted that some other prominent companies, including Home Depot, Macy's and PepsiCo, charge smokers more as part of their health plans.

Tammy Yancey, a $9.50-an-hour gas attendant at a Sam's Club in Pinellas Park, Fla., complained that she would no longer be able to afford health insurance from the company. Ms. Yancey, a smoker, said her premiums would jump to $127.90 every two *weeks—or $3,325 a year—up from $53.80 at present, when she earns $12,000 a year from her job. "I won't be able to afford the insurance," she said. "And I really can't go without insurance because I have a heart problem."*

Now I don't know Ms. Yancey and her circumstances and I don't mean to pick on her, but that last sentence captures all that has been wrong about how consumers interact with the health care system—lack of personal accountability. We expect our employers to pay our benefits and then we all blithely go around using them with nary a thought to how our own actions affect the cost of those services. I don't care how educated or self-aware you are, I bet that the last time you went to the doctor for ANY reason you did not ask what the cost of services was going to be and whether there was a less expensive alternative.

Can you imagine undertaking that kind of behavior when you stroll into Best Buy to purchase a television? I doubt it. You probably came armed with articles from Consumer Reports and reviews from some geek website, plus feedback from friends and a mood to bargain. You are going to wander around the store comparing pictures on 30 TVs as if your life depended on seeing the pores on Alex Smith's face as he throws for a touchdown. You are going to compare how the color looks on each unit like you are auditioning to be Rachel Zoe's styling assistant. And you are going to get the biggest damn screen that your car can transport at the lowest price you can wrangle and damned if you're not going to get them to throw in the fancy remote control thingy for free.

But in healthcare? Never. We go in, we say help me, we walk out, we get the bill 6 weeks later and have no idea what it says. We throw it away and hope that the next one looks better after the coverage is applied. We pay the remaining co-insurance bill when it comes in the collection agency envelope. We sheepishly admit we have no idea what just happened. And worse: we don't care that much.

Now add in the fact that we are not only engaging in making bad health care purchases, but we are acting counter to our own good health in doing so by smoking or overeating or not exercising or whatever our self-abuse of choice might be. Smoking is easy to pick on because we all know it is deadly. The problem is that before it kills you, it causes all sorts of expensive health crises—hypertension, heart disease, asthma, cancer, etc.—that your employer gets the privilege of paying for if they provide you with health insurance. If cigarettes just killed you quickly, no problem: an insurance payer's dream. The issue is that they kill you slowly and cause high expenses along the way—roughly 25%-40% higher healthcare costs than others, depending on who you ask.

Ms. Yancey, of the NY Times article described, notes that she is being forced to pay $3300/year extra for health benefits because she is a smoker. If she is an average smoker she is probably spending at least that much on the cigarettes themselves. At nearly $5/pack now, that is almost precisely the cost of a 2-pack a day habit. Worse yet, she reports that she has a heart condition, which I'm guessing can't be improved by the smoking. So are we supposed to feel angry at Wal-Mart for enforcing this clearly discriminatory rule against smokers? I don't think so.

I am quite confident that Wal-Mart offers coverage for smoking cessation programs if they are like most large employers. I am not suggesting that quitting smoking is easy—in fact I am quite confident it is not. However, there is no way in hell that we can get our nation's healthcare costs under control if there is no personal accountability here.

In health insurance programs that have provided people with clear transparency about what things cost (e.g., the cost of one type of pharmaceutical vs. another), it has been widely demonstrated that people tend to select the cheaper choice if it is clinically equivalent or less invasive (e.g., less invasive surgical procedures for cardiac conditions vs. more expensive open your chest like a bagel procedures). In fact, Wal-Mart has been the poster child for this, launching a very successful program to sell most generic drugs for $4 for a month's prescription, thus driving serious traffic into their stores by consumers who know a bargain when they see one. We know that engaging people like real consumers, such as when they are buying that HDTV, can make a meaningful difference in healthcare costs. And I am quite sure that people already know that cigarettes make healthcare more expensive. We can't force people to stop smoking, but we can make them pay for making the more expensive choice as we would in any similar situation. I mean seriously, no way Best Buy is throwing in the 3D TV option for free—they are going to charge you for it AND get you on the installation. When you choose a more expensive product, you pay. And that is what the smoking issue is to healthcare.

Let's do some simple math: the cost to employers of offering healthcare benefits went up about 9% on average this last year. Wal-Mart's U.S. sales have been essentially flat for 9 consecutive quarters. That means that overall profits are down due in part to rising healthcare costs. If this continues into next year, it's only going to get worse for Wal-Mart. It starts with health benefit reductions and ends with worker lay-offs. So by taking action to essentially penalize those that disproportionately increase healthcare costs (smokers), Wal-Mart is acting quite rationally from a financial standpoint. No one likes to hear this, particularly when the implication is "ok, smoking I get…what comes next?" Wal-Mart has not said they will increase the cost of benefits for people who are overweight or who don't exercise or who eat some of the very food that is sold at Wal-Mart (Velveeta, anyone?), but it is the logical extension of the idea.

To avoid going down this rabbit hole, people just have to become more serious about how they purchase their own healthcare and manage their own health if any of this is going to change. We need to give a damn about what that visit to the doctor costs and whether the generic drug is equal but cheaper and whether a particular MRI is really necessary. We need to start asking what things cost and bargaining with our healthcare providers. Guess what? That's how insurance carriers make money. They buy deep discounts from hospitals and health plans and pharmaceutical companies and pass it through with a mark-up. Wake up, consumer—you can play at this game and you better if you want to stay insured.

I saw a study this week by the Annals of Emergency Medicine that said that 11% of patients prefer to go to the Emergency Room of the hospital over going to their Primary Care Physician's office not because they have an emergency, but because the ER offers more services. Holy crap. I prefer to go to the Four Seasons rather than the Holiday Inn because it offers more services, but I am generally expecting to pay extra for the cabana boy, not the same fee. Unfortunately, because of the way insurance works, those 11% (who know full well it costs more to go to the ER) are probably paying about the same out of pocket for their incredibly lame choice.   Bleeding from the eyes? Yes, go to the ER. You find it handy that the ER can do all your tests in one place? Suck it up, people.

Cost of average ER visit: $1000 or so.

Cost of average physician office visit: $200 or so.

Doing the right thing: Priceless.

Oh, and one final thought. Wal-Mart, if you are listening, you are not helping yourself by selling cigarettes in your store. – LS

Road Not Taken: The Unrecognized Harm Of Excessive Regulation

The difficulty of creating new and better medicines has been the subject of extensive—at times excessive—soul searching, a process that's intensified as high-profile patents expire, along with their associated revenue streams, traditionally relied upon to support future R&D. As a result, both biopharma companies and patients awaiting new treatments find themselves struggling for viable solutions.

Predictably, industry (where I obviously reside) attributes excessive regulation, regulators say "don't blame us," and considered reporters and observers typically try to split the difference—maybe everyone is a little bit at fault.

The problem with this resolution is that it's a cop-out; while there is clearly a measure of shared responsibility, it's willful blindness not to recognize the extent to which a deliberate and very conscious regulatory policy is putting a damper on what has traditionally been the world's most vibrant drug development ecosystem.

It's not that other factors (such as the complexity of science) aren't important—in fact, it's precisely because developing new drugs is challenging, so inherently difficult, that's it's crucial to do everything within our control to work together and create an environment, an ecosystem, that stimulates and enables meaningful innovation.

The most significant—and potentially, most correctable (which is why it's especially frustrating—it's explicitly of our own making) problem—is that regulators, as others have astutely observed, seem to have misapplied the "precautionary principle," colloquially understood as "first, do no harm." The problem isn't so much the sentiment as the way it's reduced to practice.

We are far more attuned to the potential harms a new product may create than the potential harms a new product may avoid. No regulator wants to face a Congressional committee—generally a bipartisan committee, incidentally, as indignant posturing and self-righteous outrage seems easily to cross party lines—demanding to know why an approved drug was ultimately discovered to cause unexpected problems. Raise the bar for approval high enough and you reduce the likelihood of this occurring.

Unfortunately, far less attention is paid to the reverse—to the very real patients who never receive a new medication because excessive regulation resulted in prohibitively high hurdles, effectively dampening work, disincentivizing investment, and stifling progress.

Perhaps this is the policy we want: regulators face an admittedly formidable challenge (essentially, predicting the future), and in some cases, as I've explicitly noted, have been way ahead of the curve—for example, in highlighting the very real need for more investment in assessment science.

Yet, as regulators seek to weigh the potential benefits and risks of a new medicine, my own observation is that they tend to be both tentative and ultra-paternalistic; many seem to feel they must somehow protect doctors from themselves, and the result is that patients are systematically denied access to medicines that might be useful, and for whom the risk/reward, when fully understood and discussed with their physician, would be worth it.

This is a critical point: not everyone has the same view of risk/reward, and by positioning themselves on the far, far end of this spectrum, regulators effectively substitute their often extreme value judgements for the considered views of others who might thoughtfully come to a different decision.

Truth is, regulators don't trust patients and doctors to make these judgments, and take these decisions into their own hands; the result has been bad for the entire biopharmaceutical ecosystem, and most unfortunately of all, absolutely disastrous for patients—of course the very people who regulators are ostensibly trying to protect. How wonderful it would be if the many patients who are denied access to the new medicines a healthy ecosystem might have created were to enjoy the same degree of advocacy, voice, and incessantly aired late-night TV advertisements as those who claim to represent patients allegedly harmed by approved products.

But don't take my word: instead, listen to one of the most compelling talks of TEDMED2011, presented by Juan Enriquez, and available here. Enriquez presents an accessible and sensible discussion of the problem of the uncaptured costs of failing to innovate; this short video should be required viewing for anyone who cares deeply about this space—and that should be all of us. – DS

Medicine Must Allow For Customization: A Lesson For Policy-Makers—And Regulators

As appealing as it is—as useful as it is—to imagine that there exists a gold-standard way to practice medicine, and a single-best way to approach most human ailments, the reality is considerably more complex and messy, as Hartzband and Groopman's (continued) critique of so-called "best practices" makes clear.

The heart of their argument is this: "For patients and experts alike, there is a subjective core to every medical decision. The truth is that, despite many advances, much of medicine still exists in a gray zone where there is not one right answer. No one can say with certainty who will benefit by taking a certain drug and who will not. Nor can we say with certainty what impact a medical condition will have on someone's life or how they might experience a treatment's side effects. The path to maintaining or regaining health is not the same for everyone; our preferences really do matter."

This resonates (see here and here), although I've also heard distinguished health policy proponents argue convincingly that even if experts can't agree what is definitely "right," there can definitely be agreement about a number of ways of practicing medicine that are clearly "wrong," yet very common—so that while it may be harmful, and disingenuous, to insist upon a single algorithm or best approach, it could be helpful to at least provide clear guidance so that physicians would know to avoid certain therapeutic approaches.

Not only does Hartzband and Groopman's argument have implications for the current healthcare debate, it also would seem to have significant implications for the way we view medical product regulation.

Currently, in deciding whether the benefits of a particular medical product are worth the cost, regulators, as I've discussed, often deliberately adopt the most restrictive view possible, taking it upon themselves to decide that this decision is in the best interest of patients.

Yet, as Hartzband and Groopman write, "Policy makers need to abandon the idea that experts know what is best. In medical care, the 'right' clinical decisions turn out to be those that are based on a patient's goals and values."

If regulators took this admonition to heart, they would recognize the utility in offering more physicians and patients the opportunity to decide whether a particular risk/benefit is worth it, rather than impose excessively high hurdles and in many cases, take the decisions out of the hands of patients and physicians—and into their own hands instead.

Policy makers, like technologists, and like pharma companies, clearly struggle with the complexity of medicine and the nuance of medical decision making, and more generally, with the concept that as convenient, and efficient, as one-size-fits-all solutions might appear (whether a policy, a decision tree, or a new drug), it's far better to provide meaningful opportunities to individualize and customize solutions for each patient.

The challenge, and urgent need, right now is to advance a regulatory policy with the wisdom and humility to enable and support this sort of shared decision making, rather than effectively circumventing it. – DS

Can Progressive Approvals Cut Regulatory's Gordian Knot—And Stimulate Innovation?

Few topics inspire more rants among drug developers and industry watchers than regulation. To be overly simplistic, industry veterans generally seem to feel that excessively conservative regulators are squelching innovation, motivated largely by a desire to cover their own behinds. Critics (I will resist, for now, the urge to use the term pharmascolds) often contend that regulators aren't strict enough, and that medical product companies (who, critics believe, have more than earned their present enmity) warrant even greater supervision, and should be held to an even higher standard in their clinical studies. Meanwhile, patients continue to suffer, and wonder why modern science hasn't produced the medicines they desperately need.

Incredibly, there may actually be an answer to this that could potentially satisfy everyone. The basic proposal—which has been eloquently articulated by UCSF Chancellor (and former Genentech executive) Susan Desmond-Hellmann—is to turn drug approval from a discrete variable (yes/no) into a continuous one. (Others, including a group of European regulators writing for themselves, have made similar arguments—as I've previously discussed here.)

The fundamental problem with the current system, Desmond-Hellmann observes, is that regulators have only two options, when in fact, it might make a lot more sense for them to have a range of choices, permitting them to approve a drug for limited use, or use with limited promotion, following the presentation of initial evidence of safety and efficacy; permission for broader use, and less restrictive promotion, could be given after additional data are obtained.

This solution makes sense on so many levels, and acknowledges: (a) the long time it can take to become familiar with a drug and learn some of it's more subtle effects—good as well as bad; (b) the importance of accelerating the time it takes to get potentially useful drugs into the hands of patients who might need them; and (c) the technologies available now to track the performance of new drugs and assess their performance. I suspect a whole army of entrepreneurs are eagerly waiting for the opportunity to tackle this task— one can imagine a system where provisionally approved drugs are dispensed with scannable labels, and a condition for patients receiving the provisionally-approved product is the willingness to report how it working, and contribute to a database.

A particular advantage of such a system would be the emphasis it would presumably place on durable results, as full approval would likely require not just success in a clinical trial, but continued demonstration of success under "real world" conditions. Such a requirement would almost certainly stimulate the development of integrated "health solutions," a bundled assortment of patient- and physician-support systems accompanying the drug. The patient support offering accompanying J&J's lap-band is one obvious example of this sort of adjunctive program.

While such patient support systems would seem to be a good idea even now, the business case has been difficult to make. In the context of an offering that would need to succeed in order for a drug to be fully approved, the incentives are considerably more apparent, and would almost certainly stimulate interest in start-up companies striving to deliver the most effective patient support programs.

A graduated regulatory approval process such as the one discussed here would not be perfect; however, it almost certainly would represent a significant step in the right direction. – DS

Personalized Regulation: More Than Just Personalized Medicine— And Urgently Required

Regulators of medical research face the daunting task of vetting protocols, drugs, and devices to ensure that they are appropriate, meaning that the benefit/risk is reasonable.

Understandably, there has been considerable focus on better defining both the benefit and the risk here, an effort that has paralleled the focus on "personalized medicine"—the right medicine for the right patient at the right time.

The basic idea here is that if you can define more precisely (hence the term "precision medicine") exactly which patients are or are not going to benefit, you significantly increase the benefit/risk ratio, as patients unlikely to respond aren't exposed to a drug, and you increase the likely benefit achieved by patients ultimately receiving the product.

Segmenting patients can also be done using phenotypic characteristics—assessing HER2 expression level to determine whether to administer Herceptin use is a common example, but you can also think about a range of physiological or even behavioral parameters as well.

On the face of it, this would all seem to be good news—and to an extent, it is: defining with greater precision the likely benefit and risk faced by a patient potentially enrolled in a clinical study or potentially using a particular product should lead to more informed decision making.

The challenge, however, is that this conceptualization misses the fact that patients differ not only in their genetic and phenotypic characteristics, but also in the way they perceive risk/benefit, as described by Michelle Meyer, a Harvard legal scholar who offers in a recent paper perhaps the most eloquent and insightful perspective on what she terms "the heterogeneity problem." Focusing on IRBs, she writes,

"...even if all prospective participants could expect the same costs and benefits from participating in a study, they are very likely to differ in their willingness to assume those

risks in pursuit of those benefits. Yet IRBs must assign a single risk-benefit profile to each study, and then determine, for all prospective participants, whether that risk benefit profile is 'reasonable.'"

Bingo.

It's important to recognize that the key issue here is one of de-averaging, of needing to recognize that a consensus assessment may not accurately reflect the divergent views of individual participants. More concerning, as Meyer astutely observes,

"By employing a broad understanding of research risk and a narrow understanding of research benefit, IRBs tend to characterize the risk-benefit profiles of proposed studies in ways that reflect the preferences and other circumstances of often-idiosyncratic, hypothetical eggshell participants. Erring on the side of restricting research opportunities to which individuals may be invited is benign only if we assume that individuals can only be harmed, and never benefited, by participating in the research, a claim that is refuted by much of the empirical evidence discussed in this Article."

Bingo, again.

Furthermore, while Meyer's comments here are aimed at IRBs, they could just as easily apply to federal regulators of medical products as well—something familiar to anyone who's ever watched an advisory committee meeting. More often than not, individual committee members presented with the same exact information will come to very different conclusions regarding whether a product's benefit/risk profile is "reasonable."

Without question, patients would also have a range of views here, and the real challenge going forward is refining our approach to regulation to more effectively preserve patient choice. If a drug is shot down, that choice disappears.

The goal here must be what I call "personalized regulation"—an approach that preserves patient choice—at least to a greater extent than is available today.

Some might invoke a variation of what might be called compassionate paternalism, and point out that since individuals often make bad choices (a point convincingly made by Kahneman and others), it's important that wise regulators protect patients and physicians from themselves.

This is reasonable, but only to a point. It is misleading to assume implicitly that if a patient has a different view of risk/benefit than a committee's consensus, the individual's view must somehow reflect deranged thinking on the part of the patient.

To the contrary, regulation must endeavor to more respectfully, expansively, and creatively accommodate the rational preferences of diverse patients in order to avoid leaving so much opportunity on the table. If we can agree on the need for such personalized regulation, we are more likely to find a way to achieve it. – DS

Social Media: More Likely To Identify Bad Medicines—Or Tarnish Good Ones?

Every week, it seems, I come across a new story about data analysts proposing to mine data from either medical records or social media to identify potential new harmful drug side effects; often, it is asserted that the methodology could have been used to successfully identify, at an early stage, the concerning effects of Vioxx.

I worry about us heading down this road—but perhaps not for the reasons you might think.

Many cynically assume that drug developers (like me) would resist such a surveillance system because it could unexpectedly result in the withdrawal of a marketed drug, costing a company millions in lost sales.

In fact, I suspect most drug developers (like me) would thrill, positively thrill to the prospect of a robust system of post-marketing surveillance that would enable rare but important side-effects to be captured accurately and responded to quickly. No one wants to develop harmful products.

Many hurdles drug developers now face reflect the limited faith some regulators place in such post-marketing surveillance; initiatives such as the Sentinel program reflect the commitment of regulators to get this done right.

Bottom line: a robust surveillance system could make drug development faster, cheaper, and safer—a win for all stakeholders involved.

A robust surveillance system might even have an additional upside—the opportunity to detect the unexpected positive effects of drugs; such observations have played a critical role in the discovery of many important classes of drugs (especially for neuropsychiatric conditions), and it would be powerful to search for such opportunities more systematically, as discussed here.

Nevertheless, I'm concerned by some of the surveillance analytics about which I've been reading; I worry not about the sensitivity of these approaches—their ability to detect a true signal—but rather the specificity—their ability to accurately recognize the lack of a true signal.

I suspect many emerging approaches are so intensively focused on improving (and reporting) their sensitivity ("we could have found Vioxx!") that they may be neglecting to think through the consequences of an approach that has relatively poor specificity, and detects "signals" that aren't there. Similar to the problems faced in the hospital (especially in the ICU) by constantly beeping warnings, an element of alarm fatigue develops, and you may start discounting all warnings—including, unfortunately, the real ones.

By itself, the problem of sensitivity and specificity could probably be solved through appropriate selection of cutoff criteria, and optimizing the analytics. The real problem comes when you start to factor in the effects of social media (an emerging issue in medicine).

As Reddit has painfully demonstrated (nicely reported by The Atlantic's Alexis Madrigal), false information can spread on social media like wildfire, reinforcing Iago's awful, prescient observation, "Trifles, light as air/Are to the jealous confirmations strong/As proof of holy writ."

The continued popularity of the anti-vaccine movement (despite the discrediting of Andrew Wakefield—see this recent informative discussion by Phil Plait in Slate), and the remarkable sales of books such as "Natural Cures 'They' Don't Want You To Know About" (see this NYT takedown of author Kevin Trudeau) emphasize the power of suspicion and rumor to impact perceptions of health and disease.

Next, think about what happens when you layer in the "nocebo effect"—discussed with characteristic grace by the New Yorker's wonderful new science blogger Gareth Cook here. As Cook explains,

"With placebos ('I will please' in Latin), the mere expectation that treatment will help brings a diminution of symptoms, even if the patient is given a sugar pill. With nocebos ('I will harm'), dark expectations breed dark realities. In clinical drug trials, people often report the side effects they were warned about, even if they are taking a placebo."

As Cook adds, "The nocebo effect is not confined to clinical trials."

So here's the dilemma—on the one hand, powerful new big data approaches enable smart researchers to identify important faint signals, though they may often mistake noise for signal. On the other hand, powerful social media technologies provide new opportunities for the profound amplification of spurious signals, leading to their mischaracterization.

As we progressively gain our footing here, we'll learn how to sort this out all. Let's hope that important new medicines are not erroneously discarded along the way. – DS

VIII.

Gadgets, Apps, Technology

In Car Health Monitoring: Lemon Or Lifesaver?

Patient monitoring outside the hospital has been a hot topic (and also a not so hot topic) for the past 15 years. Starting back in the late 1990s with companies like Health Hero, a company whose products for patient home monitoring are still in use today, company after company has sought to bring a successful product to market. The holy grail: finding an easy, non-intrusive, and continuously reliable way to predict patients' potentially serious medical problems when it is early enough to do something about them and prevent an acute and expensive episode of illness. Some of the newer companies are focused more on the wellness and tracking side of the equation, such as helping individuals see progress from an exercise or other preventive/health-inducing regimen.

So far this whole area has been a very tough nut for businesses to crack in the US in particular. While some studies have shown great positive effect, others have not. Insurance payment for these programs has been spotty at best and nonexistent at worst; most of the current vendors are stuck in pilot hell without significant long term and widespread commitments from payers. There is a belief, veracity unknown as yet, that the proliferation of risk-based entities such as Accountable Care Organizations will change this and lead to broad adoption of ambulatory patient monitoring tools, angels will sing and a large number of hospitalizations and rehospitalizations will be avoided. That may be true, but remains to be seen.

Yet due to the growing belief (wish?) that the broadening risk base will create massive monitoring market growth, fed by the advent of smart phones and miniaturized, inexpensive mobile sensors, the number of companies focused on this opportunity has grown faster than Rapunzel's hair. And these patient monitoring tools are showing up everywhere. There are sensors that plug into home appliances that let you know grandma woke up and turned on her coffee pot; sensors in phones that can remind you to take blood pressure and glucose readings and send those readings off to be tracked; sensors in beds that help measure body parameters and whether patients are moving or about to fall. Even sensors in clothing, although none yet that detect hipness.

I saw an article this week in the *Wall Street Journal* that really made me wonder where this is all going and when and how we will determine when the sensor craze has jumped the shark. The article, entitled "A Car That Takes Your Pulse," was about a growing trend among automakers to create "technology that could feed your heart rate, blood pressure and other biometric responses into the car's computers, the better to determine when you're drowsy or overwhelmed with distracting media" among other things.

Car manufacturers such as Mercedes, Lexus and Ford have already begun building biosensors into their vehicles. Experiments are underway there and elsewhere using built-in passive sensors to measure respiration, sweaty palms, pulse rate and other signs of stress and distress that could lead you to have a car accident. I actually test drove a Mercedes that had the sensor to detect driver drowsiness in it. When it perceives you are getting too tired to drive it shows you a cute little coffee pot and suggests you stop for a rest. No word on whether they have done a joint promotion with Starbucks.

Here's my favorite example from the *WSJ* story:

Sports car maker Ferrari SpA, for one, has filed a patent application that indicates the company is evaluating technology that would embed wireless electrodes in a car seat's headrest to monitor drivers' brain waves for stress as they pilot machines capable of roaring up to 200 miles per hour. Depending on what the sensors detect, the car might try to mitigate the driver's risk by cutting power to the motor or automatically stabilizing the vehicle. As Ferrari researchers put it in the patent filing: "drivers tend to miscalculate —in particular, overestimate—their driving skill and, more important, their psychophysical condition."

I am pretty sure this technology is redundant. As the police and everyone else know without sensors, the Ferrari driver is definitely under extreme stress because their mid-life crisis drove them to buy a Ferrari in the first place, for goodness sake. They are worried no one will ever say they are young and hot again, and keeping up appearances is exhausting. Plus they are constantly being pulled over for speeding and worried about making the next payment. Stress? You betcha. Indication of poor driving in the moment? Who knows?

Ford is also working on a stress sensor program that, when it identifies extreme stress or distraction, will turn off the drivers' cell phone ringer. If they think that is the cure for distraction, I think they will be disappointed. A better solution will be to require drivers to turn their phones off completely or new technology that makes in-car cell phone use impossible at all times, because one does not have to be stressed to be distracted by the phone. We all see the texting, phoning idiot drivers on the road now, and most of them look just fine until they hit the light pole. This isn't a personal stress monitoring issue; it is a public safety issue. I really wonder about the value of this approach.

And sensors for sweaty palms as a meaningful stress indicator to suggest getting off the road? Have these scientists met teenagers? How are they going to factor in sweat baselines for those heading out on a first date or going to a job interview or whatever?

But while I can generally understand the idea of sensors that impact driving ability very directly, particularly sensors that detect blood alcohol level or falling asleep, it's the sensors designed for general health management that really give me pause. I know smart people are thinking about this so maybe there is merit, but I wonder how effective of a tool this really can be. It's hard not to think about all this without harkening back to KITT, the car in Knight Rider, which monitors Michael Knight's heart rate and other vital signs and displays them on monitors. KITT was very sophisticated and could identify not just biometric distress, but injuries, poisoning, and other factors key to crime fighting success. Same goes for the Batmobile, as I recall. So is the real audience for these products: the senior market, for whom they are currently being developed, or the middle-aged vigilante crime fighter driving a muscle car? Very different demographic.

A key idea behind biometric sensors in cars is to extend the driving lives of senior citizens who might otherwise, at least in theory, be unable to drive safely if their condition wasn't closely monitored. Yikes, is all I can say to that. There are both inherent risks in letting people drive who might pose a risk to themselves and others, and a question in my mind as to whether monitoring would prevent problems fast enough to prevent dangerous outcomes. A sensor that detects heart attacks and immediately stops the car? Uh, too late, and by the way, not a problem limited to senior citizens.

Also, let's just say your car can measure your glucose level and let you know you are in danger. I would wager that most diabetics who follow their proper regimen don't need this, and the ones that do may or may not pay attention, just like they don't now. And let's say that data is being shown on the car display. Isn't that, combined with the worry of constantly being watched and getting dashboard feedback about biometric parameters, going to itself be a huge distraction?

Plus, who is going to pay for this monitoring? As everyone in healthcare ought to know by now, the presence of data isn't valuable, it's what is done with data that creates value. If you need a risk management or care coordination system to sit behind the sensor data stream in order to let drivers know they need to get some insulin or take their blood pressure medicine, some analytics system is probably going to have to sit behind that to put the real-time data into context of the driver's existing health situation. So are we going to see Lexus SUVs integrated with the Epic EMR?

Moreover, remotely collected data that doesn't have human intervention to back it up hasn't been all that successful to date in achieving good outcomes in the monitoring game. Programs that combine monitoring with clinician engagement with the patient are far more effective. So how might this work? Is Healthways going to start an automotive division? Is Ford going to start hiring care managers to triage at-risk patients from those who stopped at Dunkin Donuts and had a glucose spike? Maybe Tom and Ray Magliozzi can start a whole new career after retiring from Car Talk where, instead of diagnosing mechanical issues, they diagnose acute exacerbations of chronic illness via OnStar.

And by the way, if history is any indicator (and it always is), if someone pays for biometric sensors to be installed in cars, they are also going to want in on the savings from avoided incidents—how does this all work? Is Toyota or BMW going to be the third wheel in some newfangled accountable care organization?

One of the issues that is not discussed enough in any discussion of passive patient monitoring is the consumer's view of the experience. Some welcome it, but some are unwilling to be watched 24 hours per day, whether it's Big Brother, their own adult child or Herbie the talking Volkswagen who is doing the watching. The *WSJ* article includes this quote:

Dick Myrick, a 63-year-old retired electrical engineer from Arlington, Mass., participated in AgeLab experiments in biometrically monitored driving. His says he would be interested in a car that kept tabs on his condition as part of its safety technology, but only if he was in control of the system. 'I need to know that the function is on, and have it not on when I want,' he says.

Having the ability to turn the system off kind of defeats the purpose, but makes clear my point. Finding the right balance between privacy and monitoring is not entirely obvious, but I can imagine plenty of people do not want to be videotaped constantly while driving, illness or not. In fact I imagine the sense of paranoia some might feel from constant surveillance could increase driver stress levels, particularly if they know they are being watched, have a runny nose and lack available Kleenex. As the saying goes, just because you are paranoid doesn't mean they aren't watching.

As I reflected on the WSJ car sensor article, I took a moment to read some of the reader comments, always the best part of any online story. If you are a real marketer with a mission to sell product, they say that you must always listen to your customer, and customers were talking (or typing as the case may be). Instead of or in addition to biometric monitors, drivers suggested the car companies invest in onboard auto technologies that administer espresso to sleepy drivers rather than just point out the sleepiness; another suggested that rather than technology that shuts off cell phones, how about gear that drowns out the sound of whiny kids asking "are we there yet?" Now that's noise-canceling technology we can all appreciate.

Besides, isn't this all about to become slightly moot if Google has their way and cars drive themselves? I guess when that comes to pass the auto manufacturers will have to outfit new cars with backseat driver monitoring technologies instead. – DS

Release Yourself From Mental Slavery

"Emancipate yourselves from mental slavery. None but ourselves can free our minds." –
Bob Marley, Redemption Song

In the July 16, 2012 issue of Newsweek there was an article called "Is the Onslaught Making Us Crazy?" The article is about mounting evidence that the connected world—the world that drives us to obsession in the pursuit of constant Internet, mobile phone, Facebook-obsessed Twitterosity—is slowly driving us insane. To quote the article:

"The current incarnation of the Internet–portable, social, accelerated, and all-persuasive–may be making us not just dumber or lonelier but more depressed and anxious, prone to obsessive-compulsive and attention-deficit disorders, even outright psychotic. Our digitized minds can scan like those of drug addicts, and normal people are breaking down in sad and seemingly new ways."

Yes, I appreciate the irony you are reading this in an online blog. You should probably take my decision to even write this thing as evidence that I have already gone off the deep end and am paddling far from shore.

As I read this article, which described large amounts of recent academic research demonstrating the potentially serious negative impacts of excessive technology addiction including ADHD type behavior and a wealth of other miseries, I couldn't help but be reminded of the funny dog character named Dug in Pixar's movie "Up." Dug wears a digitized collar that enables him to speak English.

Dug's squirrel distraction reminds me exactly of what it is like for people who have spent way too much time in front of their iPads, iPhones, iMacs, iToilets or whatever iThing they derive life from. Their attention spans are like Dug's: brief moments of intensity interrupted by countless squirrels. The result is a world of people who are constantly multi-tasking (talking to you, looking at their email, sending a text, walking, chewing gum, face-planting) instead of concentrating on the conversation or activity at hand. I am convinced this behavior is, in part, responsible for the increasing stress, anxiety and impatience that permeate the working world. "What? You can't answer my inquiry immediately by Googling the answer and texting it to me before I finished asking the question? What they hell are you squandering all that extra time on? Look, a squirrel!"

The Newsweek article goes on to say, "This life of continuous connection has come to seem normal, but that's not the same as saying that it's healthy or sustainable, as technology—to paraphrase the old line about alcohol—becomes the cause of and solution to all of life's problems." Look, a squirrel!

According to the article, the average Americans stares at some form of screen 8 hours/day and the average person sends or receives 400 texts/month, four times the 2007 number; if you're a teen it's 3700 texts/month (accidental upside: perhaps this will reduce smoking among kids since they need both hands to text). There is even a new malady known as "phantom-vibration syndrome," which occurs when you think you feel something in your pocket vibrating (hopefully a phone and not something untoward) but really no one is calling. I'm not sure if this syndrome made it into the new ICD-10, but other codes for injuries that can occur while typing/texting did. See codes Y93C1, Activity, computer keyboarding and Y93C9, Activity, other involving computer technology and electronic devices. No doubt the whole reason for the three (!) different ICD-10 codes involving running into lampposts derives from people's overutilization of mobile phones and other wireless devices.

Stanford University School of Medicine psychiatrist Elias Aboujaoude is quoted in the Newsweek article as saying, "There's little doubt we're becoming more impulsive and one reason for this is technology use." He claims that the recent precipitous rise in OCD and ADHD diagnoses is directly related to technology addiction. I'm guessing that Internet addiction is not best treated by the newly-emerging field of cyber-therapy, where therapists "visit" with patients online instead of in person. Can you imagine?

Patient: "Thanks for viewing me doctor, I think I have a problem with excessive iPhone use."

Therapist: "I'll be with you as soon as I finish this text."

Patient: "I'm sorry I didn't hear you; I was checking the Giants scores."

One of the things this whole issue made me think about in earnest is how technology, and particularly iPhones and similar metallic marvels, are becoming widely used for patient home monitoring, particularly for patients with high blood pressure, diabetes and other chronic illnesses. The whole discussion about iPhone/Internet addiction and its ills makes me wonder if this continuous remote monitoring thing is such a good idea. On the one hand, it is clearly a positive to regularly be checking patients in the context of their real lives to be sure they are staying at appropriate levels of health. On the other hand, is it really necessary or even a positive thing to **continuously** monitor people **and** give them access to the biometric readings? How obsessive, anxious and stressed out might patients become if they are constantly checking their readings on these devices and how might that affect the readings themselves? Would they interrupt texting to check their biometric levels or would they interrupt watching their glucose fluctuate with every bite to check their messages? Either way, probably not a good thing.

I remember when I was pregnant lo those many years ago and I was put on bed rest and given a fetal home monitor to check for premature contractions, as I was having some pre-term labor issues. They stuck me in bed and said, "don't get up for 3 months except to pee and every day at 5:00 we are going to call you to put this monitor on so we can see how you are doing." Yeah, that was awesome. For an already Type A person, it was not a highly practical way of living. But okay, it was for the kid and she turned out to be worth it. Anyway, I would feel pretty much fine all day and feel very few contractions, but at 5:00 when the bell tolled for me and the tracking service called to get a formal reading, my contractions would go through the roof. Correlation or causation? I am going with the latter. In my weakened and blob-like state I used to call it "performance anxiety," which is kind of correct.

Doctors are well aware of what is known as "white coat syndrome," a condition which causes blood pressure patients' readings to skyrocket when they are in the doctors' office (likely due to anxiety) but to otherwise stay in much lower ranges in other circumstances. Is there a risk that we will cause some sort of "iPhone case syndrome" if we are continuously monitoring people's biometric parameters and they are becoming more and more OCD or stressed out as a result of the constant technology interaction itself?

There are lots of people out there who check their email/texts every two seconds. Would those same addiction-oriented people check their blood pressure or heart rate or glucose score the same compulsive way, driving up stress and anxiety and thus driving up the negative readings? Would those negative readings then be the result of correlation or causation and how in the world could we possibly separate the two? Does this suggest that any continuous monitoring results be shielded from the patient's view for their own good? If so, what of the engaged healthcare consumer? It feels like a very complex issue to me, but not one I have read anything about.

Here is another quote from the Newsweek article, an article I really encourage you to read if for no other reason than to understand your own budding lunacy:

The Internet "leads to behavior that people are conscious is not in their best interest and does leave them anxious and does make them act compulsively," says Nicholas Carr, whose book The Shallows, about the Web's effect on cognition, was nominated for a Pulitzer Prize. It "fosters our obsessions, dependence, and stress reactions," adds Larry Rosen, a California psychologist who has researched the Net's effect for decades. It "encourages—and even promotes—insanity."

Clearly the mobile health movement has some monumental potential advantages, such as bringing needed healthcare to those who can't otherwise get it and making in-home care available to those who would otherwise forego it. But, if it is true that we are turning into a nation of Internet addicts and if it is also true that, "The brains of Internet addicts, it turns out, look like the brains of drug and alcohol addicts," then how do we ensure a balance between mobile health applications that help patients and those that add to their woes?

Ok, everybody... put down your iPhone and repeat after me: Om... - LS

mHealth: Hallelujah Or Bah Humbug

3600 people and I went to the mHealth Summit in Washington, DC and, having spent the better part of 48 hours listening, I am still not sure what to make of this emerging healthcare sector.

Given the incredible energy and high attendance at the conference, it would be easy to get caught up in the hype that surrounds mobile health and it's many potential uses. There were an enormous number of companies present and news of many new financings.

For those of you not yet familiar with the buzz word, mHealth is basically what you get when you cross healthcare with mobile phones. It is essentially the love child of Ma Bell, Hippocrates, Dr. Oz and Steve Jobs. For the true believers, and there are a lot of them, mHealth is the answer to the health care systems prayers. By bringing texting and Wifi and reams of personalized data to the fingertips of the masses, healthcare will right itself, costs will decrease and angels will sing. Can I get a Hallelujah?

The entrepreneurs in the mHealth space tend to be young and often new to healthcare, though of course there are the exceptions-those few old-timers who remember the days before iPhones were issued upon one's birth. The young upstarts are full of energy and absolutely certain that their product or service will be the one to change the healthcare system for the better. God knows some of them will be right. Hanging around these people can be very energizing and they are surely of a different temperament than those who preside over the traditional healthcare IT companies. These entrepreneurs are looking at healthcare unfettered by the unhelpful customs and disincentives of the past. They are not weighted to the earth by how things have always been done in healthcare, but literally floating in the so-called clouds (ha ha, get it? a cloud joke) held aloft by fresh perspective. It can be refreshing as hell to hear their stories.

On the other hand, hanging around these guys can also make one drip with cynicism. As I walked the exhibit floor with my pal Margaret Laws from the California Health Care Foundation, I think we were both feeling somewhat schizophrenic.

The conference definitely had its share of wildly enthusiastic CEOs leading companies that had devised very compelling products to improve point of care diagnosis (Alivecor, CellScope), simplify healthy eating (Fooducate), improve public health (Asthmopolis) and engage consumers in all manner of activities to prevent and manage chronic disease (lots of companies). There was some seriously cool stuff to look at and one can easily envision how some of these products can make the world a better place.

On the other hand I kept looking over my shoulder for the Ghost of eHealth past. "Scrooge, er I mean Lisa," the ghost would say,"let me take you back to the year 1999 when eHealth companies flooded the Internet, offering the promise of a much improved healthcare system only to leave behind the tattered corpse of Dr. Koop.com and the trail of a bazillion incinerated VC dollars and careers. Look upon them–the ones who thought they had it all figured out and were confident that, since everyone had Internet access, their products would become more ubiquitous overnight than that damned Lady Gaga!"

"Bah Humbug," I would say, "Anything but that! Don't make me look upon the shattered dreams of all of those companies that only aspired to be the Webvan of healthcare! I can't bear it! And please, dear God, no Lady Gaga!"

The mHealth revolution definitely has some of the feel of the eHealth bubble of about ten years back. Companies are popping up left and right, many which are carbon copies of each other but with a twist ("we are the newest weight loss app but ours uses an entirely different font!"). There is a frothy financing market despite the overall healthcare venture capital downturn, with these nascent companies commanding valuations that have little to do with traditional metrics (" I have no revenue but my idea is so cool that I'll settle for nothing less than $100 million in pre-money value and that's only if you slap down a term sheet by midnight tonight!"). Healthcare IT is hot and mHealth is en fuego.

Lots of big companies were at the mHealth Summit trying to look hip and mHealthy. Kind of weird to see Verizon and ATT represent at a healthcare conference. A friend and healthcare luminary type with whom I was watching Verizon present said to me that, in fact, these companies are perfect for the healthcare market because they are good at overcharging and bad at customer service.

As I walked the exhibit floor the one question I asked of nearly everyone I talked to was, "Can you name 3 mHealth companies that have yet achieved $10 million in annual revenue?" Crickets. No one could name me even one, even if such a unicorn does exist. Self-interest alert: I do know one, which happens to be PatientSafe Solutions, a company in the Psilos portfolio with more than twice that in annual revenue. That doesn't mean that the others won't get there, however. There is no doubt in my mind that mHealth will become a major part of the healthcare system. The question is when.

The Ghost of eHealth Present, in the form of market analysis firm ABI Research, reports that the mHealth market is growing so fast that it will more than triple to $400 million by 2016. If you are an investor like me, and I'm sorry to use such a technical finance expression, that sucks. We are trying to build companies that we can sell for $400 million. If that is the size of the whole market 3-4 years from now, it's hard to see it as a good investment today. On the other hand, you can't help but see the evidence of why some of the mHealth products have the potential to make a profound difference in the lives of patients and providers. And it makes you want to get in on the action.

There is definitely a burgeoning mass of data from successful mHealth experiments showing it is possible to improve access to care and clinical quality while saving money. Unfortunately, little of that was presented at the conference, but one presentation by Bella Hwang from Weltel, demonstrated how an mHealth project serving HIV-infected patients in Kenya used regular text messaging to dramatically improve adherence to antiretroviral drug regimens (62% compliance vs 50% in the control group) and suppress the viral load (57% vs. 48% in the control group; the project is estimated to generate $10 million in net savings over 3 years and break-even in year 2). It was an impressive analysis. I have seen other equally compelling stories, although they are largely from small pilot studies and not from large real world deployments. However, the night is young and Scrooge has not yet been out with the Ghost of mHealth Yet To Come. Just think what Tiny Tim could do with an iPhone, a compelling fitness app and an unlimited data plan!

U.S. Secretary of Health and Human Services Kathleen Sebelius actually opened the conference with a speech in which she said that no healthcare sector has innovated as rapidly as mHealth and isn't it amazing that there are over 12,000 apps related to health in the iTunes library. Amazing or scary? You be the judge. Anyway, Secretary Sebelius also said that the government is committed to supporting this sector because it is "the greatest technical breakthrough of our time to address the greatest problem of our time," by which she meant the healthcare crisis. That might be a bit hyperbolic, but Dr. Eric Topol doesn't think so. Topol, one of the world's most renowned cardiologists and now Vice Chair of the West Wireless Institute, gave a very entertaining follow-up talk on the concept of Creative Destruction and how mHealth innovation can meaningfully change the field of medicine for the better. He hilariously demonstrated his hypothesis by using several mHealth products on himself while on stage, giving us a live ECG view of his own heart augmented by use of the conference hotel room free hand lotion since he forgot to bring his own ultrasound gel.

One of the biggest impediments to the widespread adoption of mHealth is reimbursement, but even some payers were on hand and squarely on the bandwagon. Dr Richard Migliori, Chief Healthcare Officer of the nation's largest private payer, United HealthGroup said that mHealth has the most promise of any technology to create health system reform because it is a true means of connecting people to actionable information.

So in this, the holiday season, will I end up in the role of Scrooge, the mHealth pessimist or Bob Cratchit, the mHealth optimist? Tough call. I think I'm sticking with schizophrenia for the moment while I sit by the (mobile) phone waiting for a call from the Ghost of mHealth Present telling me which is the best app in the iTunes library for mental health. God bless us, everyone, who makes the leap into the mHealth rapids. I have no doubt it will be an interesting, awful, awesome ride. – LS

Medicine's Tech Future: The View From The Valley

A few quick impressions from the FutureMed extravaganza put on by Singularity University at the Museum of Computer History, a stone's throw from Google's Mountain View headquarters.

The event featured an exhibition session where emerging digital health companies (with some others) demo'd their initial products, followed by a plenary session introduced by FutureMed Executive Director (and former MGH medicine colleague) Daniel Kraft, and featuring presentations to the packed house by several leading innovators—including one of the developers of IBM's Watson, which is pivoting from Jeopardy to clinical medicine.

Given the high density of reporters there—to say nothing of innovators, would-be innovators, VCs, and assorted *poseurs* (categories not mutually exclusive)—I expect there should be lucid coverage available elsewhere on the web.

Instead, I want to capture the three sequential reactions I had, which strike me as somewhat analogous to Haeckel's Law (ontogeny recapitulates phylogeny), as each response seems to reflect a distinct stage of professional development.

The inevitable initial, and most visceral reaction to this sort of event, is that technology is wicked cool, and will deliver us all; I think this two minute introductory video captures the vibe more effectively than any description I could offer. I'm also certain any student of semiotics would find it especially rewarding.

Accordingly, even much of the informal discussion at the event seemed to revolve around Big Questions, lofty ideas, and the Next Big Thing. New technologies and approaches—artificial organs from stem cells! Computers that can read your mind! Bottom-up innovation! Exponentials!—were discussed expectantly, the key question being not if, but when. The remarkable progress many in the tech crowd had seen in other disciplines suggested that technology advances in health would be similarly achievable, and just as inevitable.

My second reaction to this event—arriving only moments after the first, and perhaps reflecting my experiences in the trenches of clinical medicine and drug development—was far more critical; it was not difficult to see the event as a celebration of technology for its own sake. For many in attendance, technology was regarded as both driver and consequence of human progress and human advancement, an almost unassailable good in its own right.

The problem with this, as I've discussed extensively before, is pragmatic: there's a huge gap between the way many technologists envision medical problems and the way problems are actually experienced by physicians and patients. For example, I am curious to see how Watson does on the MGH ward service where I trained; the discrete questions of Jeopardy will almost certainly provide limited preparation for the ambiguities and complexities of this experience.

The worry more generally is that innovators are focused primarily on developing cool technologies, rather than solving actual problems; a century and a half ago, Oliver Wendell Holmes Sr. famously commented, "If the whole *materia medica* [available medications] as now used, could be sunk to the bottom of the sea, it would be better for mankind-and all the worse for the fishes." It's tempting to speculate that the same might apply today to the estimated 15,000 medical apps now available on iTunes.

At a minimum, it's clear there remains an urgent need to more efficiently connect those with problems and those interested in developing solutions—as I discussed in this recent column, and will be working on in the coming months with colleagues at Rock Health.

Upon further consideration, however, it occurred to me that reflexive skepticism isn't really justified either. Consequently, my third perspective on the event, and the one I'm carrying with me, is that it's a great thing that so many smart people are not only developing powerful new technologies (even if currently not as powerful as typically portrayed), and seek to deliver improvements in health (even if the aim remains a bit off). What's clear is that there is a critical mass of people who are converging, and who bring a range of expertise, experiences, and capabilities—to say nothing of their war stories and battle scars.

While the vision of medicine preached at FutureMed remains far removed from the way medicine is practiced daily in the clinics right down the street, I think the worlds may be getting closer—the simple act of using an iPhone highlights the power of easily accessible personal technology, and more physicians and patients are starting to explore, and recognize, what technology might offer them.

Similarly, technologists, having learned from the experience of Amazon and Zappos, increasingly appreciate the need to listen to the voice of the customer—even while realizing that, as compellingly demonstrated by Steve Jobs—customers might occasionally want something they cannot currently imagine.

Although the future of medicine is unlikely to be either as close or as glorious as Daniel Kraft and his colleagues enthusiastically proclaim, I've little doubt that he's doing a world of good in catalyzing its ultimate arrival. – DS

Are Digital Health Companies Aiming Too Low—Or Is Incremental Improvement Underappreciated?

Breathless language about changing the world and disrupting the known universe aside, most digital health companies I know aren't proposing radical new treatments for dreadful diseases—or anything close (see this articulate critique by David Whelan, and this one by Matthew Holt). At the end of the day, most simply hope to make existing approaches somewhat faster, cheaper, or qualitatively better (i.e. improve the experience of cancer patients, rather than develop novel treatment for the underlying disease). When you think about it, this isn't much different than the way the biopharma industry (where I work) is often (derisively) described.

To the extent that Silicon Valley's leading tech investors even consider investments in the health space, they're generally not contemplating the development of profound new therapies, but rather, seem to be thinking about hot consumer trends, looking at some infrastructure plays, and wondering whether there are any opportunities to dominate access either to healthcare data or to stakeholder segments (think Sage Bionetworks, only run by SMERSH instead of Friend). This makes perfect sense from a business perspective, but may not be the sort of health-changing innovation many hoped the valley was preparing to deliver.

I see three key themes here:

1. Reports of the demise of incrementalism have been greatly exaggerated, in the context of both biopharma and digital health.

Many top-selling drugs—blockbusters, in fact—continue to represent incremental improvements on established mechanisms of action. There is still a major market opportunity for best-in-class products, and existing regulatory and commercial hurdles for these products would seem, in medical parlance, to represent relative contraindications, rather than absolute contraindications, as often assumed.

On the digital health side, anxiety about overreaching regulators, as I've discussed, has led to a profound aversion to products or approaches that regulators might need to review—hence the explosion of interest in consumer-focused opportunities, especially around wellness, and a dearth of investment in the sort of substantial efforts that could more profoundly impact patient health. Unclear is whether VC trepidation here reflects hard-won experience or reflexive aversion to uncertainty in an area outside their natural comfort zone.

2. Incrementalism isn't (necessarily) lame; this often arrogant assumption frequently overlooks the true unmet needs experienced by real-world patients.

The idea of getting the best use out of existing drug mechanisms (in the case of biopharma), and of ensuring existing available health resources are utilized as effectively and efficiently as possible (in the case of digital health—consider the goals of high profile companies such as Castlight and ZocDoc) isn't unreasonable, and can deliver significant benefit to patients (see here, here and here).

Arguably, the most significant immediate opportunity we have today is the health that could be achieved right now but isn't because existing health care knowledge and resources aren't optimally deployed. This uncaptured potential is an unconscionable waste—and of course, a tremendous opportunity. For example, the technologies of digital health could be used to measure and better define, in an increasingly granular fashion, discrete unmet medical needs in the real world, and to understand where (and for whom) current products and health providers are effective and where they are coming up short, and where better approaches are clearly needed. To their credit, regulators (as I've discussed) have explicitly called out the need for increased investments in such "assessment science."

3. Both digital health and biopharma advocates must guard against "the soft bigotry of low expectations," and at some level must acknowledge that tweaking the current system isn't the same as radically improving it.

In other words, developing new apps, or new formulations, may be better than making sugared water, but it's not the same as curing cancer—essentially what UCSF Chancellor Susan Desmond-Hellman recently commented.

Interestingly, the notion that innovation is under delivering represents an increasingly common critique not only of biopharma, but also of Silicon Valley; technology veteran Steve Blank tells Derek Thompson in the *Atlantic*, "The Golden Age of Silicon Valley is over, and we're just dancing on its grave." His point is that investors will go where the money is, and no one will be interested in "commercializing the really hard stuff;" instead, in the era of social media, "VCs are only going to be interested in chasing the billions on their smart phones." An unusual Silicon Valley investor manifesto (discussed at length in this *New Yorker* profile) makes a similar claim, as I recently discussed.

While I appreciate the concern that social media bling-bling will distract us—and investors —from the truly important, and considerably more difficult, health challenges confronting us, I'm fundamentally optimistic that the technology, the interactivity and open collaboration, the big data analytics that the social media and consumerism revolution has produced will ultimately facilitate the sophisticated study of complex biological phenotypes—ideally in vivo—and lead to the development of more predictive models that can help us design and develop impactful, radically new treatment approaches.

That's a lofty ambition—but one worthy of our best minds, and most innovative entrepreneurs.

Disclosure: as previously noted, I've co-founded a new academic initiative, the Center for Assessment Technology and Continuous Health(CATCH), together with Dennis Ausiello (who directs this effort) and several Boston-area colleagues. The basic idea is that improved phenotypic measurement—measurement of relevant parameters in a fashion more comprehensive and more continuous than typical patient data—could immediately improve care (Theme 2, above) while also advancing future science (Theme 3). - DS

Why You Probably Are Already Using The Most Powerful Digital Health App

Among the most frustrating dilemmas facing patients—and physicians—is when doctors are unable to assign a specific diagnosis. Just having a name for a condition can be remarkably reassuring to patients (and families), providing at least a basic framework, a set of expectations, and perhaps most importantly, an explanation for what the patient is experiencing.

Sara Wheeler, writing in the New York Times in 1999, poignantly described the experience of traveling through "the land of no diagnosis." Ten years later, the NYT featured a story called "What's Wrong with Summer Stiers," about another patient without a diagnosis—and about a fascinating initiative at the NIH, the "Undiagnosed Disease Program"—specifically created to meet this need.

Today, some patients and their families are taking this process one step further: when experts can't help, perhaps the crowd can.

Several years ago, Simon Turkalj's wife—herself a physician—developed seizures in the first trimester of her fourth pregnancy. Since then, she has suffered from frequent seizures at night, without obvious cause despite an extensive medical workup at a leading tertiary care center.

Frustrated, Simon decided to celebrate her birthday this year by giving her what he describes as "a different kind of gift—a diagnosis." At least he hopes so—and he's relying upon the crowd (and more generally, open innovation) to deliver.

He has set up a Facebook page devoted to the diagnosis of his wife, and including links to all of her relevant medical history, data, and information, in hopes that someone will recognize the pattern, and offer a cogent explanation, a unifying diagnosis.

Facebook has been used before to diagnosis illness—for instance, this case of Kawasaki's Disease; moreover, it seems like a pretty smart approach—assuming, of course, you don't mind the conspicuous loss of privacy.

Most immediately, I hope someone finds a diagnosis for Simon's wife; I also suspect it's only a matter of time before a clever developer sets up a website devoted to crowdsourcing medical diagnoses (perhaps even offering prizes, InnoCentive-style); it's even possible this is occurring already.

Beyond this specific use case, however, it's also fascinating to think about the many ways in which the Facebook platform could be leveraged to both learn about health and improve health; the much-publicized organ donation initiative is probably just the tip of an exceptional opportunity here—particularly for extensive real-world measurement and for behavior modification.

For all the discussion about novel technologies in digital health, it's quite possible that one of the most powerful technologies we have—certainly, one of the most promising enabling platforms—has been sitting right in front of us the whole time.

It's an attractive opportunity that's hard for anyone passionate about health not to like.

Addendum: Thought it might be useful to reiterate here my response to a thoughtful reader comment: In my view, it's limiting to focus only on how Facebook is currently used in health (whether for diagnosis, such as the example discussed above, or for physician practice marketing, such as the reader example below). Rather, thinking a bit more broadly, it's exciting to contemplate whether—using a combination of existing data (which Facebook undoubtedly collects) and compelling user engagement (which Facebook undoubtedly offers)—there are untapped opportunities to learn more about health and to drive improvements in health, perhaps in combination with additional applications or consumer devices. – DS

Handle With Care: Success Of Digital Health Threatened By Power Of Its Technology

The ability to gather, analyze, and distribute information broadly is one of the great strengths of digital health, perhaps the most significant short-term opportunity to positively impact medical practice. Yet, the exact same technology also carries a set of intimately-associated liabilities, dangers we must recognize and respect if we are to do more good than harm.

Consider these three examples:

- At a recent health conference, a speaker noted that a key flaw with most electronic medical record (EMR) platforms is that they are "automating broken processes." Rather than use the arrival of new technology to think carefully, and from the ground up, about the problems that need to be solved, most EMRs simply digitally reify what already exists. Not only does this perpetuate (and usual exacerbate) notoriously byzantine operational practices and leave many users explicitly complaining they are worse off than before, but it also misses the chance to offer conceptually original approaches that profoundly improve workflow and enhance user experience.

- In a must-read blog post in *Health Affairs*, Al Lewis (author of Why *Nobody Believes the Numbers*, my 2012 selection for "digital health book of the year") and Vic Khanna discussed the methodological limitations of workplace "Get Well Quick" schemes (my related take here), and zeroed in on the exact same fundamental problem: "consecrating standard practices without clear evidence":

"We agree that workplace wellness is a useful construct, providing morale and productivity benefits. However, where large financial incentives are offered in the hopes that health expenses will decline, measurement of health expense reductions is a critical responsibility that is almost invariably lacking in today's wellness marketplace. *If employers continue to rush to buy workplace wellness programs, they will soon find themselves doing what the health care system itself has done for so long, to its great detriment: consecrating standard practices without clear evidence drawn from sound analytics.* This will result in more money spent on services of uncertain value that produce invalid outcomes, and misallocate resources away from more valuable endeavors and discussions." (Emphasis added.)

- A study from Case Western reported that at least 20% of the information in most physician progress notes was copy-and-pasted from previous notes. As recently discussed at kevinmd.com and elsewhere, this process can adversely affect patient care in a number of ways, and there's actually an emerging literature devoted to the study of "copy-paste" errors in EMRs. The ease with which information can be transferred can lead to the rapid propagation of erroneous information—a phenomenon we used to call a "chart virus." In essence, this is simply another example of consecrating information without first appropriately analyzing it (e.g. by asking the patient, when this is possible).

Each of these three examples represents a variation of a more general theme: the ability of digital technologies to afford ready access to large amounts of information can be tremendously dangerous, due to the ease with which bad information can be pushed out and widely disseminated. It's great that a physician in a healthcare system can immediately access the data for a specific patient—but only if that information is actually correct; otherwise, it can actually lead to bad decisions that wouldn't occur if centralized data weren't available at all.

The most obvious way to respond to this concern is to focus more effort on getting the process right—making sure we're consecrating the right things—thinking about how to redesign hospital workflow before we commit to digitizing it, for example, or ensuring we appropriately vet workplace wellness programs before rolling them out. Ditto for clinical decision support tools that encourage "best practices."

But this response misses a more subtle, and perhaps more important problem: the construction of a system that seems increasingly "fragile," in Taleb's sense, with less variation and less redundancy, and more vulnerable to catastrophic failure. A "chart virus" can rapidly endanger a patient in a way far more rapidly than an error in a traditional medical chart, while enforcing strict best-practice guidelines can rapidly endanger entire populations if the guideline turns out to be a mistake (say the prophylactic use of certain antiarrhythmic agents in effort to prevent sudden death in patients who previously suffered a heart attack, to pick but one historical example).

In the case of best practices, as Recon Strategy's Tory Wolff and I have argued, it may make sense to take a firm line against demonstrably bad behaviors, but permit a greater range of acceptable practices, as well as to ensure guidelines are "living documents" that can be continuously informed and updated by new knowledge and user experience.

More generally, efforts to excessively streamline processes in the name of efficiency must be balanced against some respect for the possibility of unintended consequences, and an appreciation for the robustifying effect of redundancies and inefficiencies (in moderation).

Digital health aspires to elevate human health and the practice of medicine by enabling providers to offer compassionate care with engaged patients, care that is informed by both updated, evidence-driven guidelines and patient data of almost unimaginable richness and depth.

If this vision is to be realized, however, we must also acknowledge the risk these powerful technologies pose, and take care to handle them with the caution they demonstrably require, and with the respect they unquestionably have earned. – DS

The Napsterization Of Health Care —Coming To A Theatre Near You

I had the good fortune to be invited to the South by Southwest Conference (SXSW) to participate as a judge of a digital healthcare start-up competition. SXSW, which takes place in Austin, TX, is historically an indie music gathering that has evolved into a massive mainstream music conference as well as a monumentally huge film festival, like Sundance times twenty. There are literally hundreds of bands and films featured around town. There has now evolved alongside this a conference called Interactive that draws more than 25,000 people and focuses on technology, particularly mobile, digital, and Internet.

In other words, SXSW has become one of the world's largest gatherings of hoodie-sporting, gadget-toting nerd geniuses that are way too square to be hip but no one has bothered to tell them. Imagine you are sitting at a Starbucks in Palo Alto, CA among 25,000 people who cannot possibly imagine that the rest of the world still thinks the Internet is that newfangled thing used mainly for email and porn. SXSW is a cacophonous melting pot of brilliance, creativity, futuristic thinking, arrogance, self-importance, ironic retro rock and roll t-shirts and technology worship. One small example: It's very hard to get your hands on a charger for anything other than an iPhone 5 because, seriously, who would have anything else?

Non-sequitur alert: Despite there being legions of legitimate celebrities at SXSW, the biggest line for a "celebrity" photo op was in the Mashable tent, where literally hundreds (maybe even over a thousand) people lined up to take their photo with The Grumpy Cat of Internet fame. Really, I swear. If you ask me, the cat looks a bit like McKayla Maroney, the Olympic gymnast. But I digress.

In the last two years healthcare has become a highly featured part of the SXSW Interactive conference, particularly as digital health has risen to the forefront of the healthcare conversation. Last year there were a few events focused on this topic but this year there were many of them, including two major start-up competitions, a plethora of presentations, and even a pretty healthy group of parties put on by the likes of old school healthcare entities looking to find their seat at that Palo Alto Starbucks look-alike contest.

Aetna, Blue Cross Blue Shield plans and other carriers were well-represented. It is interesting to see our industry make an earnest attempt, at least in some quarters, to find their way into the 21st Century and beyond. It was also interesting to notice who was not yet there: the mainstream healthcare IT companies, particularly those that sell to hospitals and other provider organizations. Back to that in a minute.

I was happy to go to SXSW to see the health care companies and my colleagues in the field, but this year I was determined to get to the fun side of SXSW where the film and music festivals take place. Having completed my official duties I snuck off to catch the premiere of the movie Downloaded, which is a documentary about the rise and fall of Napster. For those of you who aren't familiar with Napster, it was the very first music sharing company on the Internet. Founded by Shawn Fanning, who invented the technology with the help of early versions of crowdsourcing and peer-to-peer networking (ideas that didn't really exist in fully-thought out form at the time), Fanning came up with the idea of MP3 file sharing of music while bored at Northeastern University, where he ultimately dropped out to pursue Napster full time, with collaborator Sean Parker, more recently of Facebook fame (definition of "made it": Justin Timberlake plays you in a movie). In 1999 the site was launched and chaos ensued. It became the most widely used Internet site with over 26 million users by 2001 when it was summarily murdered by the legal efforts of the music industry which felt that Napster threatened their very existence. They were right.

There were so many interesting lessons in this movie that apply more broadly to the interplay of industry and technology, and those were particularly pronounced when watching it in a venue where you were surrounded by the somewhat unintentional spawn of Napster, as well as the entire music industry. Napster's original intent was mainly to allow college kids to share MP3 music files around the world, but really the company ended up catalyzing so much of what drives the Internet today: social networking, peer-to-peer computing, consumer engagement, free/freemium commerce, streaming, etc. I could go on and on. These young kids did not intend to upend the traditional music industry, much less the world of computing, but they did.

Napster ceased operations, at least in its original form, in 2001 after the Recording Industry Artists Association and many musicians, promoters and major music corporations rose up with an army of lawyers and crushed them with copyright law enforcement. Legitimate as those copyright claims were, the truth of the matter was that, once unleashed, the old guard was powerless to stop it once the new guard reached critical mass—they had won the battle but lost the war. This is a very prophetic lesson here for the "traditional" health IT companies.

There was a particularly poignant moment in Downloaded where the chief engineer at Napster was told to just shut it down—turn off all the servers and create a total service blackout—after the company could not comply with the court-ordered requirement to stop passing along music that was under copyright. But even when they unplugged all the servers, they found that hundreds of mirror servers existed out in the global community that were still fueling the Napster feed, and that the lights literally could not be turned off. It is a powerful moment, particularly as a metaphor for the concept of Clayton Christensen's Innovator's Dilemma. Even though Napster literally pulled the plug, their technology and its offshoots powered on and over the likes of record companies, music stores, music publishers and artists, all of whom were forced to adapt to the new world order despite many efforts to protect their old businesses models when they should have been embracing disruption in order to thrive in the future. In fact, the SXSW conference is now a virtual shrine to this experience, chock-a-block with the technology spawn that lives at the intersection of music, software and fan-engagement.

You healthcare people who aren't big music fans might be saying, "so what?" but this could well be the story writ large for many participants in our industry too. And nowhere is this more true than in the world of traditional healthcare IT (HIT), where we are poised right at the same precipice in many ways: a few massive players dominate the provider systems industry with closed systems. And in their wake are a million small entrepreneurs, armed with iPhones and massive creativity, and on a mission to undermine the traditional HIT oligarchy while they sleep and/or rest on their historical closed system laurels.

So much effort has gone into keeping patient and provider and insurance data proprietary that the medium to large institutions host data fortresses that would give Superman's Fortress of Solitude a run for its money. Providers have been notoriously closed with their data, preferring to keep costs, patient histories and anything else they can out of the patients' hands to preserve their aging business models. In some cases the more mysterious the better, as one can read in Stephen Brill's stunning story in Time Magazine a few weeks back, where a mythical "chargemaster" rules the hospital pricing universe, shielded even from the eyes of many hospital executives. I am not going to belabor the point about how hard it is for consumers to get their own healthcare data (not to mention that they don't even own it) or to access information about cost transparency, quality, etc. Everyone knows this. But what is happening is that the kind of people who attend SXSW are rising up and going straight to the consumer end-user to find ways to work around the system, get them their data, get them pricing information, connect them with quality and provider data and do all of the things that the traditional health IT infrastructure has been turning flip-flops to avoid.

Some of the industry's leaders have already figured out, at least in small ways, that the times, they are a'changing. The landscape of health insurance carriers haven't exactly embraced true open data, but some have flirted with it, offering mobile access to limited chunks of patient data or provider information to keep consumers loyal to their brands. While a start, this doesn't exactly foster true interoperability or transparency since the data stays within and addresses only what is inside their own figurative four walls, but there are glimmers.

On the hospital side, Epic stands firm as the poster child for "Katie, bar the door." They have steadfastly refused to embrace true interoperability or open data and, since they are the dominant purveyor of healthcare IT platforms to many of the nation's most prestigious hospital organizations, they have had the upper hand. But the Epic armor may soon be subject to cracks, alongside other of their provider-focused health IT brethren. And those cracks will be driven into their armor by the upstart entrepreneurs who are figuring out how to connect consumers to the information they want anyway and to build patient profiles from free-floating data in the social networking and related technology superstructures that have become more prevalent in consumers' lives than anyone could have predicted, particularly as mobile phones have become as common as kidneys. And by that I mean that, yes, many people have two phones.

Many may have seen the recent CommonWell Health Alliance announcement from McKesson, Cerner, AllScripts, Athena Health, Greenway Health and Relay Health. In it these 6 groups announced they were banding together to form a non-profit industry association to "support universal, trusted access to health care data through seamless interoperability." It's a noble goal, but it may well be a bit like the last stand of Custer in the face of a million very mission-driven warriors. The trick lies, as former President Clinton might say, in what the definition of "is" is—or in this case what the definition of "open" is. There are true open systems and then there are open-ish systems and it will be some time before we really know whether these HIT companies are going to be the kind of pterodactyls that evolve into birds and take flight or the kind that become extinct as they fight for their ever-decreasing share of a shrinking closed systems pie.

When I saw the CommonWell announcement I had a huge case of déjà vu. In my last life I worked in the high technology (non-healthcare) industry and worked for a brief while at an organization called X/Open, which was formed in 1984 by the then international leaders in the computer hardware industry. The original list included Groupe Bull, ICL, Siemens, Olivetti and Nixdorf. They were later joined by Philips, Nokia, AT&T, DEC, Unisys,

HP, IBM, NCR, Sun, Prime Computer, Apollo Computer, Fujitsu, Hitachi, and NEC. The focus of the organization was to "specify a *Common Application Environment* (CAE) intended to allow portability of applications across operating systems. The primary aim was compatibility between different vendors' implementations of UNIX."[citation from Wikipedia]. Interoperability, not true data openness or system integration, was the goal back in the 1980s. Sound familiar?

Fast forward many years later and, while X/Open morphed into The Open Group in 1992 and is still around, a majority of the companies on that list above wouldn't land on most people's list of the 3 most important and influential technology companies around today. Many of them are dead (or just resting), some are limping along; and a few are thriving but none of them have the cache of Apple in today's blossoming healthcare IT environment. While X/Open and its cadre were ascending in the mid-1980s, Apple was descending. Today most people would classify Apple as the most important IT company on the planet. Who'd have thought? And the reason Apple saw this resurgence was because the company had the forethought to blow itself up in order to become the very company that capitalized on what Napster had created by making it acceptable to the mainstream. Enter irony, stage left.

And this all makes me wonder…who will be there as the king of the hill 20 years from now in the healthcare IT marketplace? Mobile technologies and digital health companies and consumer engagement platforms are popping up like dandelions and no amount of Current-Market-Leader Brand weed-killer can get them all. Only the big companies that embrace new business models and voluntarily self-immolate their old-school strategies will be the names we see on the hardware stacks of the future—assuming hardware stacks still exist among the fluffy clouds that house the data rooms in the sky we are starting to embrace. In a recent article John Moore of Chilmark likened Epic's closed system strategy to Wang Laboratories' protectionist approach, and we all know what happened to Wang, or everyone would if they were old enough to have heard of it. When Wang croaked in the early 1990's it was because the company was too late to recognize that personal computers would kill mainframes and that would kill the company. Bummer dude. But it is, as they say, a timeless tale. As a colleague who runs the innovation programs at AARP, Jody Holtzman, recently said to me, a perfect example of "Ye Olde Innovators Dilemma."

So what does this mean for the HIT companies we have come to know and….know? It means that they must embrace the changing role of the consumer with respect to his/her data and the rapidly expanding imperative that they get real information to make purchasing and clinical decisions. It means that interoperability must start to be seen as the price of doing business in this sector, not the evil whose name must not be spoken. It means that mobile technologies must be integrated into the product roadmap, not tacked on like a billboard on the side of the road. Here's the good news: it appears that the more open technology becomes, the more it breeds demand for more technology, so a true open systems approach may actually increase the size of the pie for everyone.

While it is a total geekfest, I would recommend that everyone watch Napster, not just because it's interesting, but because it is a cautionary tale writ large for everyone who makes their living in the technology field, including those of us in healthcare. I have included a link to the trailer here. – LS

Watson And The Valley Girl

OMG and gag me with a spoon. A Fortune article called, "Teaching IBM's Watson the meaning of OMG" gave me a pretty good chuckle. The article discusses how the "final frontier" in machine intelligence is teaching computers not just words, but the subtle differences in meaning that make language rich, powerful and specific. I have often written about the intersection of language and healthcare (one of my most popular posts ever was about the application of Rap Genius' Internet annotation concept to healthcare communication), but this Fortune article really made clear to me how far we have NOT come.

Our entrepreneurial society worships science and technology but puts so little value on the soft sciences, the communication arts. And yet, Watson has proven for us all once again that technology without humanity is incapable of solving the world's problems, trapped as it is in its own syntax without context. Yes, man may be replaced by machine in many instances—already has in some cases—but in the end someone has to teach that machine to understand the human condition in order to realize its special purpose. Yes, yes, you engineers and physicians are swell, but give me an old fashioned English major any day of the week. Like, totally.

Meanwhile a mountain of scientists, doctors and their minions are busily working away to make themselves obsolete-ish through the education of Watson, IBM's super duper computer. By filling Watson's brain with the world's array of medical literature, these dudes in lab coats can totally improve patient diagnosis and treatment planning, y'know. But not so fast white guys in white coats; turns out Watson might work great when one is speaking the King's English, but might not be quite so bitchin' when the patient at hand is speaking actual American in one of its many forms, like y'know?

According to the article: *"The biggest difficulty for Brown (aka Eric Brown—Watson's overlord), as tutor to a machine, hasn't been making Watson know more but making it understand subtlety, especially slang. 'As humans, we don't realize just how ambiguous our communication is,' he says."*

The article goes on to talk about how Brown attempted to teach Watson the Urban Dictionary, which is the Internet's current most utilized slang repository. However, according to the article, Watson wasn't able to quite connect with terms like OMG or "hot mess." Moreover, *"Watson couldn't distinguish between polite language and profanity—which the* Urban Dictionary Is *full of. Watson picked up some bad habits from reading Wikipedia as well. In tests it even used the word "bullshit" in an answer to a researcher's query."* OMG, Watson, I'm sure! No way!

The article on Watson's OMG moment suggests that the programming work being done to make Watson the hospital's uber-diagnostic & therapeutic advice tool won't require that it be conversant in Valley-speak or other versions of American slang, but I'm not so sure that's true. Patients don't come in and report they are in the throes of a myocardial infarction; they say they feel like they're gonna barf and there is a vise in their chest. Unless Watson gets caught up quickly with the subtleties of human language, there is a still going to be a human intermediary required to translate those words into something Watson can understand; and thank goodness for that, because a little empathy and a pat on the hand are also nice touches in the ER. No one wants to look up at their attending and see the computer spinny wheel of death in the place of eyes.

But I have to admit I love the idea of teaching Watson slang so it can commune with the people on their own terms. Can't you just picture the perfection of Watson, ensconced in a San Fernando Valley area hospital, exclaiming these immortal words:

> *Okay, fine*
>
> *Fer sure, fer sure*
>
> *She's a valley girl*
>
> *And there is no cure* - LS

IX.

Behavior, Design, And Translation

The Behavior Gap

Remarkable advances in biology and genetics offer the promise of understanding disease at the molecular level, enabling a healthful future where physicians can offer "personalized medicine"–the right treatments to the right patients at the right time–perhaps even before disease symptoms are present. However, unless this technological progress is coupled with advances in understanding of human behavior, our dreams of improved health may fall far short of the mark.

Characterizing illness at the molecular level has radically expanded our view of disease, allowing us to recognize that many of the terms we typically use–hypertension, cancer, etc.–actually obscure a dizzying array of disease subtypes that are distinguished through molecular fingerprints or "biomarker profiles." Paul's hypertension may not be the same as Judy's hypertension–they may have profoundly different molecular causes and respond best to very different types of treatments. Understanding the different categories of disease, and segmenting a large patient population into smaller, more precisely defined classes, enables medical researchers to discover new, tailored treatments and considerably improve chances of survival and quality of life.

Of course, those suffering from devastating conditions such as pancreatic cancer or ALS would embrace such targeted medicines immediately; for these patients, the new treatments would represent the difference between life and death.

For most patients, however, the individualized therapies promised by personalized medicine represent incremental improvements in the treatment of asymptomatic conditions such as hypertension, high cholesterol and osteoporosis; will patients in the future embrace tailored treatments with more enthusiasm than patients diagnosed and treated today? Will a more personalized, more definitive risk assessment improve a patient's willingness to adhere to a particular regimen? What will be the response of patients who learn about their susceptibility to cancer and heart disease years before these diseases show up?

We've already learned that behavioral improvement is urgently needed even when effective medications are available. While patients with acutely life-threatening conditions such as cancer and HIV are understandably quite diligent about their medicines, many of us tend to be more cavalier, especially if the condition seems relatively unobtrusive, such as high blood pressure or low bone density. Despite effective monitoring and treatment options, diabetes remains the leading cause of blindness, kidney failure and amputation in the U.S. Similarly, while detection and treatment of high cholesterol has been clearly demonstrated to be of enormous benefit, less than half of patients who start on a statin even refill their prescription.

The best medicines only work if you take them. And many patients require cholesterol or diabetes medicine in the first place because they are unable to adjust their unhealthy eating and exercise habits. The bottom line is that changing behavior is as difficult as it is essential. Consequently, our ability to harvest the benefits of personalized medicine may depend upon our ability to meaningfully change our behavior.

The "behavior gap," as we call this, is likely to increase as scientific advances create new, more precise risk assessments and expand our diagnostic tools. Many people will suddenly discover they are "at risk," well before pharmacological treatments are available. In some cases the diagnostic testing may suggest the person is in a segment of patients for whom existing therapies have lower chances of success. Consequently, technological advances may actually further fuel the need for improved behavioral options.

The ability to monitor progress more precisely, and identify treatment response earlier, can allow for a fine-tuning of therapeutic approach, and can also help patients adapt to individual approaches. Monitoring could also help patients stick with treatment regimens, since the benefits of positive actions might yield rapid reinforcement, while unhelpful behaviors could be identified quickly and avoided in the future.

Information technology can also help close the behavior gap. The widespread adoption of electronic medical records will facilitate the organization of important health data, and will help patients and doctors connect behavior to outcome. Online communities of patients are also providing compelling behavioral support options, emphasizing both the increasingly important role of the Internet in healthcare as well as the trend for patients to play a central and more active role in the management of their own conditions.

For all the advances of modern science, the future of medicine will look a lot like the present, and will provide physicians and patients with many of the same challenges. While sophisticated science may yield a more precise segmentation of disease states, and a few magic bullets, we'll likely still be left with many more diseases than drugs, and our health will likely continue to depend upon our ability to modify our behavior, whether that means passing on dessert or taking our medicines regularly.

Fortunately, the same medical technologies that enable us to gauge our risk may also provide us with opportunities to develop more effective behavioral strategies that can be targeted with exquisite precision. But if we let our excitement about molecular advances obscure the pressing medical need to improve our understanding of behavior, we may be surprised by how difficult it is to translate biological progress into something the really matters–improved health outcomes for patients. – DS and Sarah Cairns-Smith

Design Can Improve Health Care; Can It Also Lead To New Cures?

Of all the areas of human endeavor touched by Steve Jobs, perhaps few stand to gain as much as healthcare, where the design principles he popularized and demonstrated remain so urgently needed. Yet, his tragic death at the age of 56 also challenges us to ask whether design principles can help drive medical science itself, and identify novel therapies.

The greatest legacy of Steve Jobs—as many have observed (see here, here, and here) may be in design, and specifically, his ability, in the words of Steve Gage, "to take this enormous complexity and make something a human being could use." While Steve Jobs did not discover design thinking, he is probably the one person most responsible for our visceral appreciation of the concept.

Tim Brown, founder of the design consultancy IDEO, describes (PDF) design thinking somewhat formally as "a discipline that uses a designer's sensibility and methods to match people's needs with which is technologically feasible and what a viable business strategy can convert into customer value and market opportunity."

Brown also offers a more useful characterization of design thinking: an "approach to innovation" that is "human-centered, creative, iterative, and practical." Design is at once an approach and a sensibility (see this [PDF] useful "bootcamp bootleg" from the Stanford D-school, or most anything written by Donald Norman).

While in some circles (radiating concentrically from Palo Alto, one imagines), design is, if not quite passé, at least associated with irrational exuberance and extravagant expectations (see this 2009 posting by Peter Merholz, founder of the user experience consultancy Adaptive Path, and the energetic dialog his remarks engendered), these principles have made only very preliminary inroads into medicine and healthcare.

For starters, medicine is far less "human-centered"—that is, patient-centered—than most observers appreciate. In the exact same way that well-intentioned engineers often go awry by creating features based on their own perception of what they perceive users must want, medicine has spent a lot of effort focused on a physician's idea of a patient, rather than developing a more nuanced view of life from the perspective of the patients themselves.

Physicians have surprisingly little visibility into a patient's day to day health experience—doctors typically have no idea whether a patient actually took their prescribed medication (data suggest the level of adherence can be shockingly low), took their medication correctly (video studies of patients taking injectible or inhaled medicines reveal remarkable variability), or adhered to behavioral recommendations (you have to ask?).

Doctors also have little sense of a patient's daily experience with their disease—their daily blood pressure, say, or ability to inhale deeply—to say nothing of less concrete but arguably more important parameters such as mood or quality of life. The physician's episodic assessment of a patient's health, an occasional snapshot, may not always capture all, most, or, in some cases, almost any of the patient's actual experience with disease. Worse still (as discussed here), the absence of more granular knowledge of patients means that doctors have virtually no idea of whether they are providing effective care or not—are patients even following their advice, is the advice doing any good, and are the doctors even focused on the issues most important to patients?

To be sure, some change is in the air; device makers are focusing more intently than ever on the user experience; equipment makers are trying to focus on the use of affordances to reduce human error; a number of hospitals are trying to pay more attention to the holistic needs of their inpatients; and a slew of mobile health companies are developing products that offer the promise of more continuous monitoring and assessment.

I've no doubt that design principles can—and, hopefully, soon will—help us all do better utilizing the resources (personnel, institutions, therapeutics) we currently have: an enormous accomplishment.

But Steve Jobs didn't die at the age of 56 because he didn't like his hospital johnny, or because he accidentally took the wrong pill, or because he wasn't getting the levels of some hormone assessed frequently enough. He died because he had cancer, and he needed an effective drug—or similar intervention. What does design thinking have to offer here? Can it lead to transformative medical discoveries, to an implementable cure for a particular disease?

The honest answer is that we really don't know yet. The jury's still out.

My hope—and at this point, it's only a hope—is that the more detailed analysis of patients could yield the sort of transformative insights that areas such as oncology so desperately need. I can imagine that if we could more carefully monitor a range of parameters in cancer patients and engage their participation in open data platforms (in a fashion similar to PatientsLikeMe, and as championed by organizations such as Sage), perhaps we would have a greater chance of discovering unexpected relationships, of finding hints of new uses for existing drugs, of developing a deeper appreciation for the underlying networks and relationships driving health and disease.

It's also likely that the opportunity to get closer to patients could help improve the total care we provide, a human-centric, iterative, pragmatic approach that is credited for playing a pivotal role in progress in diseases such as pediatric cancer and cystic fibrosis, where a magic bullet has remained elusive.

Perhaps most important, a design approach would ensure that we keep our focus on patients, rather than on dubious animal models that are often far more effective at generating research grants and advancing academic careers than they are at providing meaningful insight into a disease afflicting patients. It might also stimulate some of our smartest and most creative basic medical scientists—researchers who have traditionally been drawn to reductive, highly simplified systems—to start innovating around patients, trying to develop a far more detailed and relevant understanding of disease as it exists in the organism that ultimately holds our greatest interest and investment: ourselves.

Revolutionizing fundamental medical research may be an unreasonably audacious goal, but figuring it out—finding a way to incorporate in a meaningful fashion the principles of design thinking in the approach and strategy of basic scientists—is a worthy ambition, and one I suspect Steve Jobs would have felt proud to inspire. Let the conversation begin. – DS

A Translational Innovator Career Track To Support Health Entrepreneurs

I was having coffee recently with a bright endocrinology fellow who had a passion for digital health, and was struggling as he thought about career paths. Specifically, he loved clinical medicine and working in a university environment, but didn't see himself either as a traditional researcher or a clinical educator, the two main tracks for faculty advancement and promotion at most major academic medical centers.

Rather, he saw himself putting together start-up companies to address the specific clinical problems and opportunities he saw, and (after much negotiation) had evidently managed to set up a non-profit enterprise involving assessment of mobile health information for his fellowship research project (something that reportedly didn't sit all that well with the traditionalists in the department).

In my view, this young physician represents, or should represent, the tip of the spear, and is pursuing a career direction that we should strongly encourage, as it would represent a profoundly constructive and hopeful direction for academic medicine in general, and for the pursuit of real-world translational research in particular.

Here are four reasons why the idea of an inquisitive clinician pursuing academic medicine by starting companies within the university seems smart and appealing:

Evolving Health Information Technology (HIT) Creates Opportunities As Well As Challenges

As care becomes more regimented, physician choice becomes progressively restrained—that's the idea, after all. EMR systems that enforce such regimentation (Epic most prominently) are frequently cited as culprits.

I share many of these anxieties—see here, here, here; however, I also appreciate that as care is delivered in a more consistent and transparent fashion, it should be easier to measure what physicians (and ideally patients) are actually doing, and figure out what's working better and worse.

In theory, improved HIT should enable just the sort of deliberate experiments that thoughtful researchers have always done, and that many individual clinicians have pursued on an N-of-1 basis; with improved HIT, there should be the opportunity to explore hypotheses more rigorously, and to identify opportunities for improved care.

Field Discovery Essential for Medical Innovation

I'm admittedly a bit obsessed with idea that physicians are ideally positioned to drive the revolution in digital health—a revolution that to my eyes seems largely driven by the technologists, who tend to provide tools in search of application, rather than by doctors, who routinely encounter problems but don't always have the experience or ability to see these as important opportunities, problems that might be solvable (easily, in some cases) with the right technology.

Eric von Hippel of MIT, as I've discussed, has highlighted the importance of "field discovery"—practitioners working on problems they encounter—in driving medical innovation. In contrast, many medical products companies are largely solution machines in search of a problem, and might really benefit, at the earliest stages of project selection, from input from clinicians on the front line, as the gap between illness as understood by R&D groups and as experienced by patients and the physicians who treat them can be both profound and alarming.

Not surprisingly, leading innovation catalysts seems to have figured this out; you can't spend five minutes with Rock Health's Geoff Clapp, or Aenor Sawyer of UCSF's Clinical and Translational Science Institute, without hearing them preach the urgent need to bring clinicians and technologists together.

Academic Mission Is Best Served by Pressure-Testing Ideas in Real World

Fundamental academic research is often described as curiosity-inspired—learning for the sake of learning. At the same time, at least in biomedicine, much of this work is funded, and justified by researchers, as advancing knowledge that will lead to improved treatments. The problem is that you can publish hundreds of papers about a system or process you believe to be involved with a disease such as CF or Alzheimers, and conclude your papers with a gauzy sentence about implications for future treatments, but still—ultimately, sadly, tragically—have essentially zero impact on patients with this disease. Data continue to accumulate highlighting the difficulty of replicating, and generalizing from academic results (see here for my recent discussion of this topic).

Similarly, in clinical medicine, physicians offer recommendations all the time with little sense of whether they are actually helpful.

In this context, start-up companies might be thought of as a vivid expression of the translational ideal—which is how I described it here in 2005; the goal of a company is to take an initially promising finding and figure out a way to translate it into a real-world application.

While some view the value of entrepreneurship to academic centers as based on the financial rewards of a successful effort, I suspect that there's remarkable intellectual value to be captured from the (often unsuccessful) pursuit itself. On the basic research side, you learn so much about the fragility of science, and difficulty of even taking the first step towards implementation. On the clinical/digital health side, I suspect there will be vital learnings around the difficulty of user engagement, and the challenge of actually changing behavior and improving health.

Right Time and Place

While traditionally, start-up formation was something envisioned as occurring outside of academic medical centers (even if using insights or technologies developed by university-associated researchers), this seems to be changing. Today, an increasing number of leading academic centers host incubators for emerging health-focused companies

This co-localization may have started as a response to the much-discussed challenges faced by early-stage life-science companies, and more generally, the difficulties of "bridging the translational gap." By incubating emerging companies internally, the logic goes, these start-ups may have greater opportunity to get their footing in a relatively protected environment, and achieve the convincing demonstration of value required to garner more significant funds (which are probably more likely to come these days from strategic investors vs traditional VCs—see this characteristically smart, recent post by biotech COO Laura Strong).

Digital health startups would seem as likely as life-science startups to benefit from incubation within academic health center; moreover, the idea that it's possible to make a difference with a small, focused start-up has been demonstrated (in tech) by Dave McClure and others, and seems especially attractive in the digital health space.

Translational Innovator Track?

If start-ups are going to be an increasingly prominent part of the academic medical center landscape—as I hope they are and believe they should be—then there should be a meaningful career opportunity for faculty members who focus their efforts on advancing this translational interface.

More generally, while some translational innovators might choose to pursue careers in industry, I suspect many, like the endocrinology fellow with whom I spoke, might envision a professional life in the university, and there should be a career path designed to recognize, support, and encourage this vitally important trajectory.

Yes, the requirements for a "translational innovator" would look different from those of traditional physician-scientists or of clinician-educators, and yes, this would require some adjustment of traditional beliefs.

But if academic medical centers are going to continue their historical role of leading biomedical innovation, if they are going to create health's future rather than just be carried along with the tide, then a good first step would be supporting and enabling the careers of the translational innovators who are willing to work across disciplines and domains, and use startups as an innovation vehicle to drive change, catalyze progress, and improve human health. – DS

Keen To Drive Science Into Medicine? Four Lessons From An Innovation Conference

I participated in an engaging and highly interactive translational research innovation symposium at Duke University put together by Dr. David Epstein at the Duke Eye Center and Chancellor Victor Dzau, and featuring both University faculty and invited external speakers. Four key themes emerged:

Theme 1: Driving science into application remains difficult but desirable

I was struck by the range of participants eager to push science into the clinic, from PhD chemists and biologists to internists and surgeons (and, of course, ophthalmologists). A vigorous entrepreneurial spirit was apparent, a determination to do something outside the usual academic practice.

I was equally struck, however, by the challenge of giving form to this spirit, something I appreciate is a more general concern: how does a university (or any organization, although for now I'm thinking particularly about academic centers) capture and channel this visceral but relatively inchoate yearning?

From what I heard at this conference, it sounds like the three basics may be culture, coordination, and capital.

Culture: As sick as I am of hearing the phrase, "culture is everything," I understand the point. Culture really matters—and academic leaders can play a vital role either passionately encouraging and supporting entrepreneurship (Susan Desmond-Hellmann and Tom Byers stand out in my mind here), or offering only tepid lip service. Arguably the most valuable aspect of culture are the presence of positive examples, faculty members and students who've actually done this—developed a product, started a company, pushed an innovation into the clinic and changed medical practice.

This also suggests an opportunity to initiate a virtuous cycle—once you have a nucleus of entrepreneurs, a critical mass, the excitement can spread virally (case in point: I suspect that almost every undergraduate at Stanford has considered forming a company at one time or another), and following the success of Mark Zuckerberg, the same may now be true at Harvard.

Coordination: While the idea of forming a company, or developing a technology for licensing, may sound sexy, the reality tends to be more complex, and (in the case of start-ups) typically involves far more work than the participants had originally anticipated. It's also clear that while there may not be a formula for innovation, there are discrete structural activities that can be done in an environment to support, nurture, guide and sustain innovation, as several faculty members from Duke's Fuqua School of Business Emphasized. Some learning is inevitably didactic (learning the rules of road), but most is experiential, and a crucial element seems to involve learning how to work as team, to transform the germ of an idea into something concrete. The best learning, clearly, is real world experience; seeing and solving the real-world challenges experienced as you try to transform an idea into an actual (often commercial) product or service likely represents the most useful training of all.

Capital: This wasn't discussed extensively at this week's meeting, but was an important subtext. Capital plays a vitally important role in driving innovation, and the availability of capital can be transformative—just as the lack of same can be a problem. New York's recent arrival on the national entrepreneurial scene is arguably a testament to the power of the capital, intelligently deployed, to ignite a primed innovation community.

Theme 2: Think differently

Exhorting people to "think differently" seems about as useful a hollering at your microwave to "cook faster." Yet, several examples from this meeting suggested that are actually approaches to deliberately think about problems in slightly different ways.

Dean Nancy Andrews, for example, presented interesting social science data I hadn't previously seen highlighting the value of diversity in innovation; it turns out that heterogeneous teams tend to solve difficult problems more effectively and apparently more creatively than teams with less diversity. This ties in nicely with the suggestion (that I've heard frequently, though I can't speak to the evidence base) that breakthroughs tend to occur at the intersection of disciplines.

Keynote speaker and legendary MIT bioengineer Robert Langer emphasized the value of multi-discipline collaboration as well; such interactions have been a defining characteristic of his career, and also the foundation, beginning with his decision to pursue his post-doc not in a chemical engineering division, but rather in the lab of a pediatric surgeon, the late Judah Folkman.

The emphasis on unexpected ideas tied in very well with a second point Dean Andrews also made, about the unique value of students on entrepreneurial teams; not only do they tend to be energetic, of course, but they are also relatively naïve, and can ask the fundamental, vital questions overlooked by those with more experience.

The idea of thinking differently was a key message of my talk (which also highlighted the broad transformative potential of robust phenotypic measurement), and also a significant theme of the talk given by Geoff Duyk, a physician-scientist by training, and currently managing director of TPG's in-house biotech VC fund; not surprisingly, Duyk is a big believer in the concept of intellectual "cross-training."

Both Duyk and I highlighted the need to look beyond the traditional model of early stage innovation (pathway -> target -> drug), and consider other types of innovation that could improve health—including innovation in devices, services, processes, and care delivery (topics I've also discussed in previous commentaries—for example here, here, and here). Of particular interest, Duyk highlighted the unique healthcare needs and opportunities associated with countries in Central and South America, as well as Asia, providing an often underappreciated global perspective, and an important reminder of the value of thinking outside the border as well as the box.

Theme 3: Pharmascolds still have academics running scared.

As impressed as I was by the interest of university researchers in moving their research out of the university and into practice, I was even more struck by their fear (articulated to some extent publically, and to a far greater extent privately) of the pharmascolds, an anxiety that took many forms. Junior faculty were concerned that working with industry in any way might jeopardize their relationship with the NIH, and introduce a prohibitive array of complications and requirements into their already busy lives.

To a person, everyone emphasized the need to be completely transparent and open; there was unanimous agreement here. The problem, rather, was the seemingly excessive and gratuitously onerous requirements associated with this transparency, a level of micromanagement (one might argue nanomanagement) that was perceived at times to be absurdly heavy-handed, and more likely to inhibit university/industry collaboration than enhance it.

There was also a strong sense that partnering with industry is still viewed in many academic circles as collaborating with the enemy, a relationship that threatens to stigmatize the researcher—a disgraceful phenomenon, in my view: we should be celebrating, not castigating, the researchers who seek to drive their science into practice, not just into papers and prestige.

The view from a subset of the many senior leaders with whom I spoke was, if anything, even more concerning—though hardly surprising. Several senior faculty members strongly believed that the media had their crosshairs fixed squarely on academics who work with industry, and any academic leader who tried forcefully to defend or support these relationships was likely to be taken down. Paranoid as it sounds, I've heard this from a number of academic leaders at a range of institutions, highlighting the perceived ferocity of the pharmascold attacks, as well as the courage of the rare academic leaders —such as Desmond-Hellmann—willing to stand up and forcefully make the case that driving science into application (a) is core to a research university's public mission, and (b) can be powerfully facilitated through well-structured collaborations with industry. (See here as well.)

Theme 4: Role of the champion and the opportunity to make a difference

The two highlights of the symposium were the first talk of the day by Langer, and the last talk of the day, by Y.T. Chen. Each seminar highlighted the tremendous impact of an impassioned innovator.

Langer's talk discussed the arc of his career, including the initial challenges he faced as he struggled to get a new technology patented. It's often said that the mark of a true scientific breakthrough is that it seems obvious—but only after someone suggests it. The trouble, of course, is that if you're the one who suggests it, a patent reviewer can then decide it seems obvious, which was the trouble he initially encountered (he persevered and eventually received his patent).

He also highlighted the excitement and many challenges of developing new products and forming new companies, and you are reminded that just being brilliant and uncommonly creative—as Langer is (see this brief profile I wrote for Boston Magazine several years ago)—isn't enough; success also requires exceptional persistence, and a lot of gritty work.

Chen's talk, to close the symposium, offered a poignant and modestly-presented reminder of why translation is so essential; Chen is a physician-scientist (pediatric geneticist) who, motivated by the searing experience of a patient's memorial service, ultimately developed the first treatment for Pompe Disease, a rare, devastating, historically fatal lysosomal storage condition that afflicts muscles leading to debilitating weakness and frequently death; following the development of a enzymatic replacement strategy by Chen—and its subsequent development and commercialization by industry (Synpac, later Genzyme, now Sanofi)—many children with this disease have a significantly improved chance of living a much better—in some cases, relatively normal—life, especially if treatment is initiated very early.

As I listened to Chen's talk, I found myself wondering about this model of innovation, this narrative of the intrepid, determined physician-scientist successfully shepherding a discovery from the lab into the clinic. It's a compelling vision—it's what I had in mind when I decided to pursue an MD/PhD, and I know it's what many of my colleagues were thinking as well.

But now, I'm torn: part of me worries that while this model has great narrative appeal, it may be more the exception than the rule; more often, progress may involve a number of discrete, and often disjointed advances, that over time are integrated into a more complete picture, and ultimately give rise to novel therapies. Moreover, by holding up these sorts of dramatic exemplars, we may not only be misleading future researchers but also encouraging the wrong behaviors—celebrating the iconic crusader, rather than the conscientious collaborator (although notably Chen was apparently both), the charismatic entrepreneur rather than the boring but relentlessly effective CEO (see here).

The thing is, I can't escape my fundamental belief—and it really is just a belief—in the absolute primacy of the clinical champion, the inquisitive physician or scientist who is determined to drive science into application. I believe deeply in the unique ability of highly motivated champions to walk through walls, and accomplish what other, more grounded researchers might never attempt. I recognize the narrative of the intrepid entrepreneur, but I also believe in it.

I hope we continue to highlight the accomplishments of clinical champions like Y. T. Chen, like Judah Folkman, like Peter Pronovost (incidentally a nice example of a champion pursuing systems innovation). These exemplars may not be representative of everyone who has contributed impactfully to medical progress and scientific translation, but they offer an inspirational reminder of the power of what can be achieved with a focused mind, a committed heart, and little bit of luck. – DS

Closing The Translational Gap: A Challenge Facing Innovators In Medical Science—And In Digital Health

The gap between model or potential solutions and solutions that work in the real world—the translational gap—is arguably the greatest challenge we have in healthcare, and is something seen in both medical science and in digital health.

Translational Gap in Medical Science

The single most important lesson I learned from my many years as a bench scientist was how fragile most data are, whether presented by a colleague at lab meeting or (especially) if published by a leading academic in a high-profile journal. It was not uncommon to watch colleagues spend months or even years trying to build upon an exciting reported finding, only to eventually discover the underlying result was not reproducible.

This turns out to be a problem not only for other university researchers, but also for industry scientists who are trying to translate promising scientific findings into actual treatments for patients; obviously, if the underlying science doesn't hold up, there isn't anything to translate. Innovative analyses by John Ioannidis, now at Stanford, and more recently by scientists from Bayer and Amgen, have highlighted the surprisingly prevalence of this problem.

An invaluable function of industry (as I've argued) is pressure-testing academic results, and seeing if they are as robust and generalizable as the authors hope and expect. One reason early-stage VC funding in the life sciences is so hard to come by these days is that investors have learned through painful experience not to take hot published data at face value.

The challenge of data reproducibility also represents an opportunity—if you can demonstrate your intriguing results are robust, and achievable by others, you've effectively differentiated yourself from a lot of the competition.

That's the logic, anyway, behind an effort called the Reproducibility Initiative, which aims to provide a mechanism for scientists to show their results are reproducible by paying a third party to replicate them (see this Reuters article by Sharon Begley, the science journalist who I suspect has done the most to focus attention on the need for better translation). A PLoS journal has committed to publishing such validation studies, and Nature journals that publish original studies have indicated (according to this excellent Carl Zimmer article in *Slate*) that they will link to subsequent validation publications.

I'm a bit skeptical that this initiative will actually catch on (and I also wonder what fraction of academic studies are even amenable to this approach); however, the very existence of this effort highlights the magnitude of the challenge we now face in bridging the gap between a self-sustaining academic enterprise that thrives on journal publications and a struggling medical products industry that requires a far higher (and underappreciated) standard of proof in order to be successful.

Translational Gap in Digital Health

The most significant gap that I've seen in digital health is between the seasoned clinicians and other healthcare providers who arguably have the best sense of the problems that need to be solved, and the enthusiastic but medically naive technologists and entrepreneurs eager to offer solutions.

Most of the digital health entrepreneurs I've met—even those who see themselves coming from the clinical side rather than the technology side—have remarkably little medical experience, something that comes across not only in the problems described and solutions envisioned, but also more generally in the failure of many entrepreneurs to grasp the gravitas of medicine, and to appreciate the range and depth of fears and concerns experienced by patients contending with serious or chronic conditions.

Meanwhile, the truly experienced physicians and providers immersed in patient care tend to be consumed with—that's right—patient care, and often haven't either the time or inclination to consider entrepreneurial solutions to the problems they encounter. They may have a comparatively full and nuanced appreciation of the problems to be solved, but may be disinclined to leave their established comfort zone and think about new, technologically-enabled solutions.

Ideally, this challenge should also represent an opportunity; I suspect experienced clinicians encounter specific problems every day that could be solved, perhaps in a generalizable and widely-applicable fashion, by a competent entrepreneur.

Failure to involve such seasoned physicians more fully in digital health will result in a lot more of what I'm seeing now—cutsie, tractionless health apps that might appeal to a young kid's (or inexperienced tech VC's) idea of what doctors do, rather than addressing a real pain point experienced by doctors and other medical providers. (See also this excellent recent post by Dr. Jay Chyung of the consultancy Recon Strategy about the need to ensure health data analytics efforts are focused on actual problems. [Disclosure: I've previously co-authored several EMR strategy articles with Recon Strategy partner Tory Wolff.])

Enterprises seeking to catalyze digital health are doing a great job drawing in young entrepreneurs, energized medical and graduate students, and junior med school faculty members—a tremendous achievement.

However, I suspect durable success in digital health will also depend upon the ability to access the insights of the experienced physicians who are less focused on disrupting medicine, and are consumed instead with the profound, worthy responsibility of delivering it. – DS

The Mentalists: Behavioral Psychology Delivered Votes; Can It Now Deliver Health

Obama's most significant healthcare-related accomplishment this year may well have been his campaign's demonstration of the effective use of analytics and behavioral insight—strategies that also offer exceptional promise for the delivery of care and the maintenance of health.

For starters, of course, there's the widely-reported "big data" success of the Obama campaign. In unprecedented fashioned, they collected, mined, analyzed, and actioned information, microtargeting voters in a remarkably individualized fashion.

Imagine if health care interventions could be personalized as effectively (or pursued as passionately).

Another example: according to the NYT, the Obama campaign hired a "dream team" of behavioral psychologists to burnish their message and bring out the vote, using a range of techniques the field has developed over the years.

According to the article, the behavioral experts "said they knew of no such informal advisory committee on the Republican side."

This idea of focusing intensively on behavior change is without question an idea whose time has come.

Recently, for instance, a colleague (with similar training in medicine, molecular biology, and business) and I were surveying the biopharma landscape, and were struck by the extent to which classic biology hasn't (yet) delivered the cures for which we had hoped; physiology turns out to be extremely complicated, and people, and communities, even more so.

We were also struck by the remarkably low adherence rates for many drugs, abysmal whether you look at this from the perspective of clinical care or commercial opportunity (imagine if Toyota lost half their cars on the way to the dealership).

We joked that biopharmas might not be worse off (at least in the near term) if they got rid of all their current basic scientists, and instead hired a bunch of behaviorists, to figure out how to enable patients to best utilize existing products. (As Lisa Suennen has recently written, it appears many medical device companies already are focused on just this sort of innovation. I appreciate the rationale but hope we continue to strive to develop entirely novel products as well.)

While it's far too early and much too facile to attribute the success of the Obama campaign to the involvement of the behavioral psychologists, it's hard not to applaud the thinking, and appreciate the implications for health care.

Currently, there's a tremendous focus on translational medicine, generally understood as the need to ensure molecular advances in the laboratory are turned into better care at the bedside. Clearly, this remains vitally important.

At the same time—as Sarah Cairns-Smith and I argued in 2009—it's equally important to focus on what we termed "the behavior gap," and ensure we also pay attention to translating the advances from behavioral psychology into practice.

The good news here is that digital health is growing up, and may provide many of the enabling technologies required for both actionable analytics (companies such as GNS Healthcare and Predilytics, among many others, come to mind) and behavior modification (Ginger.io, Omada Health, many others).

Astute use of data analytics and behavioral science demonstrably improved the health of the Democratic party; the question now is whether this integrated approach can evolve do so something arguably even more important: improve the health of the American people. – DS

Corporate Wellness Programs: Better For Waistline Than Bottom Line?

The WSJ (VC Dispatch) features an informative post about corporate wellness initiatives (a related Venture Wire story ran the year before), programs offered by employers to improve employee health and well-being.

The WSJ article notes wellness programs can help employers reduce not only absenteeism but also "presenteeism" (you're at work but not maximally productive), habits that collectively cost U.S. employers an estimated $36B a year in lost productivity.

Here's where it gets interesting: given the huge numbers wellness companies tend to throw around to describe the "epidemic" of absenteeism and presenteeism, you'd figure that if the problem was really so large, and the interventions offered were really so effective, then linking payment to performance would be the best way to optimize alignment, and clearly would be in everyone's best interest.

While some wellness companies assert they save employers money, and most insist they deliver improved wellness, the fact remains that most wellness programs are offered as a benefit to employees, something HR provides to help recruit and retain workers.

Nothing wrong with that, of course. But the point is that payment for wellness activities seems rarely linked to any measure of productivity or cost-savings—in other words, the wellness company gets paid for helping workers feel better (and sometimes for activity participation or weight loss), rather than delivering any measurable benefit to the corporation's bottom line.

If wellness companies really do save healthcare costs, and make workers more productive—great and great: let employers pay these companies on the basis of actual health care savings delivered, and for demonstrated evidence of improved performance.

Understanding what wellness companies are or are not delivering to employers has several key implications for understanding the economics of digital health more broadly.

First, the corporate wellness example highlights just how unbelievably difficult it is to deliver true cost savings; I've previously described what I've termed the "Milstein Metric"—the goal of developing innovations that improve health while reducing costs within a five year period. Sounds simple, but in practice, this bar turns out to be exceedingly high.

Second, this example highlights the difference between:

(a) Soft, consumer outcomes—a product needs to make consumers feel good (perhaps there should be a term "wellfulness," akin to Stephen Colbert's "truthiness");

(b) The higher expectations that have traditionally defined the medical products space—a product must demonstrate efficacy in a rigorous, controlled clinical study;

(c) The explicitly higher expectations that are increasingly expected of medical products, enforced by regulators in the EU, and by payors in the US—a product must show not only that it works, but that it is cost-effective, increasingly in "real-world" situations.

Wellness companies generally aspire to, imagine, or genuinely believe they are in the third category, but most are firmly planted in the first (although some, such as Weight Watchers, likely merit inclusion in the second).

To be sure, developing offerings that help employees feel good about their health is a savvy strategic decision on the part of wellness companies, enabling them to be paid by established, well-resourced employers for delivering what is essentially a consumer offering.

But let's reserve our highest praise for behavioral health companies that not only promise more productive employees and reduced healthcare costs, but are confident enough in their ability to achieve these goals that they are willing to be paid on the basis of the ROI they actually deliver. – DS

Three Tensions In Medical Innovation To Watch For In The Next Twelve Months

As we anticipate unprecedented interest in healthcare innovation, pay particular attention to the following three emerging tensions in the space.

Tension 1: Preventive Health vs Excessive Medicalization

A core tenet of medicine is that it's better to prevent a disease (or at least catch it early) than to treat it after it has firmly taken hold. This is the rationale for both our interest in screening exams (such as mammography) as well as the focus on risk factor reduction (e.g. treating high blood pressure and high cholesterol to prevent heart attacks).

The problem, however, is that intervention itself carries a risk, which is sometimes well-characterized (e.g. in the case of a low-dose aspirin for some patients with a history of heart disease) but more often incompletely understood.

As both Eric Topol and Nassim Taleb have argued, there's a powerful tendency to underestimate the risk associated with interventions. Topol, for example, has highlighted the potential risk of using statins to treat patients who have never had heart disease (i.e. primary prevention), a danger he worries may exceed the "relatively small benefit that can be derived." (Other cardiologists disagree—see this piece by colleague Matt Herper).

In his new book *Antifragile*, Taleb focuses extensively on iatrogenics, arguing "we should not take risks with near-healthy people" though he adds "we should take a lot, a lot more, with those deemed in danger."

Both Topol and Taleb are right that we tend to underestimate iatrogenicity in general, and often fail to factor in the small but real possibility of potential harm.

At the same time, I also worry about external experts deciding categorically what sort of risk is or isn't "worth it" for an individual patient—a particular problem in oncology, where it now seems fashionable to declare the possibility of a few more months of life a marginal or insignificant benefit.

Even less dramatically, a treatment benefit that some might view as trivial (for hemorrhoids, say) might be life-altering for others. For these sufferers, a theoretical risk that some (like Taleb) find prohibitive might be worth the likelihood of symptom relief. Ideally, this decision would ultimately belong to patients, not experts asserting to act on patients' behalf.

Tension 2: Relentless Standardization of Medicine

Every day, I feel like I'm witnessing two parallel, completely different narratives about the current and future state of medicine. One view—which might be termed the "Cheesecake Factory" perspective—is that medicine is currently practiced in an absurdly capricious fashion; medical care is wildly and unjustifiably variable. Instead, medicine should be standardized like other business processes, so each patient will receive the best known care for their particular condition, rather than be subject to the whims and caprices of the treating physician.

The other story I hear is that in the evolving standardization of medicine—as physician visits become more focused on EMR data entry and adherence to mandated algorithms—something vital is being lost. From this point of view, the advice of the efficiency experts and technologists is seen as dangerously reductive, representing a naïve caricature of medicine, where patients report symptoms, receive a diagnosis, and are assigned a treatment. The reality, say many physicians (see here, for example), is so much messier —symptoms are often vague, reasons for the visit are often complex, there is no clearly-defined "best practice," and the problem to be solved is often so much more nuanced that "what's wrong with my car."

Cheesecake Factory advocates stress they aren't seeking to remove the nuance from medicine, and instead wish only to standardize what is already known, collect data and determine best practices so that physicians can focus on the interpersonal interaction while knowing they are treating patients in context of all available data. It's a compelling vision.

Yet it's hard not to worry that if medicine goes in the direction of the Cheesecake Factory, where care is administered on the cheap by customer-service technologists plugging data into an algorithm, then an ancient and noble profession will face extinction because of an inability (some might say a haughty unwillingness) to adequately contemplate and communicate its essential value proposition.

I am overwhelmed by a feeling of tragic sadness as I see the pervasive sense of dissatisfaction that has settled over medicine, leaving so many honorable, brilliant, well-intentioned doctors in a near-state of shock, asking whether this could possibly be the profession they had dreamt of all their lives, and worked so hard to enter.

On optimistic days, I am hopeful that the process improvements and advances in digital health will inspire, not dishearten, inquisitive physicians, who perhaps will appreciate the opportunity to more fully leverage information and deliver a higher level of care.

I'm also certain that if medicine does continue to become as excessively standardized and depersonalized as many fear, this will create important disruptive opportunities for entrepreneurial physicians with a different—call it old-fashioned—vision of the value of a more substantial doctor-patient relationship.

Tension 3: Industrialization of Drug Discovery

The most significant problem facing the biopharma industry today is that large biopharmas depend upon products they have little idea how to reliably discover. It's a strange concept, when you think about it—and a huge challenge for the industry, since most of what large companies do very well—industrialize processes, produce products at scale—just don't map all that well to the skills and capabilities required for discovering new drugs.

It's not a new problem, of course, but one big pharma R&D execs continue to struggle with—and paeans to open innovation aside, it's not clear they've landed upon any sort of viable solution.

Instead, large biopharma companies continue to emphasize the importance of "line-of-sight" thinking, the idea of discovering compounds with a precisely determined commercial profile in mind.

The concept of designing-to-specification makes a lot of sense in many businesses, but it's not clear to me it works especially well for drug discovery, where the combined uncertainties of scientific discovery and a commercial landscape that can evolve significantly in the decade or more it can take to move from scientific idea to approved drug, create profound challenges for meaningful strategic planning.

Yet, large biopharma's deep-seated need for centralized planning arguably leads to precisely the sort of false precision Taleb and I discussed in 2008, and the fragilizing strategic planning fallacy he critiques at length here and elsewhere.

Ideally, large biopharmas would be schooled by small agile upstarts, who might be willing to pursue a greater range of approaches, and consider a wider range of potential indications.

Yet, I'm not sure this is really happening—instead, big pharmas (really, the blue chip management consultants they employ) are defining the priorities, and the rest of the ecosystem is dutifully trying to respond.

Why? The answer, perhaps somewhat ironically, is that in part because of all the critiques and concerns about Big Pharma, drug development has become so intensively regulated, and so astronomically expensive, that large biopharma companies are almost the only players who can afford most full-on clinical development efforts (see this provocative discussion by Avik Roy).

The challenge, going forward, is whether progressive regulatory reform (including greater use of digital health technologies—see this encouraging example) can reverse the current trend and make drug development faster and cheaper, or will the process instead become only more burdensome, slow and expensive. If this happens, the stodgy, fragile, central planning of research by large biopharmas will remain dominant—in spite of their strategy, not because of it.

Unless or until agile competitors can figure out a significantly faster and cheaper way to develop drugs (the successful application of a personalized medicine strategy remains attractive but largely elusive), it's difficult to envision the current innovation climate improving very much—bad news for innovators, and worse news for patients. – DS

Can A Graduate Of Rock Health's First Class Democratize Diabetes Prevention?

In 2002, a revolutionary paper was published in the NEJM reporting the results of the Diabetes Prevention Program (DPP), a NIDDK-sponsored, multi-centered study asking how patients in danger of developing type two diabetes could reduce this risk.

In addition to a control arm—patients receiving standard education and counseling—there were two medication arms of the study: a group of patients who received metformin (a medication that's been used to treat diabetes for decades—even as scientists still are working out the details of exactly how it works), and a second group of patients who received a medication from a newer class of drug called thiazolidinediones—though this arm of the study was discontinued early on due to concerns about liver toxicity. Finally, there was a fourth arm of the study, called "lifestyle" intervention, which involved trying to motivate patients to diet and significantly increase their exercise, to achieve and maintain a 7% reduction of body weight.

In clinical medicine, diet and exercise is always the initial recommendation, but often fairly *pro forma*, and typically done with an air of resignation—physicians typically don't expect patients to really improve, but nevertheless want to give the approach a chance before moving on towards medical therapy.

Indeed, in the DPP, it turned out that metformin reduced the risk of progressing to diabetes by 31%, a significant benefit. Yet, the incredible shocker of the study was that the lifestyle intervention resulted in a whopping 58% reduction in progression to diabetes, an outcome so profound that the study had to be cut short as a result—given the clear benefit of this intervention, it would no longer be considered ethical to maintain patients in the other arms of the study.

A recent follow-up outcomes study, examining persistence of results after ten years, was also encouraging; according to study chair David M. Nathan of MGH,

"In 10 years, participants in the lifestyle changes group delayed type 2 diabetes by about four years compared with placebo, and those in the metformin group delayed it by two years. The benefits of intensive lifestyle changes were especially pronounced in the elderly. People age 60 and older lowered their rate of developing type 2 diabetes in the next 10 years by about half."

The first question raised by the DPP was "how'd they do it?"—more specifically, how did they get achieve such profound results with lifestyle modification where so many others failed.

The answer, it turns out, is essentially that all lifestyle recommendations are not created equal; while most doctors might half-heartedly encourage patients to eat less and exercise more, the care coordinators in the DPP were intense, engaging, and persistent, their level of involvement remarkable, some might say heroic; a huge amount of effort was required.

The next question was whether the lifestyle intervention used in the DPP could be done at scale; some pilot experiments suggest the answer may be yes—for example, a study run by researchers at Indiana University and delivered by the YMCA (Y-DPP) using group counseling demonstrated weight loss results similar to the DPP.

The question now is whether DPP-style approaches can be delivered in an even more cost-effective fashion; bay area startup Omada Health, who announced their official platform launch today, hopes to convince payors the answer is yes.

Omada, a member of the first Rock Health class, seeks to replace in-person group counseling with virtual group counseling, using a deliberately-designed interface (not surprising since Omada has roots in IDEO) and leveraging what it claims to be a proprietary approach to sort users into groups. The product also ships plug-and-play wireless scales to facilitate participation.

Omada reports promising initial results; the key questions they face now include (1) whether the success of their pilot will replicate; (2) how they will achieve adequate distribution; and (3) proving the program is either so unique or so far ahead of the game that others can't quickly employ similar approaches.

The best thing Omada has going for it is that it's looking in the right place, both scientifically (it's seeking to emulate one of the most effective behavioral inventions described in the medical literature) and economically (there are significant cost-savings associated with delaying or preventing type 2 diabetes, unless of course offset by the cost of administrating a disease prevention program).

The key question for Omada is also a critical challenge—or opportunity—facing digital health more broadly: can an online support group be as durably effective as individualized, face-to-face attention? Is there even a chance that over time it could evolve to be even more effective? After all, while participants in the lifestyle intervention group of the DPP lost an average of 15 lbs the first year, they regained 10lbs over the next decade; perhaps an ideal engagement platform could help better sustain the original weight loss.

Success here would effectively democratize the DPP approach, providing a relatively economical route to DPP –level results.

I'm excited by the possibilities here, but confess I remain somewhat skeptical: having developed a feel for the DPP approach (my diabetes training was in Nathan's MGH clinic), I appreciate just how intense and personalized it was. The approach and mindset is perhaps most evocative of Dr. Warren Warwick, the off-the-curve cystic fibrosis physician Atul Gawande so memorably described.

On the other hand, it's also important to recognize that the real-world choice for most pre-diabetics probably isn't between the original DPP and a digital DPP, but rather between a digital DPP and the current, fairly discouraging, standard of care; hence there's clearly a huge opportunity for a digital DPP, even if imperfect, to offer significant value. – DS

Three Lessons A Hot Midwestern Weight-Loss Startup Can Teach Us About Digital Health

Not long ago a Chicago-based personal weight-loss company Retrofit announced that it had raised an $8M series A round, an investment nicely covered by my Forbes colleague Kelly Reid, who also wrote a terrific profile of Retrofit several months back.

In short, the company sells a highly-personalized, digitally-enabled weight loss coaching service, at $250-$350/mo with a one-year commitment required. As Reid described, each Retrofit client is paired with an experienced team that includes a dietician, an exercise physiologist, a behavior coach, and a program manager, who regularly and directly interact with the client (often via Skype). Progress is also monitored electronically, both through a wifi-enabled scale and a FitBit wireless activity monitor.

Retrofit targets a weight loss of 10-15%; in the view of founder Jeff Hyman, most diets fail because they promise rapid weight loss that even if achieved, is rarely sustained—95% of "successful" dieters regain the weight (or more) within a year, and 99% within 3 years. In contrast, Retrofit aims to deliver a more "realistic" or achievable goal that can be sustained, and is said to be associated with significant health benefits.

Retrofit's growth and traction offer three key lessons for digital health.

1. Tangible revenue model. Among the most significant issues plaguing the digital health space is the absence of a viable revenue model—a solid answer to the question "who is going to pay for this?" (As my Forbes colleague Brett Nelson shared in a memorable column, "Generating positive cash flow is one of the f—ing hardest things in the world.")

Retrofit has this covered, via a hefty subscription fee—perhaps it's not a coincidence that early adopters seem to include a Chicago law firm and a Silicon Valley venture fund.

They have also focused on the workplace, and try to leverage network effects there; if several colleagues are subscribers, and seem to be succeeding, others might be tempted to join as well. With their recent raise, they've also announced a "Retrofit My Company" contest specifically to drive this segment.

2. Realistic health goals. Many digital health companies I encounter are fired up about their potential to change the world (a laudable goal), yet often overpromise the dent in the healthcare universe their enterprise will deliver. Retrofit seems to take the opposite view, evidently believing that successfully delivering on a seemingly more modest goal is a ultimately a better proposition.

That said, Retrofit certainly promotes their benefits to employers by suggesting a benefit to the bottom line, a premise that I've recently argued tends to be more theoretical than realized—a conclusion shared by disease management guru Al Lewis, who has written an entire book, "Why Nobody Believes the Numbers," deconstructing the questionable math associated with many health and wellness revenue claims.

3. Technology plays a supportive role. This is perhaps the single most important lesson of Retrofit, which is basically a high-end coaching service. While digital health monitoring devices figure prominently in the offering, they are explicitly used in service of the customized advice developed and delivered by real people.

There may be a real parallel here in the success of Up-To-Date , essentially an e-textbook that has nevertheless become indispensible for many if not most physicians (as I've discussed here). The key to Up-To-Date's success aren't fancy algorithms that collect data or generate advice, but rather the many expert physicians who distill the literature and offer interpretations and recommendations, insight with far more credibility (at least at this point) than what faceless algorithms seem likely to offer.

Rather than replace expert health advice with computer-generated and delivered suggestions, Retrofit seeks to enable experts, allowing them to provide the most useful input possible (I've made a similar case for digital health enabling, not replacing, physicians).

It's still early days, and far too soon to designate Retrofit a "success story." Their price point is conspicuously high, and it's possible that a well-designed offering could deliver a similar benefit for less using fewer experts, sophisticated algorithms, and great design— and many startups are explicitly working on this.

But I'm inclined to believe there's an important lesson about health and technology here: at the end of the day, so much of health (as I've incessantly argued) is about people and connection, and the best digital health technology will support, not supplant, human relationships.

One final observation: it's interesting to note that there seems to be a rise of digital health investors in the Northern Midwest—the "Cold Coast," as I've termed it. While Retrofit's latest round was led by Silicon Valley-based DFJ, previous investors included New World Ventures and the I2A fund, both based in Chicago. Chicago-based Apex Ventures joined New World and others in funding Analyte Health to the tune of $22M this summer, while Wisconsin-based Lemhi Ventures announced (also this summer) that they had raised their second fund, $150M, to focus on "disruptive new business models" in healthcare.

With the ascent of intrepid healthcare investors, the emergence of promising startups, and the established dominance of Minnesota-based Epic (see here and here), the Cold Coast may be one of the hottest regions for innovation in digital health. – DS

Online Mothers Groups: Powerful, Unheralded Influencers Of Family Health Care Decisions

For all the interest in reputation apps (Yelp, Angie's List, etc.), I've been struck by the number of household decisions across the country that seem to be powerfully influenced by another, less-well-appreciated force: online mothers groups.

I've been especially impressed, more specifically, by the number of professional women I know—a prominent healthcare consulting executive in D.C., for example, or a top VC in SF—who immediately cite such groups as a key source of information, whether for choosing a pediatrician or selecting child seats for the car. In fact, these groups often seem to be both the first and the most trusted source of such referral information.

Perhaps we shouldn't be surprised; after all, "Data show that women are at the center of health care decisions in the family unit," according to Sue Siegel, former Partner at MDV and now CEO of GE's Healthymagination division.

In the Bay Area, leading examples are the Golden Gate Mothers Group, the Burlingame Mothers Club, the Parents' Club of Palo Alto and Menlo Park(PAMP), and the Berkeley Parents Network (BPN). These groups generally started as a resource for mothers, though some have expanded to include fathers. The Berkeley group appears unusually integrated, including (according to a BPN administrator) an estimated 35-40% men, a fraction that has reportedly increased in recent years. Most groups appear to have far less (if any) participation by fathers, however, and I've deliberately used the term "mothers groups" to emphasize this point.

The Palo Alto-Menlo Park group—as you might have imagined—produces an elegant, data-rich annual report, including informative demographic details (although interestingly, not the gender split of its members; a request for this is pending). According to the 2012 report, half the members report annual household incomes above $250k, half work outside the house full-time and another quarter work part-time, about 2/3 have an advanced degree. And the most common reason cited for joining—more important than playgroups, activities, or member discounts? To be part of the online community.

The influence of mothers groups raises a host of important, and in some cases, vexing questions:

1. What is the relative importance of trusted peers (vs objective metrics) in service recommendations (and are improved healthcare metrics likely to change this)?

2. Is there an underappreciated opportunity to positively impact the health of families by improving our understanding of real-world influence patterns (a thesis of startups such as Activate Networks, for example)?

3. Conversely, what is role of influence patterns in promulgating dangerous misinformation, leading to inadequate childhood vaccinations, for example?

4. Have we adequately appreciated the enabling function of social networks to broaden the reach of busy professional moms, many of whom clearly still value interactions with other moms, even if they might not have the time to engage off-line as fully as they might like (a motivation for startups such as Alt12, for example)?

5. The obvious question begged by Question 4: What about the professional dads? While some fathers participate in online parents groups, most, it's safe to say, do not. Are they gathering input relevant to family decisions from other sources, or just not collecting as much information at all? Is there an effective way to reach them, and motivate their involvement?

6. How is it that even absurdly busy professional moms are often still responsible for so many of the key household decisions, including around health? Is there early evidence —such as the conspicuously active involvement of fathers in the Berkeley parent group—suggesting a broader societal change may be underway? – DS

X.

Big Data, Measurement, and Metrics

Analysis Paralysis

Last year 37,000 of my closest friends and I attended the HIMSS Conference in Las Vegas. For those of you who don't have a propeller permanently implanted in your head, HIMSS stands for the Health Industry Management Systems Society. It is an industry association self-proclaimed to be focused on "transforming healthcare through information technology."

Despite the fact that I have worked in and around healthcare information technology ("HIT") for nearly 25 years (since I was 7), I had never been to HIMSS before. When HIT has become the new, new thing once again, I decided I should check it out.

Have you ever gone to the park where there are a hundred kids attempting to co-exist in the sandbox with one shovel? As you would expect, there would be a lot of screaming, pushing, shoving, cajoling, cringing and toddler-on-toddler contact as everyone jockeyed for control of the shovel. That's what HIMSS felt like to me. There was such a cacophony of noise, information and activity that I went into sensory overload the minute I stepped into the conference area. In Las Vegas, that's saying something. I have become somewhat accustomed to the lights, noise and human insanity that is Las Vegas, as I do go there relatively frequently for fun; but stepping from the Venetian Casino into the Venetian Expo Center (where HIMSS was housed) was like transforming from an observer outside the sandbox to becoming the shovel itself. It was bedlam. Think about the mind-numbing noise of a Nirvana concert combined with the technology-adoring throngs who would show up at a free giveaway at the Apple Store. I have dubbed officially dubbed HIMSS "Nerdvana."

Yes, it was great to see old friends and acquaintances at HIMSS and to meet with longstanding partners and new colleagues. But I went in part to see what was hot and worth watching in the space and, as it turned out, this was not the place to do it. The signal to noise ratio was far too low.

What you couldn't help but notice by walking the exhibit floor, which was 3 stories tall, each larger than an airplane hangar, was the sameness of it all. It was almost impossible to see the meaningful differences between the thousands of exhibitors showing their HIT wares. Through the incredible din what you could pick out from the chatter were a few choice buzzwords used more frequently than the word "the": cloud, SAAS (software as a service pronounced by the twitterati as "sass"), big data, analytics, coffee and blister were the big standouts. Actually, I think it was me saying "coffee" and "blister" over and over again. Everyone else was screaming the other words at the top of their lungs as if saying them louder would give them real meaning. I found it to be somewhat the opposite. The more times someone would say "big data" and "analytics" and that they were delivering "SAAS in the cloud" the less meaning the terms started to have, and here's why: there is an avalanche of talk about how technology can transform healthcare by harnessing all of the data and using it for good not evil, but almost no talk about how organizations are going to change their cultures to make it actually happen.

During the course of the show, my attention was drawn to this schematic, created by Nuance Communications:

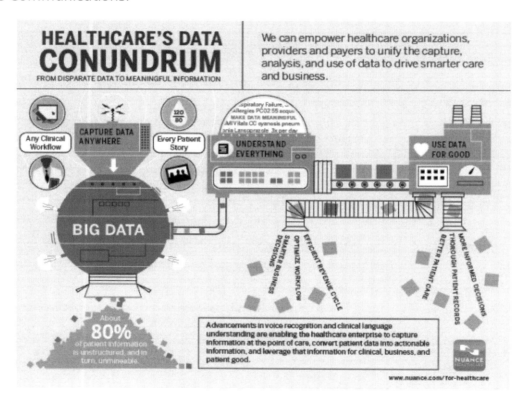

What I noticed from this picture was the section between the two green boxes on the top right: "understand everything" and "use data for good". And what particularly stood out, aside from the cute little heart beside "use data for good," was that there was nothing in between point A and point B saying how to do that. It reminded me so much of a the underwear gnomes in South Park who say that their business is this: steal all the underwear, reap profits; unfortunately there is no step in between that says how they are going to do this.

The McKinsey Global Institute ("MGI") recently wrote this in a May 2011 report:

"The amount of data in our world has been exploding, and analyzing large data sets—so-called big data—will become a key basis of competition, underpinning new waves of productivity growth, innovation, and consumer surplus, according to research by MGI and McKinsey's Business Technology Office. Leaders in every sector will have to grapple with the implications of big data, not just a few data-oriented managers. The increasing volume and detail of information captured by enterprises, the rise of multimedia, social media, and the Internet of Things will fuel exponential growth in data for the foreseeable future."

MGI goes on to say that if US health care were to use big data creatively and effectively to drive efficiency and quality, the sector could create more than $300 billion in value every year. Two-thirds of that would be in the form of reducing US healthcare expenditure by about 8 percent.

Well, that is obviously a good thing. In a sector where costs are rising at 2-3 times the rate of inflation, technology that reduces healthcare costs is a great thing. I am just worried that there is a huge amount of talk accompanied by a huge amount of technology spending and little attention being paid to how enterprises must psychologically, culturally and organizationally transform themselves to meaningfully take advantage of this opportunity.

Here's what I mean. I attended a breakfast put on by McKesson, a leading HIT company, which featured talks from three of their hospital customers, each clearly very smart people committed to using data to improve hospital system operations. They each spoke about the products they were buying and the money they were spending and the objectives they were after (mainly improved efficiency, lower cost). However, none of them spoke about how they were re-orienting their organizations around a concept of continuous quality improvement, in the true sense of the words, to ensure that the data received could actually be applied to create change. I asked a specific question of the panel: "what are you doing from a human resources and corporate culture change standpoint to make best use of this big data?" What I got back was not much.

One of the hospital CEOs said that his senior management team was spending a lot of time learning and talking about how big data could help the organization. But to me that's only one part of a correct answer. It's the rank and file, the hundreds or thousands of middle managers and line employees of healthcare organizations that have to be retrained to use data to root out the cause of errors and inefficiencies and then take action to achieve real change. If you take an organization of people who have worked in a particular way for a long time and suddenly give them a lot of new information, particularly information that points out where they have created systems that produce inefficiency, mistakes and poor outcomes, what happens if you don't train them that it's ok to find your mistakes, publicize them and invest in correcting them for the greater good? Here's what happens: they take the data, rationalize why it's not correct, put it in the bottom desk drawer and move on with their normal way of doing things. I fear that this lack of cultural change is going to be the virtual missing link between the promise and the reality of big data and its friend, data analytics. Yes, analytics turn data into information, but people turn information into action.

So what does this mean for entrepreneurs trying to tackle the big data opportunity? To me it means you need to provide more than just the information, and there are probably two ways of doing this. 1) You can augment your analytics technology with a companion service offering that specifically makes use of the data to solve a problem; or 2) you can provide a consulting service that helps your data analytics client transform their organization into one that understands exactly how to take the stream of information you are providing them, integrate it into their workflow and use it for good.

At the conference I met with several entrepreneurs who are building analytics businesses, each of which promised to "turn data into information" (another overused phrase) for their clients. The question so few of them could answer was "so what?" The corollary questions are: How do you turn information into action? Now that there is all this information, who actually needs it for what specific purpose and to what specific end? Who at the client organization will be responsible for taking this information and acting upon it to achieve cost-savings and what is the expected savings to be thus produced? How will all this information, once delivered, be applied inside the operation to produce exactly what change in behavior? Unfortunately, if you are an entrepreneur and you cannot answer these questions, you risk ending up hanging with the Underwear Gnomes–waiting for profits without a clear view of what makes them show up. – LS

Our Metrics Fetish—And What To Do About It

"How'm I doing?"

It's not just [the late] NYC mayor Ed Koch who's been asking. At some level, we are all preoccupied with this question, and ask it not just of ourselves (are we winning?), but also of those with whom we work, and of the businesses we choose to patronize.

We're fairly obsessed with rankings, when you think about it—what restaurant scored highest on Yelp? Which college (or, for those living in NY or the bay area, pre-K program) was ranked highest? How's my book faring on Amazon? Find me an author who doesn't monitor his ranking compulsively (or for that matter, a blogger who doesn't keep track of her pageviews).

Presumably, there's something in our nature that's hardwired to be comparative.

Of the many reasons for keeping score, the most important reason—or at least, the one most frequently cited—is to motivate improvement. A restaurant with a poor Zagat score for décor, for instance, might invest in new wallpaper, a student who gets a "C" on a math test may decide to study harder, and a hospital that's found to rank poorly on infection prevention might institute more stringent practices.

Businesses are especially keen on quantitation in general, and on metrics in particular, as these would seem to offer an objective standard against which improvements can be measured. Process modifications that accelerate inventory turns or reduce days sales outstanding are likely to improve the bottom line. Similarly, if doctors had information telling them that they weren't providing specific patients with the optimal care, these physicians might modify their practices (see here for a useful discussion of an effort along these lines in Sweden).

We intuitively use and value metrics, and view metrics as important and powerful tools that allow us to start making sense of a complex world, and permit us to make the many decisions that define our personal and professional lives. Metrics enable us to prioritize time, resources, and mindshare.

The problem with metrics, scoring, and rankings is directly related to their instinctive appeal: once there's a number affixed to something—a process, a business, and yes, a person—it can be prohibitively difficult to move beyond that; in our minds, we tend to replace the complexity of something with a number or rank; in fact, that's very much the goal and the point.

This may be reasonable if the number that's been derived effectively captures the aspects and qualities you are most interested in; if you want the fastest car, you should compare the maximum speed each model can demonstrate. If you are trying to lose weight, it makes sense to compare calories.

More often than not, however, we tend to overreach—and in a fairly predictable way. First, we measure things that are easy to count (even if of dubious relevance), and then we roll these up into a grand score and ultimately, a final rank list.

Perniciously, this process offers something for almost everyone: let's say we're talking about a business. In this case, managers have objective parameters to track, workers have objective performance goals towards which to strive, consultants have balanced scorecards to create and deliver, and investors and other stakeholders can compare these results to industry best practices. What's not to like?

The Achilles heel of this whole process is the assumption that the parameters you are tracking are truly relevant to the outcomes you are trying to achieve. I worry—deeply worry—this often is not the case. Far too frequently, we track the factors that most easily lend themselves to counting, rather than thinking deeply about whether they are truly the most important.

I remember vividly an example from the pharmaceutical industry, where a newly-formed division of a very large company, in an effort to gain credibility with senior management, instituted an elaborate series of process metrics, to the point where department members seemed to spend almost as much time recording and tracking these metrics as they did designing clinical protocols. Moreover, the plan worked: senior management was delighted that the new department "got it." Unfortunately, these metrics didn't speak at all to the most relevant concerns: were the right studies being done, were the right questions being asked, were the new department's efforts ultimately helping the company? In this case, the metrics were able to assess how fast the department was moving, but not whether it was heading in the right direction.

This habit of testing first and asking questions later (if at all) has also impacted the way we think about competency and achievement. Consider that almost every profession now, from medicine to law to massage therapy to motorcycle repair, has increasing numbers of proficiency exams, tests designed to signify a particular level of achievement and competence. Almost invariably, the professional societies responsible for these assessments make serious bank administering these exams, yet it's often unclear or not known whether these tests have been demonstrated to exhibit content validity (the right things are being measured), appropriate measurement properties (another key factor), and predictive validity. We take comfort from the fact that practitioners of all stripes have been duly "certified," yet rarely ask whether this certification process has either meaning or value. To have been tested, it seems, is enough.

One organization that has given considerable thought into just these sorts of questions is a group within the FDA known as SEALD (Study Endpoint and Label Development); they've put together a much-discussed document summarizing what medical product companies (disclosure: including mine) must do to ensure that the appropriate patient parameters are monitored, and in the right way. The guidance developed by this group—available for download here; Figure 3 on p.7 is the money shot—strikes me as generally relevant to the way most metrics should be developed. Without question, the process (as medical products companies are discovering) is extremely rigorous, and certainly not for the faint-of-heart. Yet, in focusing on the relevance of the questions as well as the measurement qualities of the instrument, the process offers the promise that the metrics produced from this exercise will be something worth counting on.

Moreover, as we strive to improve the quality of health delivery by increasing the amount of data that is collected, analyzed, and disseminated, it's essential that we take the time and care to develop the right measures, and resist both the pressure (particularly from consultants) and the temptation (notably within ourselves) to settle for the metrics that are easiest to create. – DS

Improved Measurement: A Path To Better Health For Real People

I had the opportunity to speak at the Open Science Summit at the Computer History Museum in Mountain View, CA not long ago. The meeting featured a number of interesting and unusually diverse talks, and many thoughtful questions. Like the annual Sage Commons Congress, this attracted an unusually involved (and articulate) group of participants.

My talk, entitled "Improved measurement: a path to better health for real patients," aimed to present a concise, high-level overview of the key opportunities and challenges in the health space (nothing like modest ambitions). I'll try to hit the high points here, many of which will be familiar to readers of this column; I would specifically highlight this four-part series on topics in healthcare innovation, and this recent post, co-written with MGH Physician-in-Chief Dennis Ausiello.

Goal: Better health for real people: *health*, not just disease; *people*, not molecules, cells, or rats; *real*, not only clinical study subjects (though I believe this is a critically important first step), but also real patients, in the real world.

Tool: Improved measurement—it's difficult to improve what you can't measure (see here, also here). However, can be two-edged sword—must avoid fetishization of metrics; many of the most important parameters are things that we can't measure, and it's important not to lose sight of or devalue these vitally important qualities.

Thesis: medicine's greatest need is closing the feedback loop. Currently, patients are seen episodically (at best) by physicians then sent on their way. As discussed here and here, doctors have very little idea about what happens after patients leave the office, which is bad for both the patients (obviously), and for the doctors, who don't have the opportunity to learn professionally and improve. Interestingly, Bill and Melinda Gates make similar points in the context of education in a recent WSJ essay. Without a functioning feedback loop, we are missing the essential opportunity to iteratively optimize and improve patient care.

Framework: As a product of BCG, I naturally conceptualize things via a 2×2 matrix; one axis = time horizon (short, long), the other axis = activity (research, application). Of course, real life is continuous not discrete, but the framework may be useful nonetheless.

On the long-horizon side of things—what can we do to generate truly breakthrough innovation?—I'd put my money on Eric Schadt-style systems biology, which I know is thirsty for more data, and would also hope to see the rebirth of human physiology as a more tractable—and hence more attractive –basic science.

On the short-horizon (where I think there is a particularly sizable opportunity to have significant impact), I argue that on the research side, our two greatest needs are improved technologies (obviously—and there is already a significant amount of effort in this space) and improved science, specifically "assessment science," a term I first heard used by the FDA, who I believe has been ahead of the curve on this important issue (see discussion of SEALD towards the end of this piece). The point is that all measurement isn't created equal, and it's important to have confidence in the measures used, as well as ensuring that they capture the aspects of a clinical condition most important to patients. The goal of measurement remains not to maximize the volume of data collected, but to deliver relevant, actionable information.

Still on the short-horizon, there's a tremendous challenge even after data is collected to ensure it is actually utilized. Virtually all physicians genuinely seek to deliver the best care possible, yet changing their behavior is notoriously difficult, as Peter Pronovost and others have discovered (discussed here and here). There's a compelling case here to apply design thinking (defined provisionally as innovation that is human-centric, creative, iterative, and practical) to both how we think about patients (we need to get a much better understanding of their real lives so that we can do a better job of both assessing health and suggesting useful solutions) and also, and perhaps less obviously, how we think about physicians. Almost every doctor I know (and it's a very high "N") feel utterly pressed for time—most feel there already is far more to squeeze into a 15 or 30' session than is reasonable or even possible. Collecting all the measurements in the world is not going to be useful unless it can be presented in an obviously useful fashion for physicians, and make their jobs easier (a lesson learned the hard way by many Silicon Valley initiatives in this space, discussed here). The idea isn't to oversimplify—the complexity is real, and in some sense appropriate; rather, the challenge is to deal with the complexity on the back end of applications so that the user experience is as clean and accessible as possible (a concept I've borrowed, perhaps imperfectly, from Donald Norman).

These are the highlights, although there are several other benefits of improved measurement worth touching on as well, including:

- Identify new uses for existing drugs, the ultimate example of real-world phenotypic screening, which appreciates the value of a true, integrated read-out rather than a highly-reduced simplification (see this Boston Globe op-ed, co-written with Mathai Mammen, from earlier this year).

- Contribute to the identification and reliable quantification of real world needs, providing important opportunities for innovative medical products and protocols to demonstrate the value they are delivering (arguably the single most important way to improve the practice of medicine, especially if it includes approaches to assessing the associated economics).

- Enable sophisticated segmentation (especially if the measurement incorporates a range of phenotypic and environmental attributes), extending the thinking we now apply to genetic markers, and use this information to help physicians target different types of treatments to the patients most likely to benefit from that particular approach. This de-averaging could be extremely powerful—for example, it's been very hard to show that classic disease management is profitable (discussed here); however, if you could select the patients most (and least) likely to benefit from a nurse phone call, for example, you could be more selective in your efforts, and use your limited budget more wisely.

Bottom line: improved patient-focused measurement, while not perfect, could be profoundly enabling in the short term as well as beyond—but capturing this potential will require thoughtful science, involved patients, and inquisitive physicians, as well as the shared commitment to iterate and optimize around the common goal of improved health for real people. – DS

What A Casino Executive Can Teach Doctors And Job-Seekers

Quick: what large corporation's chief executive—a former Harvard professor—said: there are three ways my employees can get fired: steal; sexual harassment; or run an experiment without a control group?

Answer: not a pharma company, not a medical products company, but Caesar's Entertainment Corporation, which it turns out is run by a former academic economist named Gary Loveman.

I heard this story on a recent episode of Planet Money, and the complete podcast makes for fascinating listening. Two aspects of his story particularly jumped out at me, and seemed especially relevant.

First, Loveman seems to run his business in a highly empirical fashion, using small, controlled experiments whenever he can to guide decision-making and boost revenue. He might test a range of incentives on food servers to determine how best to motivate customer drink orders without driving the servers to be overly pushy, or evaluate which of several potential incentives might make first-time visitors down on their luck more likely to return.

The concept of serial experimentation isn't new, of course, and retailers such as Wal-Mart have developed highly sophisticated systems to adjust and optimize the revenue-generating potential of each inch of shelf-space. Success requires two important factors: the drive to experiment and the ability to measure how you did.

As I've frequently pointed out (see here and here, for example), this sort of optimization approach that's employed routinely at Caesar's and Wal-Mart is, sadly, shockingly, not generally incorporated into modern medical practice—and not because physicians aren't curious. Instead, the more significant problem is that doctors really don't have the ability to meaningfully and systematically measure most of the outcomes from patient visits, and thus aren't able to make the adjustments and modification in their approach that could potentially enable them to be far more effective.

Worse, since most physicians are keenly interested in providing the best care, and generally pride themselves on both learning from experience and offering highly individualized care to each patient, doctors tend to generalize excessively from either their most recent experience ("my last patient seemed to find this helpful so maybe you will, too") or from a particularly salient experience ("after I saw a patient develop a horrible rash in response to this medication, I never used it again").

Bottom line: by relying on N-of-1 anecdotes rather than a more systematically gathered dataset from their own patients, physicians miss out on profound learning opportunities, and patients miss the opportunity to benefit from the collective experience of each other.

The second highlight of the Loveman interview relates more to careers in general than to healthcare in particular. Loveman, it turned out, never intended or expected to be a casino company CEO. Rather, he was teaching classes at Harvard, and on the side, he was apparently asked to provide some instruction for a group of business people. Evidently, within this group, there were a few casino managers who never showed up for their classes. When he tracked them down and asked them why, they basically told him they felt that a tweedy academic had little to teach them about their business. Almost immediately, according to Loveman, he recognized this as an exceptional opportunity for "intellectual arbitrage," as he realized his systematic analysis could represent a competitive advantage in this field that seemed to be populated by luddites.

I love his term—intellectual arbitrage—as it seems to capture the essence of a career-making role: a role where you can leverage a distinctive personal trait—which certainly doesn't have to be intellectual—to great advantage. Since everyone is so different, the key part of all this may not be having a leveragable trait, but rather in figuring out—or potentially even creating—the optimal arbitrage opportunity for it.

This may also highlight the value of branching out professionally beyond your original specific discipline or comfort zone—you open yourself to discovering opportunities to utilize your strengths and experiences in unexpected ways.

There are no guarantees, of course—but it seems like a bet worth making. – DS

Decoding Phenotype: The Holy Grail For Today's Medical Scientists

Starting with the elucidation of its structure by Watson and Crick (PDF) in 1953, medicine has been captivated by the power of DNA, by the ability to understand our health and treat disease based on subtle differences in the four-letter code that comprises our genetic information—our genome.

The technology of DNA sequencing has progressed to the point that the readout of an entire human sequence—a feat that just a decade or so ago was considered medical science's holy grail, worthy of a massive, Manhattan-Project style mission, and ultimately celebrated by a Presidential press conference—has evolved into an almost routine activity for a number of technology companies, at a cost now closing in on $1,000 per genome, and dropping fast.

Perhaps not surprisingly, the spate of data emerging from sequencing efforts has not only revolutionized our understanding of disease, but has also highlighted fundamental limitations in our scientific understanding. As we try to wring meaning from the petabytes (that's over a billion million bytes) of data, it's become increasingly clear that sophisticated—and actionable—understanding of biology and disease requires not only a parts list, but also a nuanced readout of how the parts operate together in the context of a cell, an organ, a person. In a word: phenotype.

Phenotype is how something looks, acts, or behaves; in contrast to DNA sequence, which is fundamentally discrete and universal, phenotype tends to be much "messier," more challenging to reliably assess. Two investigators across the world can easily agree on the exact DNA sequence within a specific cell, say, but might come to very different conclusions about how the cell behaves in culture.

The greatest challenge may also be the most important: measuring complex human phenotypes, such as how a patient is experiencing a particular disease, or responding to a given treatment. Too often, and quite understandably, the approaches used by physicians and medical researchers have been relatively simple, episodic assessments—measuring a patient's blood sodium, or blood pressure, for example, at the time of an annual physical. Such evaluations can provide important and useful information, but rarely capture the complexity of a patient's health and experience over time.

We envision improved measurement of phenotype as the underlying basis for the next generation of medical progress. Improved measurements of patients can guide—immediately—the treatment approach used by physicians, who often have very little visibility into what happens after a patient leaves the office. Better measurement can also guide medical product development, focusing attention on a patient's true unmet needs.

The FDA, to its credit, has recognized the need for improved measurement, and has been an early champion of the need for better "assessment science." Speaking at a conference on the subject last year, the director the FDA's Center for Drug Evaluation and Research, Dr. Janet Woodcock, noted (PDF, p.13) that "the identification, development, and qualification of new clinical trial outcome assessments has not been aggressively pursued by the scientific community," adding that "the consequent lack of assessment tools has been impeding, I think, the development of new drugs because we really, in many cases, don't know how to measure the impacts, both for good and ill, of the drugs we test in people."

The ability to measure with greater precision the real-world impact of a patient's illness would also enable improved assessment of the impact of both treatment approaches and of the providers themselves, giving us an opportunity to better assess the value of each, and to enable the iterative improvement of patient care and health delivery.

The improved measurement of complex patient phenotypes will also provide enormous benefit to basic researchers, enabling them to link this new information with existing, rich genetic data to form coherent datasets that can help identify key underpinnings of disease, and enable researchers to develop more targeted, and in many cases more personalized, interventions. Integrated datasets will also fuel increasingly sophisticated computer-driven "in silico" modeling approaches, capturing the benefits of empiric, "big data" technologies and approaches already used to great effect in other industries and disciplines.

The improved assessment of phenotype will be profoundly enabled by the explosion of mobile technologies, and the rapidly growing field of "mHealth." At the same time, we also recognize that technology and data collection alone are unlikely to provide the robust, integrated insight that science demands and patients deserve. While it's essential to understand the performance characteristics of the technology, and be sure it is reliable and robust, it's even more important that we're measuring the right things, focusing on the aspects of disease most troubling to patients, rather than simply the features we are able to quantify most easily.

This brings us to our final and perhaps most important point about phenotypic measurement: While it's essential for medical researchers and mHealth technology developers to view patients as partners in discovery, we must also recognize that most patients want to spend their time living their lives, not thinking about their health. Perhaps the most substantial design challenge for assessment science, and for mHealth in particular, will be delivering improved health without creating new burdens—liberating patients from their illnesses, rather than dominating patients' lives with disease monitoring and management.

An approach to phenotype assessment that's sensitive enough to capture the real-world experience of patients, powerful enough to enable actionable change leading to improved health, and wise enough to do this without being intrusive—this is the holy grail for today's medical scientists. – DS + Dennis Ausiello

Why The Fragility Of Health Outcomes Research May Be A Good Outcome For Health

Durably improving health is really, really hard.

I've discussed this in the context of drug discovery, which must contend with the ever-more-apparent reality that biology is incredibly complex, and science remarkably fragile. I've Discussed this in the context of patient behavior, focusing on the need to address what Sarah Cairns-Smith and I have termed the "behavior gap."

Here, I'd like to focus on a third challenge: measuring and improving the quality of patient care.

I've previously highlighted the challenges faced by Peter Pronovost of Johns Hopkins in getting physicians to adhere to basic checklists, or to regularly do something as simple and as useful as washing hands, topics that have been discussed extensively and in a compelling fashion by Atul Gawande and others.

Several recent reports further highlight just how difficult it can be not only to improve quality but also to measure it.

Consider the recent JAMA article (abstract only) by Lindenauer et al. analyzing why the mortality rate of pneumonia seems to have dropped so dramatically from 2003-2009. Originally, this had been attributed to a combination of quality initiatives (including a focus on processes of care) and clinical advances. The new research, however, suggests a much more prosaic explanation: a change in the way hospitals assign diagnostic codes to patients; thus, while rates for hospitalization due to a primary diagnosis of pneumonia decreased by 27%, the rates for hospitalization for sepsis with a secondary diagnosis of pneumonia increased by 178%, as Sarrazin and Rosenthal highlight in an accompanying editorial (public access not available).

Why did the coding pattern change? Multiple explanations were proposed by the authors; possibilities range from the benign—changes in diagnostic guidelines, greater awareness of sepsis, etc.—to the cynical (and quite likely)—utilizing different coding to maximize reimbursement.

One key take-home is that reliable measurement of health variables is so much more of a challenge than is typically appreciated, and ensuring that we're robustly measuring what we think we're measuring, rather than a paraphenomenon, is going to be very important. We're learning this lesson the hard way in so many areas of science, and health outcomes research is unlikely to be the solitary exception.

A second and equally important lesson is to remember that in many cases in health outcome research, the people who are doing the measurements and assessments often have a significant stake in the results, introducing the very real possibility of data distortion.

More explicitly: a tremendous priority of every hospital I know is protecting their bottom line, and a key element of this is maximizing billing. This is business as usual in medicine. Just this week, for example, I received an email from a professional medical society, inviting clinicians to attend a webinar entitled "Maximizing Reimbursement for the Treatment of Diabetes."

While "maximizing reimbursement" is probably not what most recipients of this email were thinking about when they applied to medical school (and please treat yourself to this wonderful TechCrunch essay by Avado CEO Dave Chase entitled "Patients Are More Than A Vessel For Billing Codes"), it's also a fact of life, and essential to the viability of most medical practices (an increasingly difficult struggle for many—see here).

When you impose quality metrics, you introduce a powerful incentive to behave in a way that optimizes apparent performance—to game the system. This could potentially manifest itself not only through the selective adjustment of diagnostic codes, but also through a range of other questionable activities; for example, I've heard stories of hospitals contriving reasons to transfer failing patients (especially transplant patients) to other facilities to preserve their own survival statistics. (Fortunately, I never saw or heard of this happening at any hospital where I trained or practiced).

Given the evident utility of financial incentives, you might think that tying these incentives to quality measures would at least improve measures of health outcomes. However, even this turns out to be tricky: a striking study by Jha et al. in the NEJM found that the pay for performance approach did not reduce 30-day mortality rates, obviously the outcome of most importance to patients.

The most likely explanation: hospitals are graded mostly by their performance on process measures—how they do a variety of specific tasks thought to be associated with improved care, even though the evidence for a relationship between most of these process measures and improved outcomes is weak at best. The system works in that policy makers seem to be getting the behaviors they incentivize; unfortunately, these specific behaviors don't seem to result in improved patient outcomes. (I've discussed this exact issue—tracking what you can, not what you should here; I'd also note that similarly suspect process metrics are routinely imposed by management consultancies upon their unwitting—or perhaps complicit—clients.)

In an interesting accompanying commentary, Joynt and Jha challenge the utility of what at first blush seems to be a useful (and increasingly popular) outcome measure, the 30 day readmission rate (how often discharged patients are readmitted to the hospital within a month), a key component of the Affordable Care Act (poor performing hospitals are to be penalized), and argue that, in fact, only a small fraction of readmissions are likely truly preventable.

This matters, because as Joynt and Jha point out, "The metrics that policymakers choose to use in rewarding and penalizing hospitals have a profound effect not just on what hospitals do but on what they choose not to do." They conclude, "the most important consequence of this policy [penalizing hospitals with high 30-day readmission rates] is the improvements in quality and safety that hospitals will forgo, and those will be far more difficult to measure." In other words, by insisting that hospitals focus on an outcome measure that may largely beyond their control, policy makers may actually make it more difficult for hospitals to identify parameters they truly can control and improve.

It is painfully obvious by this point that that no matter how you approach it, durably improving healthcare represents a daunting challenge. The underlying science (from biology to outcomes) is inordinately complex, the actors (scientists, patients, physicians, administrators) are distinctly human, and even collecting a basic and adequate set of robust measurement and underlying facts is surprisingly challenging.

It's also, of course, a great opportunity—these are truly *important* problems that have now captured the attention of some of our best minds. I'm heartened by the exceptional entrepreneurial interest that's been attracted to health care, I'm thrilled by the diversity of talent that's now started to think hard about these problems and approach them from so many different perspectives, and I'm gratified by the way so many stakeholders—including big pharma and leading payers, but also forward-thinking universities and health organizations—have recognized the urgent need to re-envision their traditional models, to move outside their usual comfort zone, and to collaborate in a more open, ambitious, and daring way than most might have contemplated even a decade ago.

It's the shared recognition of the enormity of our task that ultimately will compel us to challenge our most fundamental assumptions, embrace novel possibilities, stimulate innovative collaborations, drive organizational change, inspire creative entrepreneurs, and in the end catalyze the evolution—perhaps even revolution—of our healthcare ecosystem.

What a great time to be part of—or to join—this audacious effort. – DS

Epic Challenge: What The Emergence Of An EMR Giant Means For The Future Of Healthcare Innovation

Medicine has been notoriously slow to embrace the electronic medical record (EMR), but, spurred by tax incentives and the prospect of cost and outcomes accountability, the use of electronic medical records (EMRs) is finally catching on.

There are a large number of EMR vendors, who offer systems that are either the traditional client server model (where the medical center hosts the system) or a product which can be delivered via Software as a Service (SaaS) architecture, similar to what salesforce.com did for customer relationship management (CRM).

Historically, the lack of extensive standards have allowed hospital idiosyncrasies to be hard-coded into systems. Any one company's EMR system isn't particularly compatible with the EMR system from another company, resulting in—or, more fairly, perpetuating—the Tower of Babel that effectively exists as medical practices often lack the ability to share basic information easily with one another.

There's widespread recognition that information exchange must improve—the challenge is how to get there.

One much-discussed approach are health information exchanges (HIE's), defined by the Department of Health and Human Services as "Efforts to rapidly build capacity for exchanging health information across the health care system both within and across states."

With some public funding and local contributions, public HIE's can point to some successes (the Indiana Health Information Exchange, IHIE, is a leading example, as described here). The Direct Project—a national effort to coordinate health information exchange spearheaded by the Office of the National Coordinator for Health IT—also seems to be making progress. But the public HIEs are a long way from providing robust, rich and sustainable data exchange.

In their stead, private HIEs—serving collections of collaborating hospitals and providers —seem to account for the lion's share of growth in the HIE space. In particular, one company—Epic(discussed recently by Forbes colleague Zina Moukheiber here)—seems to have emerged as top dog in the large hospital space, winning contracts from most of the nation's most prestigious centers, and many of the nation's largest; a deal with Boston powerhouse Partners Healthcare was recently announced. (Another leading EMR contender, Cerner, is profiled this week by another Forbes colleague, Matthew Herper.)

Notably, Epic is built on a traditional client server model, and does individual, customized installations for each client; a reputation for near-flawless implementation—derived by tightly constraining how much idiosyncracy is engineered in each install—has been a prime driver of growth. While Epic systems seem to be able to communicate with other Epic systems with relative ease, communication outside of Epic seems more problematic.

The ambulatory practice space, on the other hands, appears to remain highly fragmented and largely up for grabs, as a number of competing companies—particularly SaaS-based approaches such as AthenaHealth, PracticeFusion, and eClinicalWorks seek to gain traction.

Add to the mix the observation that medicine is undergoing a general consolidation, as solo practices and small practices increasingly find themselves in the arms of larger hospital systems, which are also merging. No wonder so many practices are still reluctant to adopt EMR given all the uncertainty (why buy or upgrade a system if we are going to sell the practice?) and confusion (which system to buy given the cacophony of brands, acronyms and regulations we don't understand).

So how is all this likely to play out? The first question, as we see it, will be whether Epic, essentially a private system, will be able to dominate the EMR space (hospital and outpatient) before alternatives—likely utilizing SaaS and leveraging an expanding array of national interoperability standards, can gain traction; the second question is what are the likely consequences of Epic winning—and of Epic losing.

Let's assume Epic's march though large (and increasingly mid-sized) hospitals continues and synergizes with the flight of small practices into delivery systems, ultimately enabling Epic to achieve a clear dominance (especially in the presence of highly fragmented competition) and effectively set the standards going forward; with enough physicians using the system, there will be significant pressure on the laggards to adopt it.

Epic will effectively be health IT's (HIT's) Roman Empire: establishing the laws and the language for "known world", as well as the underlying infrastructure, and ends up shaping information flows, IT architecture and—potentially—the eventual configuration of provider systems.

From an industrialization perspective, rolling out solutions systematically into a closed Epic system should prove to be cost efficient, and may deliver enormous value if, as some believe, the most significant opportunity for improving health care is supporting the consistent and reliable delivery of care.

However, if solving major health care delivery problems requires innovation—on the frontier of evidence-based medicine, in clinical practice, in workflows, in practice models —as many believe, then it starts to get very interesting, as such a tightly-controlled system could be either good or bad.

The optimistic scenario would be that Epic could take inspiration from Apple's approach to apps, using its dominant market position to provide a clear set of operating standards and expectations, and cultivate a far-flung innovation ecosystem based on its established platform. In this scenario, Epic could keep its products relevant and stay on the leading edge by adapting quickly to evolving market needs.

Alternatively, if Epic (already based on an antiquated technology—MUMPS) decides to maintain an essentially closed system, and to drive all innovation internally, this could prove stultifying, limiting the development of novel ideas, and forcing the many high-profile adopters of Epic to accept stagnation or pay the staggering costs of switching. The restrictive mindset might drive determined innovators—entrepreneurs, developers, and eventually even clients—straight into the arms of competitors.

The second group of scenarios—we call them "Open Data"—assume that progress on interoperability standards, together with Epic's focus on convincing large clients to adopt its functional but hardly delightful software, will create an opportunity for an agile competitor to compete effectively for the long tail customers, especially those who've deliberately avoided participation in a large hospital system, and might especially value an EMR system that offers a great user experience, and doesn't distance the physician from the patient the way most EMRs tend to do.

The optimistic scenario here is that the widespread adoption of standards leads to a flourishing ecosystem based not on exclusionary access to data, but rather on the ability to utilize these data in the most appealing and useful fashion, ideally making it easier to deliver care and demonstrate value. (Epic may continue to build out its market share within hospitals, but it will have to do it without the exclusivity-based network advantage derived from its previous installations).

On the other hand, the long history of entrenched legacy systems, coupled with slow adoption of standards, could result in a long tail that remains highly fragmented. And, if the primary drivers of EMR adoption remain carrots (incentives) and sticks (penalties and accountability) rather than transparent market dynamics that drive innovation (substantive improvements to patient care), then there is a particularly high risk that the long tail will remain highly fragmented.

But this scenario is not stable. If ambulatory HIT solutions, as a whole, fail to deliver, long tail providers will be at a significant competitive disadvantage, and may be more tempted than they already are to throw in the towel and sell to hospital systems—not because it's the best care delivery model, but because it's the only viable option. We may end up with big integrated blocs by default.

How the evolution of health information systems may impact future innovation

		Standards regime	
		Private / Epic	**Public / Open**
Impact on innovation	**Positive**	Imposed standards, structures provide robust framework for innovation Example: Current Apple ecosystem	Shared standards provide common language and enable innovation to flourish Example: Android ecosystem
	Negative	Closed system excludes external contribution and stifles innovation Example: Blackberry	Slow adoption of universal standards results in perpetuation of Tower of Babel Example: Status quo (at least until recently)

D. Shaywitz + Recon Strategy

There's plenty of skepticism within the HIT community about Epic's current model, and many doubt Epic will emerge as the Apple of healthcare innovation. Epic's "capture all the information" approach certainly feels at odds with a distributed world; moreover, if Epic manages to dominate the market using their existing approach, they will enjoy significant "locked-in" revenue, and may simply not see a lot of incremental profit in rapidly changing.

A SaaS-based, "Open Data" approach seem theoretically where health information systems should, and will, eventually wind up—the architecture provides flexibility, is nimble, and is low cost. But if the industry is unable to consolidate around, advance, and aggressively operationalize interoperability standards, we may wind up spending a lot more time enduring the current chaos.

Finally, it's interesting to wonder what Epic will do as it contemplates the future, especially the very real possibility that its current dominance will be disrupted.

While one approach is to focus on growing as rapidly as possible, it's intriguing to speculate whether they'd consider the acquisition of a leading SaaS-based provider. This could enable them to compete more effectively for long-tail customers immediately, could provide an opportunity to expand and diversify their current system, and could also serve as a useful hedge, so that if—or when—the world changes, they're not stuck with what are essentially mainframes in a cloud-based world. It would need to do so soon, before its organically derived market share would make the FTC approvals a barrier to any meaningful acquisition. – DS + Tory Wolff

Is One Company About To Lock Up The Electronic Medical Records Market?

Silicon Valley entrepreneurs and investors have never quite been able to figure out health, and they know it.

For years, the clever technology fixes dreamed up by engineers have largely failed to take hold, their well-conceived rationality no match for the complexity of medical care, the persistence of clinical habit, and the counter-intuitive impact of existing incentives. Many of the Valley's most audacious VCs have become leery of the space, electing instead to pursue innovation elsewhere.

The new battlefield is on the technologists' home turf: information systems for electronic medical records (EMRs). Will this time be different? Are technology entrepreneurs finally ready to disrupt medicine?

Here's the context (please see our last commentary, available here, for more details). Most of the nation's largest and most prestigious medical centers seem headed towards a relatively closed health information system, driven by a single dominant private company, Wisconsin-based Epic, which excels at the near-flawless, customized installation of their client-server platform in big hospitals.

While Epic is meticulously working its way through the largest hospitals, the long tail of stand-alone ambulatory practices operate largely on a jumbled mess of EMRs, using many emerging vendors (such as AthenaHealth and PracticeFusion) with a multi-tenant model, similar to salesforce.com.

Since medical care as a whole is consolidating, the basic question is whether emerging EMR vendors will gain enough traction and offer enough capability to enable stand-alone practices to remain independent. Or will platform fragmentation put unaffiliated practices at such a competitive disadvantage that they'll be even more motivated to join up with larger hospital systems (the most important of which will rely upon Epic)?

What makes Epic particularly interesting is that its success seems to fly in the face of how so many of us—Silicon Valley technologists in particular – have come to view innovation; it also contrasts with the much-celebrated, widely accepted strategy of open innovation.

"No matter who you are, most of the smartest people work for someone else," Bill Joy's law goes, and so much of the current Silicon Valley innovation ecosystem relies upon the ability to leverage the insight and wisdom of others. Let good ideas bubble up, find ways to capture creativity from everyone.

From the perspective of most technologists, Epic epitomizes the exact opposite of how a health information system should work (which is also why many of these same technologists feel it's bound to fail). Ideally, according to the technological experts, there should be a common, robust and open set of standards governing healthcare information, easing its accessibility. Companies would then compete for the most effective way to exploit the information, almost certainly via a multi-tenant platform.

According to the smartest people in the Valley, Epic shouldn't be winning. But it is. How is this possible, and what does it mean?

Epic's success suggests that it has locked onto something that its key clients – academic medical centers and large health systems—need most right now. This burning need, it turns out, isn't the capacity for bubbled-up innovation. What they need is the quick and flawless imposition of structure – pushed down from above, and proprietary if necessary.

The tertiary hospital is a vast enterprise with incredibly complex array of care delivery, with a wide web of participating – and very vocal, idiosyncratic – stakeholders involved. It faces long-term pressures – e.g. care shifting from the hospital to ambulatory settings – and shorter-term pressures with more uncertain endpoints – e.g. reimbursement changes, regulatory requirements. They need someone to step in and define the information sharing processes for the system, providing a reliable way to capture, transport, receive, and use information, as a path towards measuring and incrementally improving the quality and efficiency of care.

It turns out Epic has been paying attention—a lot of it—to successful technology enterprises, and appreciates better than anyone else the most important lessons of two of the nation's most successful entrepreneurs, Amazon's Jeff Bezos to Zappos' Tony Hsieh: know your customers.

As one articulate reader of our recent commentary (and former physician informaticist at Epic), Craig Joseph, observed ,

"Epic is successful for many reasons, but possibly chief among them is their CEO's laser-like focus on the customer. Judy Faulkner knows what large health systems need, and she gives it to them. Often, she knows what they need before they do. Further, Epic figured out long before its competitors that the vendor usually knows best—not the customer. While this sounds paternalistic (and probably is), the truth is it works."

Epic's credibility—built up from installations across many of the biggest brands in hospital care – allows it to say what can and can't be done. Even places like Partners in Boston – as unique a medical system as any, and a long-time investor in home-grown solutions – has recently announced that it, too, will move to Epic.

Competitors earnestly contend that Epic's approach locks clients in to a platform that is neither agile nor open, hence it lacks adaptability. Epic is viewed by many in the health information space as a canonical example of an established player who will be disrupted by nimble innovators—and there are no shortage of eager contenders who lay claim this mantle.

Is the story so simple? How much of it is wishful thinking (or sour grapes) on the part of Epic's competitors?

The great paradox here is that by imposing a specific and relatively strict structure on a large health system, Epic provides an "industrialization" function that enables not only process efficiency but also the comprehensive capture of clinical decisions and the assessment of quality and costs, which can then be iteratively improved; the availability of a robust clinical data set can also support the research mission of an academic medical center – or at least, can help those investigators who are able to obtain access to the data. This can accelerate progress in several key areas:

- Evidence-Based Medicine : The ability to collect and easily share extensive medical information from the large patient populations served by major medical centers means that hospitals may be able to develop a robust dataset upon which to guide evidence-based decisions – they can start to segment and track both patients and physicians, and develop, and iteratively improve, best practices

- Medical Research : Access to a coherent, longitudinal medical record will enable inquisitive physicians to generate hypothesis which can be explored in *silico*, providing an important opportunity to accelerate knowledge development and advance clinical science. These observations can also form the basis for both basic molecular research and rigorous prospective clinical studies. (See here for recent discussion of phenotype as medicine's next frontier.)

Importantly, these are two types of innovation AMCs are relatively good at today. Well structured systems like Epic will make them much better.

And, to the extent that Epic-enabled hospitals do become the center of a broader care delivery model (e.g. through provider practice acquisitions), it should also support greater coordination of care: In the current system, care can be highly fragmented, with patients providing the same information multiple times, and multiple providers often entirely unaware a patient's basic medical history. A well-implemented EMR system will integrate the information and make it readily available to all relevant providers who can deliver better care as a result.

On the other hand, there's a risk with an IT system that fits all too comfortably with the current practices of providers at the top of the healthcare food chain – it will serve to reinforce the "big hospital" style of medicine, and (through hard-to-remove technology) create a hefty sunk-cost barrier to change. Given the consolidation of practices into hospitals, the leverage of these players is only getting stronger.

What sorts of innovation might get left behind? Precisely the sort many believe medicine urgently needs – radically new approaches to care delivery, to primary care, to the fundamental way doctors and patients relate and interact. It's not so much that Epic can't provide any given aspect of this, but rather, Epic isn't designed to facilitate a series of explorative forays. And these areas are outside the traditional terrain of academic medical centers.

A ubiquitous Epic platform may also reinforce many unwelcome ways medicine is practiced. Already, many physicians complain about the poor user interface, driving a wedge between provider and patients. Relying on best practice algorithms may standardize care but not optimize it (see here and here); it may be more difficult for doctors to customize care for patients, and to explore new approaches. It's especially important to recognize the lack of good data behind many best-practice recommendations, and it would be especially disappointing to undermine the doctor-patient relationship in order to impose formality for its own sake, informed only by false precision.

In contrast, imagine a world in which all medical information utilized robust and common standards; in this scenario, innovators could easily explore more disruptive approaches, could look at completely different ways to deliver care, or to address very specific pain points within an existing system.

The consumerization of medicine – the explosion of gadgets and apps representing the one area of health in which Silicon Valley has demonstrated a serious and abiding interest – would especially benefit from a more open system. There is unquestionably an urgent need for better patient engagement, and it's easy to see how existing efforts in this busy space could support this important mission – especially in the challenging area of behavior change.

While it's difficult to see how this ecosystem could develop without more robust standards (though some in the Valley envision consumers ultimately replacing physician-based healthcare), it's also easy to see the attraction of a compelling EMR, beautifully designed and offering delight as well as function to patients as well as doctors. Such an approach might appeal both to unaffiliated "creatives" – hacker-practices—who see themselves as thinking differently, and to the patients who seek these exact qualities in their doctors.

Starting to sound familiar? It certainly seems like there's a ready-made opportunity for a progressive, patient-focused, design-centric upstart that could cast itself as the Apple-inspired alternative to Epic's stodgy, impersonal, PC-like brand.

All innovators like to see themselves as Steve Jobs (see here), and there's an opportunity for Epic to step into this role as well – by permitting the construction of an innovation ecosystem on its platform and expanding its customer set to providers and care settings outside the big hospitals, practices who are driving the leading edge of ambulatory care centered solutions and patient engagement. It must first decide, however, whether such an effort is more likely to rock the boat or deliver value to its core customers.

Given Epic's s precise sense for what its customers need – together with Silicon Valley's consistently poor understanding of the realities of healthcare – you'd want to think twice before betting against Epic. It's just possible they understand better than anyone else not only how much innovation medicine says it wants in principle, but also how much disruption medicine demonstrates it can stand in practice.

But it's even harder to bet against the urgent need for profound new thinking in healthcare.

Imagine a world effectively split into two systems of care – a system comprised of today's large medical centers, build upon the Epic platform, and a second system that explores the use of truly disruptive, patient-centric models of care delivery, build on platforms that are cloud-based. Here, disruptive change in clinical practice would be led not by academic physicians treating patients out of university medical centers, but rather by a motley collection of concierge doctors, involved patients, and savvy technologists. Meanwhile, the big integrated players, dependent as they are on Epic, could risk locking themselves out of medicine's next great revolution. – DS + Tory Wolff

A Database Of All Medical Knowledge: Why Not?

The progress of modern applied science has been defined by a series of outrageously ambitious projects, from the effort to build the first atomic bomb to the race to sequence the human genome.

For scientists and engineers today, perhaps the greatest challenge is the structure and assembly of a unified health database, a "big data" project that would collect in one searchable repository all of the parameters that measure or could conceivably reflect human well-being. This database would be "coherent," meaning that the association between individuals and their data is preserved and maintained. A recent Institute of Medicine (IOM) report described the goal as a "Knowledge Network of Disease," a "unifying framework within which basic biology, clinical research, and patient care could co-evolve."

The information contained in this database – expected to get denser and richer over time —would encompass every conceivable domain, covering patients (DNA, microbiome, demographics, clinical history, treatments including therapies prescribed and estimated adherence, lab tests including molecular pathology and biomarkers, info from mobile devices, even app use), providers (prescribing patterns, treatment recommendations, referral patterns, influence maps, resource utilization), medical product companies (clinical trial data), payers (claims data), diagnostics companies, electronic medical record companies, academic researchers, citizen scientists, quantified selfers, patient communities – and this just starts to scratch the surface.

The underlying assumption here is that this information, appropriately analyzed, should improve both our potential and attained health, pointing us towards future medical insights while enabling us to immediately improve care by optimizing the use of existing resources and technologies.

As the IOM report concluded, "realizing the full promise of precision medicine, whose goal is to provide the best available care for each individual, requires that researchers and health-care providers have access to vary large sets of health and disease-related data linked to individual patients.

As daunting as this task obviously is, companies and academic researchers are bravely taking up the challenge, generally by focusing on some subset of the problem, typically at an intersection of two or more domains (clinical information plus biomarkers, say, or provider data plus claims). The selection may reflect what they bring to the table (clinical data in the case of medical centers, claims data in the case of payors) or where they think the greatest value can be found.

In addition, both established information companies (i.e. Google) and emerging companies (such as Palantir) are also key players; their fundamental business is based around their ability to approach problems of this dimension and complexity; Google famously asserts that their mission is "to organize the world's information, and make it universally accessible and useful."

One industry that seems underrepresented at the table is big pharma; evidently, many large drug companies have decided that big data informatics are not a core competency, and have elected to outsource this as a service. Perhaps this represents a savvy assessment of the current state of the art. However, it's also may be a miscalculation on the order of IBM's failure to appreciate the value of the operating system Bill Gates originally developed, or Xerox's failure to appreciate the value of the PC their PARC engineers had created, and which Steve Jobs immediately recognized and leveraged. Arguably, if you really want to build a company that is going to deliver the health solutions of the future, your first and most important investment might well be in recruiting a Palantir-level analytics group.

At the same time, you can understand big pharma's hesitation. Despite all the promise of big data in health, the results to date have been surprisingly skimpy; putting existing data in a vat and stirring has yielded a slew of academic publications, and a number of pretty pictures, but few truly impactful changes in health, at least so far.

Critics contend, "it's faddish, way overhyped, and not ready for primetime." Consider a recent big data project, that concluded that an easily observed clinical indicator, jugular venous distention (enlarged neck veins) is a bad prognostic sign for heart failure patients. That's something a third-year med student could just as easily have told you.

Advocates, meanwhile, point to early successes and plead for patience and resources; they point out that the scale of data required to build good predictive models has only recently become available, and has already led to promising advances.

For instance, system biologists such as Mount Sinai School of Medicine's Eric Schadt (a friend and previous collaborator) and Stanford's Atul Butte have already used big data analytics to identify and prioritize drug targets – though it remains to be seen whether these yield clinically useful products, and whether the associated approaches are truly generalizable.

Meanwhile, the latest issue of Cell reports the first computation model of a whole cell, a model of a bacterium that "includes all its molecular components and their interactions" and, according to the authors, "provides insights into previously unobserved cellular behaviors" while leading to new predictions that were subsequently experimentally validated.

There are at least two profound challenges that big data advocates will need to overcome en route to analytical nirvana.

First, the data have to be available. Relevant information is currently stored in what are essentially thousands of different silos. Sometimes, the data are considered off-limits due to privacy regulations; in other instances, they are considered proprietary, hence unsharable; in still other cases, the data are considered open and liberated, and there's a lot of effort among research groups and patient organizations to move more data into this category.

The privacy concerns make intuitive sense: while some may be eager to share their personal data with the world, most of us would demand and expect robust guarantees of privacy – though it's not clear to what extent this is even possible, as the deanonymization of Netflix challenge data suggests.

The reluctance to share proprietary data also makes sense, although there's a bit of a prisoner's dilemma twist: data from any one domain is of only limited value by itself; the real opportunity comes when you are able to combine data from multiple domains. Most likely, strategic coupling (data-sharing) between organizations representing different domains will precede the development of the grand, unified data set.

This highlights the second key challenge: even if you're able to gain access to data, how do you organize and assemble it once you have it? As Schadt says, "getting to a data model that represents the great diversity of data, across a great many different domains, and interrelates it so that it can all be efficiently queried and mined has never really been achieved because it is a really hard problem."

Schadt adds, "I think those who have tried to make one master data model, make it fully self-consistent and representing all data across a diversity of knowledge domains will fail.

The grand data model of everything in biology has been tried over and over again and ultimately it comes crashing down because once you lock in a model, you constrain the types of questions you can ask of the data. The information half life is short, and we know and understand so little about what the data can actually tell us that we don't really understand the questions that ultimately will be the most useful."

So where, exactly, does this leave us?

It seems clear that if there ever is a single, useful dataset, we're going to arrive there in an incredibly messy way, likely through the combination of a number of disparate datasets built to serve a range of different needs.

Schadt anticipates that in the end, these data will not be organized using a highly structured formal data model (although some components will likely benefit from such an approach), but in a less structured way that enables broader engagement of the data via simple, natural query interfaces, much like Google today manages the digital universe of information and makes it broadly accessible and useable via a very simply natural language interface.

It's also not clear whether the smartest move is to try to build broadly – focusing on collecting information across as many domains as possible—or to build deeply, by relating a small number of comprehensive data sets (and if so, which datasets do you choose?) For reasons of convenience, more companies and academics seem to be pursuing the second strategy, though it's still unclear which will produce the greatest payoff.

What I suspect healthcare big data needs above all is a dramatic win – an immediately actionable, compelling, non-intuitive recommendation that by virtue of its successful implementation will announce the arrival of the discipline.

Until then, physicians, patients, and all the other stakeholders in our healthcare system must muddle forward as best we can. It's clear from the scope of the problem just how much muddling is involved—and how unreasonable it is to expect any one individual to integrate and evaluate all the available information.

I don't think this means physicians are destined to become obsolete (as some Silicon Valley technologists seem to believe), nor do I envision a future where we rely solely upon machines and algorithims for our health care. I've seen that medicine at its best is as much about connection and understanding as it is about arriving at a diagnosis and formulating a treatment recommendation.

At the same time, I suspect that a kind word plus an individualized, optimized therapeutic plan based on the comprehensive integration of all existing health data would go a lot further than a kind word alone. – DS

Nate Silver's Prediction Was Awesome—But Don't Build Statues To 'Algorithmic Overlords' Just Yet

The morning after Obama won re-election, my twitter stream was awash in praise of math, cheering Nate Silver's exceptional forecasting ("Triumph of the Nerds: Nate Silver Wins In Fifty States", Chris Taylor wrote), and celebrating the victory of math and big data over pompous punditry. Jeff Greenfield tweeted, "I, for one, welcome our new Algorithmic Overlord."

At some level, I thrill to the ascendancy of math, and of math nerds—and I write this as a proud former math team captain (and math team T-shirt designer), and as someone whose very best summers as a teenager were spent in math (and writing) camp at Duke University. It's also one of the reasons I love Silicon Valley so much—it's where nerds rule, and where even emerging VCs promote themselves as "Geeks."

However, before we turn all of life over to algorithms, as some are suggesting, it's important to place the election prediction in context.

The accomplishment of Silver's splendid forecasting was to intelligently aggregate existing data, to accurately summarize the current, expressed intentions of the national electorate. And we've learned that careful analysis is far more useful than blustery experts—something Philip Tetlock has been trying to tell us for years.

At the same time, all forecasting challenges are not created equal, and summarizing current public opinion is a much lower bar than predicting events far into the future—and Silver has been clear about this; it's others who seem to be leaping ahead.

In many (arguably most) domains, and the further out you go, uncertainty likely swamps the ability of either experts or algorithms to make reasonable predictions—as Taleb, and more recently Mauboussin have discussed.

Discrediting expert predictions seems like real progress—but not if we believe the enduring lesson is to replace one group of fortune tellers with another. We should certainly strive to use big data and rigorous math whenever we can—but let's be careful not to fall into the trap of letting down our guard, and trusting all experts who come bearing algorithms. – DS

It's The Platform, Stupid: Capturing The Value Of Data In Campaigns—And Health care

If you've yet not discovered Alexis Madrigal's fascinating Atlantic article(#longread), describing "how a dream team of engineers from Facebook, Twitter, and Google built the software that drove Barack Obama's re-election," stop right now and read it.

In essence, a team of technologists developed for the Obama campaign a robust, in-house platform that integrated a range of capabilities that seamlessly connected analytics, outreach, recruitment, and fundraising. While difficult to construct, the platform ultimately delivered, enabling a degree of logistical support that Romney's campaign reportedly was never able to achieve.

It's an incredible story, and arguably one with significant implications for digital health.

(1) To Leverage The Power of Data, Interoperability Is Essential

Data are useful only to the extent you can access, analyze, and share them. It increasingly appears that the genius of the Obama campaign's technology effort wasn't just the specific data tools that permitted microtargeting of constituents, or evaluated voter solicitation messages, or enabled the cost-effective purchasing of advertising time. Rather, success flowed from the design attributes of the platform itself, a platform built around the need for inoperability, and guided by an integrated strategic vision.

It's no secret that the greatest problem in health IT may be the challenge of interoperability, and the difficulty of sharing and accessing information in an easily actionable way (see here and here). It also seems apparent that without seamless communication, and a clear view of what each end-user wants and requires, many of the powerful benefits of big data are certain to be lost. It's possible that established and emerging standards will be enough to enable robust sharing; if not, it's easy to envision how a platform that successfully integrates a range of mediocre functionalities might easily drive out competitors offering more elegant but "stand-alone" functionalities.

(2) Drive Key Enabling Technologies, Don't Wait For Them

As companies watch new and potentially important technologies come down the pike, they're faced with an important decision: do they try to develop the capability internally (build), or should they purchase it from a vendor (buy)? It's clear from Madrigal's article that a pivotal decision made by the Obama campaign was to build, and to recruit the world's best developers to their organization.

I've previously argued that while big pharmas might benefit from this exact strategy— recruiting A-league players in big data—they instead seem prepared to watch from the sidelines, content for now to outsource this capability to large vendors. Although ostensibly safe, this sounds suspiciously similar to the campaign strategy adopted by another seasoned corporate executive; his story did not end well. While it would be imprudent to generalize from this one example, and it would be equally foolish to believe you can or should build everything from scratch, the contrasting campaign decisions, and fates, certainly highlight the risk of waiting for key enabling technology, rather than driving its development.

(3) Technology+Purpose=Awesome

It's clear that while the team of engineers started the campaign project with mad tech skills, they were elevated and inspired by the sense they were working on something important and meaningful. "They learned," wrote Madrigal, "what it was like to have— and work with people who had—a higher purpose than building cool stuff."

It's hard to imagine a more compelling purpose than using digital technologies to improve health. – DS

Turning Information Into Impact: Digital Health's Long Road Ahead

A leading scientist once claimed that, with the relevant data and a large enough computer, he could "compute the organism"—meaning completely describe its anatomy, physiology, and behavior. Another legendary researcher asserted that, following capture of the relevant data, "we will know what it is to be human." The breathless excitement of Sydney Brenner and Walter Gilbert—voiced more than a decade ago and captured by the skeptical Harvard geneticist Richard Lewontin [1]—was sparked by the sequencing of the human genome. Its echoes can be heard in the bold promises made for digital health today.

The human genome project, while an extraordinary technological accomplishment, has not translated easily into improved medicine nor unleashed a torrent of new cures. Perhaps the most successful "genomics" company, Millennium Pharmaceuticals, achieved lasting success not by virtue of the molecular cures they organically discovered, but by the more traditional pipeline they shrewdly acquired (notably via the purchase of LeukoSite, which ultimately yielded Campath and Velcade).

The enduring lesson of the genomics frenzy was succinctly captured by Brown and Goldstein, when they observed, "a gene sequence is not a drug."

Flash forward to today: technologists, investors, providers, and policy makers all exalt the potential of digital health [2]. Like genomics, the big idea—or leap of faith—is that through the more complete collection and analysis of data, we'll be able to essentially "compute" healthcare—to the point, some envision, where computers will become the care providers, and doctors will at best be customer service personnel, like the attendants at PepBoys, interfacing with libraries of software driven algorithms.

A measure of humility is in order. Just as a gene sequence is not a drug, information is not a cure. Getting there will take patience, persistence, money and aligned interests. The most successful innovators in digital health will see the promise of the technology, but also accept, embrace, and ideally leverage the ambiguity of disease, the variability of patients, and the complexities of clinical care.

We'll also need to incorporate four key lessons of the genetics experience:

- *Don't confuse data with insight*: it can be difficult to extract robust, clinically-relevant conclusions from reams of data;

- *Don't confuse insight with value*: many solid scientific findings, while interesting, do little to inform existing practice or significantly improve today's outcomes;

- *Don't overestimate your ability to forecast from data*: even the best data often afford only limited insight into health outcomes; a lot may depend upon chance or other factors;

- *Don't underestimate the implementation challenges:* leveraging data successfully requires a care delivery system prepared to embrace new methodologies, requiring significant investment of time and capital, and the alignment of economic interests.

Digital health will ultimately revolutionize medicine, but it will get there through a series of evolutionary phases. These won't be tidily sequential—some disease areas and some delivery systems may offer more fertile ground initially and see early successes.

But for the health care experienced by the vast majority of providers and patients and influencing a meaningful share of the dollars spent, the process will take much longer. Ten to fifteen year adoption cycles are typical (even rapid) in healthcare, and digital health is well advanced in only one domain (digital capture of data in today's workflows through electronic medical records [EMRs] and digital diagnostics) of the many required for far-reaching impact.

As a whole, we anticipate the revolution happening in three broad phases:

Phase 1: Consolidating gains so far

The ongoing digitization of today's clinical information will—over time—create a clearer understanding of how medicine is currently practiced; it will provide a coherent longitudinal record of each patient's health and enable codification of existing treatment practices.

True, most EMRs are still piecemeal, incomplete, and inaccurate—and resisted by many physicians. But the short-term benefits—simple, descriptive analytics to evaluate basic measures of quality, such as whether specific patients are getting necessary treatments, or whether interacting drugs have inadvertently been prescribed—are attractive. Many companies (from startups to behemoths) are pursuing data consolidation—to make records increasingly complete and "analyzable"—as well as clinical decision support—to expose and harvest the obvious departures from acceptable clinical practice.

Nor do the opportunities to exploit digitally captured data have to be strictly clinical: addressable unforced errors may be as basic as hospital supply chain optimization—an area where best practice is already well understood outside of health care. Not surprisingly, the "internet of things" is dramatically revealing how far health system logistics often are from best practice.

A key challenge that healthcare will need to address in this phase might be termed "algorithm creep," the tendency of well-intentioned "best practice" initiatives to become artificially precise, recommending and often mandating a specific course of action when a range of alternative approaches may be equally reasonable.

Insisting on a uniform approach is instantly recognized by patients and providers as artificial, and imposes a dangerously fragilizing solution that is neither required nor ultimately beneficial. Health Care will need to reign in the algorithm mania of some hospital executives who think more like capacity managers than physicians, a problem likely to only get worse as the industry consolidates. Rather than aggressively force providers into contrived boxes, health system leaders would do well to consider the "*via negativa*" strategy discussed by Taleb, and focus more on eliminating the clearly wrong than on dogmatically designating a single approach as definitively right.

Working out the right balance between computer driven and physician insight represents an ongoing challenge healthcare must wrestle with as it seeks to fully exploit the multiplying new data streams from digital health. Approaches to care improvement that emphasize continuous evolution and iterative improvement, and are explicitly designed around active physician participation—such as the SCAMPs program at Children's Hospital in Boston—or ones which (like UpToDate) offer such compelling value that even computer-phobic physicians embrace them, point to the path forward.

Another major challenge will be getting economic incentives aligned: digital health will ideally take aim at unnecessary, potentially harmful procedures, meaning fewer dollars for those who perform them. Success requires the continued transition to a reimbursement system that rewards quality rather than volume—an incentive structure that is arguably taking shape for larger delivery systems, perhaps less so for the remaining small, unaffiliated practices. As digital health places new demands on providers to invest in new capabilities and adapt practice patterns which may turn procedure-focused revenue-generating stars into occasional consulting specialists, widespread buy-in is likely to occur only after the transition to meaningful quality-based reimbursement reaches critical mass.

Phase 2: Learning to Drink From The Digital Firehose

After digitizing today's data flows, the next phase of digital health will drive towards dramatically denser physiological measurement exploiting winning models coming out of today's explosive investments in health data acquisition approaches, especially "intelligent sensors."

The idea itself is compelling: right now, physicians have very limited visibility into the health of most patients—care is episodic, and there's usually not much solid data on what a patient is doing in the real world; granular physiological data would seem helpful.

Yet turning more measurement into better health will require significant advances in data analysis and care delivery.

On the data front, existing and emerging predictive analytic platforms will help distinguish signal from noise, and ultimately deliver scientifically significant insights, a small fraction of which will actually have the potential to improve patient care in a meaningful way. This journey from raw data to demonstrated clinical benefit, however, promises to be long, difficult, and expensive, with a number of false starts and many dead-ends.

Nevertheless, the ready availability of more comprehensive measurements, especially if tied to more precise characterization of different interventions, will enable the crafting of better, more effective treatments by supporting iterative clinical learning and the rapid evolution of improved clinical practices.

Inevitably, a significant limitation in this phase is implementation: New instrumentation, data flows, interventions and patient adherence will impose a compounded "last mile" problem, characterized by three major obstacles: figuring out which data are likely to be dispositive; processing these data so that a provider or patient can easily understand and act upon it; and continuing the redesign of healthcare workflows and delivery system to support, communicate and implement the new clinical procedures.

These are difficult challenges: how in the world are already overwhelmed and overworked care providers supposed to even begin to think about, the dizzying amount of new information, much of still-to-be-determined clinical value? We will be reminded again and again in this phase just how hard behavior change really is, for providers as well as patients.

The good news is that digital health innovators recognize and are starting to concentrate on these challenges, as evidenced by both the intense entrepreneurial interest in user engagement (signaled by the ubiquitous invocation of Stanford social scientist B.J. Fogg), as well as the progressive recognition that health care urgently requires design thinking—an approach to innovation that, in the words of design guru and IDEO founder Tim Brown, is "human-centered, iterative, creative, and practical."

Phase 3: Integrating genetic and physiological data streams

The most exciting opportunity associated with digital health also, from a scientific perspective, may be the most difficult: integrating the new physiological data with emerging genetic data and evolving biological understanding to achieve profound new insights into the underlying basis of important diseases.

Today, we are surprisingly ignorant, and lack a fundamental understanding about what causes most human diseases. Integrating physiological measurement and genomic data in a consolidated network representation of physiology might offer an original perspective on health and disease, suggesting potentially unique portfolios of targets and perhaps bringing us a step closer to realizing the powerful scientific vision that originally inspired Brenner, Gilbert, and so many others.

In addition, the opportunity to better segment patients by combining genetic with physiological, and ultimately even social (see here) characteristics, could represent an important opportunity for disease management by making interventions more precisely focused, and hence much more cost effective, while also maximizing the likelihood of clinical impact.

As digital health affords medical researchers the ability to approach science in a less reductive fashion, more readily incorporating insights at the level of the whole organism, frontline care providers—and patients themselves—are likely to find themselves an increasingly central part of the scientific process, often providing the pivotal data and generating the animating insights. Progress in science will also bring further challenges for the healthcare system, as the benefits of more comprehensive monitoring must be balanced against the privacy issues and fundamental inconvenience. A whole new infrastructure of liability and regulation will need to be developed.

Concluding Thoughts

While we believe deeply in the promise of digital health, our optimism is tempered: human health is complex, our understanding is incomplete, and change—for both individuals and systems—is very, very hard. While media reports often focus on exceptional examples of early adopters, we would be foolish to use these to calibrate our expectations (a specific example of a more general publication bias).

We are likely to discover that even if we could acquire all the data we could imagine, there are fundamental limits on what this might reveal. It's unlikely we'll ever be able to "compute the whole organism."

Even so—and with humbled mien—we should push digital health technologies hard, and leverage the resulting data as best we can to improve the human condition.

Notes:

[1] Lewontin reference (including his explanation of "compute the organism") is from the "Genes and Organisms" essay in The Triple Helix; see also Lewontin's "Dream of Genome" essay, originally in The New York Review of Books, and reprinted in part in Biology as Ideology, as well as more completely in It Ain't Necessarily So.

[2] Digital health can be defined (via the World Economic Forum, 2012) as "applying the most advanced information and communication technologies to the collection, sharing and use of information that can improve health and healthcare." – DS

We Have A Winner! Quick Take On The Humedica Acquisition By UnitedHealth

According to the Boston Business Journal, the Boston-based digital health company Humedica was acquired by UnitedHealth Group for "hundreds of millions of dollars."

The appeal of this transaction is easy to see: Humedica is a promising data consolidation/descriptive analytics company that has two major lines of business: first, they sit on top of a large health system's EMR and extract and organize data. Humedica claims a natural language processing (NLP) capability as well, although I'm not sure, at least today, how well developed this is, and much it contributes to Humedica's overall value proposition.

The beautiful thing about the Humedica business model, as I understand it based on conversations with VCs who are not investors, is that first, Humedica gets paid by the health systems for crunching the data and generating output that is used to measure and improve operational performance—a key near-term priority for these health systems. Second, Humedica gets to keep the de-identified but extremely valuable, comprehensive longitudinal patient data, package it, and sell it to interested third parties (e.g. payors and pharmas). Nice work if you can get it—and now UnitedHealth has.

When Tory Wolff and I recently outlined our vision for the likely three step evolution of digital health, Humedica was the example at the front of our minds for "Step 1: Consolidating Gains So Far." We wrote:

"True, most EMRs are still piecemeal, incomplete, and inaccurate—and resisted by many physicians. But the short-term benefits—simple, descriptive analytics to evaluate basic measures of quality, such as whether specific patients are getting necessary treatments, or whether interacting drugs have inadvertently been prescribed—are attractive. Many companies (from startups to behemoths) are pursuing data consolidation—to make records increasingly complete and "analyzable"—as well as clinical decision support—to expose and harvest the obvious departures from acceptable clinical practice."

I first encountered Humedica when I was looking into data analytics companies in the broader context of big data. Surprisingly, Humedica was originally described to me by several experts as in some ways the least mathematically sophisticated company in the group, focused more on "descriptive" analytics (aimed essentially at incrementally improving the present) rather than on "predictive" analytics, that seek to make connections to enable important insights about the future.

The distinction isn't quite fair, of course, and most analytics companies claim to be in both spaces. Yet, I think it's accurate to suggest Humedica's focus has consistently been extremely practical—aggressively pursue relationships with large health centers, extract data and immediately provide something useful back. It would appear this comparatively grounded strategy has worked well for them.

Arguably the most encouraging news for the digital health space as a whole may be not only a strong exit (notably, not via IPO, and also notably, to a payor), but also the fact that the company was backed by a diverse group of investors, ranging from blue chip VCs such as General Catalyst (also Bain Capital Ventures and North Bridge Venture Partners, among others) , to corporate VCs, such as Merck's Global Health Innovation Fund (again, the only pharma VC at this digital health party), to nonprofits, such as the West Health Investment Fund; the Kraft Group is also an investor, so I guess they're 1 for 2 this week. Notably, both Merck and West were among the most active digital health investors in 2012.

I suspect this acquisition may help heat up the digital health innovation ecosystem, highlighting that for a well-conceived, persistent digital health company with a timely value proposition, it's really possible to find a there there. – DS

Medicine By Metrics : The Digital Revolution Is On, But Patients Need More Than Operational Efficiencies

Having spent decades in search of the next wonder drug, American medicine has starting to think about improving the way care is actually delivered, and has begun to dig deeply into the processes of health care. The science of operational improvement is on the rise. There's been an explosion of interest in measurement, metrics, and analytics, as researchers try to figure out how best to improve the quality of care.

The pursuit of quality is powerfully enabled by the emerging "digital health" sector, which develops the tools and technologies that enable improved health data collection and sophisticated analysis, and permits us to contemplate the transition of medicine from an episodic, symptom-driven practice to a more holistic vision focused on presymptomatic care and a more continuous assessment of health.

The rapid evolution of digital health has been driven by an impassioned cadre of entrepreneurs hoping to bring the dazzle of tech start-ups to the challenges of contemporary health care. The recently reported acquisition of Humedica, the Boston-based clinical informatics start-up, by insurance giant UnitedHealth highlights the value accorded to innovation in this space, and offers a useful lens into the way many digital health startups are thinking about problems.

Traditionally, medical information—physician notes, diagnostic images, lab tests, and prescription orders—has been dispersed in manila folders scattered in offices and file rooms across a sprawling care network. As providers (led by large hospital systems) embrace electronic medical records, these disparate data are increasingly stored electronically; however, extracting the stored data points and organizing them in a useful and actionable way remains a significant challenge—which is where analytics companies such as Humedica come in.

Humedica is hired by large hospitals to extract information from their electronic medical records system and perform fairly basic analyses that assess the quality of patient care and suggest areas of improvement, pointing out instances, for example, where patients inadvertently have been prescribed medications known to interact, or where a provider forgot to order a key diagnostic test or veered significantly from accepted best practice. By identifying and correcting these problems, hospital systems hope to ensure each patient receives the best care possible while avoiding unnecessary, potentially harmful treatments.

Digital health entrepreneurs hope that through the right combination of improved measurement (often using "smart" sensors), sophisticated analytics, and user engagement, they can help find ways to make the best use of today's treatments, and ensure each patient consistently receives the best and most cost-effective care available. Entrepreneurs also hope to progressively raise the bar, applying the empirical intelligence of operational improvement to further elevate the quality of health care delivery.

As lofty as these aspirations are, we worry this view of quality—ambitious as it is—isn't quite ambitious enough.

Consider how today's community of digital health entrepreneurs would likely respond were polio still unpreventable and widespread: Start-ups would focus on refining the design of the iron lung, increasing the efficiency of scheduling, improving the transparency of costs, and analyzing the operational performance of each unit while tracking its location by GPS.

Without question, these tweaks would significantly improve the patient experience, and might reduce the cost of care. However, none of these approaches would have either the clinical or the economic effect of a radical new therapy—in this case, the polio vaccine.

Even as we strive to incrementally elevate health care quality through gradual operational improvement, our audacious goal must include figuring out how to use digital health's technology, data, and computational tools to increase our fundamental understanding of disease and generate profound new treatments.

Sound familiar? It should: Medical scientists held out similar hopes for genetics, only to discover that, as Nobel laureates Brown and Goldstein famously observed, "a gene sequence is not a drug," and getting from one to the other was far more difficult than many experts had anticipated—though the occasional success story reminds us of the promise.

Similarly, turning digital data into profound clinical impact will not be easy. However, combining genetic and digital data—integrating our knowledge of the building blocks of life with a dynamic picture of how the pieces are behaving—may prove particularly powerful, offering unprecedented insight into health and disease, and enabling us to develop radically improved therapies.

By then, our operationally improved health care system should be ready to efficiently deliver these treatments to patients, who have waited far too long to receive them. – DS + Dennis Ausiello

Epic Faulkner Interview: SV Should Show Judy More Love; We Shouldn't Let Hospitals Off The Hook

Two quick reactions to my colleague Zina Moukheiber's fascinating interview with Judy Faulkner, Founder and CEO of EMR powerhouse Epic Systems.

1. **Judy Faulkner should be a tech hero in Silicon Valley**. While Epic tends to be smugly dismissed in silicon valley as offering an "old-school" solution to problems that could be delivered in a more modern fashion (e.g. Practice Fusion), it's hard not to come away from the interview feeling that technologists should regard founder/CEO Judy Faulkner with more resonance, and accord her far more recognition. From the way she describes herself, she seems like a geek's geek, telling Moukheiber, "I was an undergrad math major, and a grad student in computer science. I'm hugely introverted, not atypical of math majors. " She used her brains, persistence, and ability to recognize true customer need to build the world's most significant EMR company, and generated a personal net worth in excess of $1B in the process. Perhaps if she named her company after a Tolkien character, had been funded by VCs, or was spun out of Stanford rather than University of Wisconsin, Silicon Valley would be more receptive. Based on some of the dodgy digital health efforts I've seen emerging in the Valley, I'd think her grounded perspective might be especially worthy of emulation.

2. **Interoperability issues associated with Epic may reflect tacit preferences of hospital systems**. Tory Wolff and I have discussed the interoperability challenges associated with Epic, and it's potentially negative impact on the innovation ecosystem (see here and here). Faulkner's comments don't particular assuage my concerns, but certainly highlight Epic's laser-focus on delivering what customers want—and make no mistake, *the customer isn't the patient but the hospital*. This is critical to appreciate. Thus, while it's easy (and appropriate) to critique Epic for impeding data sharing, it's

probably also important to remember that if hospitals were all that keen to share data better, I suspect Epic would rapidly find a way to accomplish this. It's almost as if Epic provides hospitals with plausible deniability. While it may be convenient to blame EMRs in general, and Epic in particular, for data access challenges, I suspect we also need to dig deeper, and hold hospital systems themselves far more—what's the word?—accountable. – DS

XI.

VCs And Other Investors

Seriously: Is Digital Health The Answer To Tech Bubble Angst?

As an ever increasing amount of money seems determined to chase an ever greater number of questionable ideas, it's perhaps not surprising that inquiring minds want to know: (1) Are we really in a tech bubble? (2) If so, when will it pop? (3) What should I do in the meantime?

I'm not sure about Question 1: I've heard some distinguished valley wags insist we're not in a tech bubble, and that current valuations are justified, but I also know many technology journalists feel certain the end is nigh, and view the bubble as an established fact of life—see here and here. The surge of newly-minted MBAs streaming to start-ups has been called out as a likely warning sign of the upcoming apocalypse as well.

I have the humility to avoid Question 2: as Gregory Zuckerman reviews in *The Greatest Trade Ever*, even if you're convinced you're in a bubble, and you're right, the real challenge is figuring out when to get out. Isaac Newton discovered this the hard way in the South Sea Bubble, leading him to declare, "I can calculate the motions of heavenly bodies but not the madness of people."

I do have a thought about Question 3, however—what to do: reconsider digital health—serious digital health.

Here's why: Instagram and similar apps are delightful, but hardly essential; most imitators and start-ups inspired by their success are neither. It doesn't strain credulity to imagine investors in these sorts of companies waking up one day and experiencing their own Seinfeld moment, as it occurs to them they've created a portfolio built around nothing.

I confess to believing that health is different: I'm overwhelmed by the extent of real, unmet need—by the need for meaningful innovation to impact the lives of people and patients. The fundamental human need is there—and a market for innovative products exists; there's real money here, and real business opportunities for companies that are able to deliver and demonstrate value.

To this point, as I've previously discussed (see here and here), a lot of the activity in digital health seems to have taken inspiration (understandably) from the efforts in the tech space more broadly—there's a lot of interest in consumer tech and wellness apps, and what seems to be an ever-increasing number of incubators that have popped up to support this emerging ecosystem.

The emphasis of health entrepreneurs and incubators on what I'd describe as "small ball" is understandable; the upfront investment tends to be small, and the initial development cycle time tends to be short—you often can go from concept to prototype extremely rapidly (not a bad thing, incidentally—see here). You also avoid a lot of the complexity of healthcare, the potential need to deal with multiple stakeholders including regulators and hospital systems that seems to have frightened so many VCs.

The real challenge and exceptional opportunity here, however, is to see if digital health (which I use to encompass everything from mobile health to healthcare IT) can move from these well-intentioned but often fairly primitive efforts to something more serious, and of more enduring value.

The dilemma here is almost certainly figuring out where to start. On the one hand, some of the initial forays seem so flimsy that it's difficult to imagine them evolving into a breakthrough offering—but presumably that's what people also used to say about thefacebook.

On the other hand, efforts that start off intending to disrupt the entire healthcare ecosystem and rebuild it anew seem destined to fail, given the entrenched and enmeshed players; my sense is this has been the experience of a lot of Sand Hill Road's tech investors to date, which is why so many are leery of this space. Navimed Capital's Bijan Salehizadeh has a good point when he observes there are "too many outside forces."

I've got to believe there's a middle ground here—opportunities for creating (and subsequently investing in) digital health companies tackling problems serious enough to be worthwhile, but focused on an existing pain point, and grounded enough to achieve success and returns without requiring the wholesale reinvention of the entire healthcare system (at least at first....).

Castlight Health (which seeks to introduce transparency to health care costs) is perhaps the most advanced example of how this approach can work, addressing a significant pain point with a service it can sell immediately to business customers, while offering the possibility of profound disruption down the road. Significantly, Castlight focuses—you might say leverages—the complexity of the healthcare system, rather than gingerly avoiding this important fact of life. Perhaps not surprisingly, investment in Castlight has been led by several of the Valley's leading healthcare investors, including Venrock's Bryan Roberts and Maverick Capital's David Singer (I know both but have no conflicts to disclose).

If the growth of tech continues unfettered, everyone stands to do well. But if the bubble should burst, I'd suspect investors who own companies like Castlight Health may be best positioned to weather the storm. Unfortunately, there's doesn't seem to be nearly enough companies like Castlight Health to go around.

There should be. – DS

Why 500 Startups-Style Small Bets Could Be Next Big Idea In Digital Health

In a previous post, I discussed the painful honesty of Silicon Valley tech VC Dave McClure's much-discussed meditation, "Late Bloomer, Not a Loser." I've since had a chance to read more about McClure's unconventional investing philosophy, reflected in his firm, 500 Startups, and the approach seemed worth discussing as well—particularly in the context of whether it might be relevant to companies in the digital health space.

(As I mentioned in my previous post, I don't know McClure either personally or professionally—I'm simply captivated by his thinking.)

What I find most intriguing about McClure's investing approach is that he seems to be doing exactly what you'd do if you read Nassim Taleb's *The Black Swan* (see my *WSJ* review here) and really took the key messages to heart. In particular: (a) make a lot of small bets with limited downside; (b) take advantage of the cognitive biases that lead investors to cluster for comfort.

McClure's approach seeks to make unusually small bets in a number of mostly tech startups—$50K-$250K, according to this recent, useful Gigaom profile. The logic is that most startups fail, but the winners can yield disproportionate returns—and you can eliminate most of the contenders without needing to sink more cash in. (Only an estimated 20% of the startups survive, and earn another round of investment, according to Gigaom.)

The math is appealing: rather than obsessing over whether one specific opportunity or another is likely to be groundbreaking, the way most VCs do, here, you try to eliminate the real dogs, and then simply roll the dice (and administer some TLC), hoping that a few of these bets yield an outsized payoff. The key premise is the humility to believe at the start that neither you nor anyone else really knows which opportunities will win big.

There are a few obvious problems with this approach, of course. For starters, you risk running out of money, and hence not realizing your payoff because you can't afford to stay in the game. This is a classic dilemma faced by undercapitalized seed-stage investors—they put in a ton of sweat equity, but then can't contribute adequately to subsequent financing rounds and thus get diluted out.

The second problem is that success for a venture investor may not depend simply upon the number of opportunities, but also upon the degree of involvement with each investment. Or not. Most VCs believe they add a significant amount of value this way, while most entrepreneurs I know have a more mixed view, at best. While the investment team of 500 Startups is known for their boundless energy, it's still hard to envision it's physically possible for them to devote the time and attention to each of their portfolio companies that a more focused VC could—at least in theory.

A related feature of McClure's investments are that he specifically—and provocatively —states he's not looking for groundbreaking innovations, companies that will "change the world" (in stark contrast to many other VCs, who may be running far larger funds). Rather, he seems to be looking for small wins in defined niches—narrow customer segments that larger players have overlooked. Of course, this probably also impacts the size of return a successful investment is likely to deliver (unless you really believe there's absolutely no correlation between scope of original ambition and the size of the company that develops from this vision).

McClure's investments also appear to be informed by a deep commitment to diversity (see this recent TechCrunch interview), for what I'd call all the right reasons. The idea— which I've also heard well-articulated by Dean Nancy Andrews at Duke University—is simple: most tech VCs (so it is argued) have a fairly similar idea of what an entrepreneur looks like and where to find him. For McClure and others, this represents what is effectively an outstanding arbitrage opportunity—by embracing a less restrictive view of what talent looks like (on parameters such as geography and gender), these investors in theory have easy access to a relatively untapped pool of exceptionally talented entrepreneurs who have been overlooked by traditional investors, but who can deliver substantial innovation nonetheless.

McClure is absolutely on target here, as I've touched upon in two different WSJ book reviews. In my discussion of Malcolm Gladwell's *Outliers*, I note that the book,

"offers an implicit message for companies as well: There is great competitive advantage for the organization recognizing that the work environment can nurture talent—and also suppress it. The best companies will not only seek to provide their employees with enrichment but will also have the insight—and courage—to identify and recruit exceptional though neglected talent that could flourish under the right conditions."

Similarly, in my WSJ review of George Anders *The Rare Find*, I write, "The real challenge may not be so much identifying talent as getting serious about seeking it." Clearly, McClure is both serious and expansive in his pursuit of talent—and it's difficult to envision this as anything but great.

The last question to think about is whether McClure's approach has implications for investments in digital health, an area he has placed only a handful of bets (and that's counting generously).

First, the bad news: McClure's approach seems very poorly suited for the one area I can think of where it is most needed: biopharmaceuticals. It's incredibly difficult to know whether an emerging compound, or an emerging company (frequently the same thing) is going to succeed or not, and unfortunately, it takes scads of money and a lot of time to find out—even if you employ the lean and/or virtual approaches that proponents advocate.

The truth is that what you really would like to do in early stage drug development is place a lot of small bets, and quickly kill all but the most promising products—and everyone knows this. Moreover, all consultants recommend this approach—and then invariably blame leaders for their unwillingness to kill favored programs.

The reality, unfortunately, is a lot more messy. In most cases, I don't think you can make intelligent and accurate early decisions about which compounds are clearly going to fail, and which might eventually succeed—it's just not that obvious. Most blockbuster drugs that I know of—including Lipitor—could easily and rationally have been killed for one reason or another at some point in their development.

Hopefully, and through improved science, we can get smarter about killing drugs earlier, but at least right now, the truth is you have to do a lot of work to figure out what will work and what won't—and it's expensive and time consuming.

I'm considerably more optimistic about the prospects of McClure's approach for digital health. To date, my sense is that the thinking around digital health bounces between a laudable but abstract vision to "disrupt everything," and a number of pretty trivial apps that are technically clever but which don't really address an unmet need.

I suspect that a McClure-style approach that preached a relentless, iterative focus on the customer, and which was comfortable concentrating on a narrowly-defined segment of customers, could ultimately be extremely impactful, and represent a compelling way to channel entrepreneurial passion into improved health. – DS

Dyson And McClure: Two Investors One Theme—VC As Auteur

I was especially excited to have the opportunity at Rock Health's Health Innovation Summit to moderate a panel discussion featuring angel/seed-stage investors Esther Dyson and Dave McClure.

Dyson and McClure have conspicuously different stories, and radically different approaches to investing. At the same time, they share an underlying and inspiring idealism, authenticity, and sense of mission that seems to set them apart from many of their investing peers, and put them in a category shared by few others: VC as Auteur.

Dave McClure, *500* Startups

The son of an elementary school music teacher, McClure grew up in West Virginia and Maryland, studied engineering and computer science at John Hopkins (as discussed in this recent TechCrunch profile), and spent a number of years as an programmer, entrepreneur, and marketing at several Silicon Valley companies including Mint.com and PayPal, where he evidently became a made man in their Mafia.

More recently, through his innovative VC fund 500 Startups, he seeks to leverage portfolio theory, and put a relatively small amount of money ($50K-$250K) to work in an unusually large number of narrowly-focused tech companies. As McClure recently told TechCrunch, "There are thousands of 'small' businesses, $10M-$25M revenue businesses that solve real problems."

To date, McClure has made very few healthcare-related investments, and it will be interesting to learn how (or whether) going forward he sees healthcare opportunities fitting into his investment strategy.

Esther Dyson, *EDventure*

Dyson's story is a bit different: the daughter of two world-renowned scholars (her father is the theoretical physicist Freeman Dyson, her mother is the mathematician Verena Huber Dyson), she studied economics at Harvard and then began her career as a fact-checker and later a reporter at Forbes. She then became a technology analyst on Wall Street, eventually running her own newsletter and conference company, which she ultimately sold to CNET.

Dyson currently operates as an angel investor (and as a journalist-turned-investor, she's in good company—see here). She is active in "Air/Space 2.0" (again, in good company) and in IT, especially as it relates to health. She typically makes investments on the order of $25K-$50K, and has invested in a number of healthcare companies including 23andMe, PatientsLikeMe, Healthtap, Keas, Genomera, Omada, and Organized Wisdom.

Dyson is a strong believer in "preemptive" health, and it will be interesting to learn how she views the balance between the potential benefits of preventive care and the potential harms of excessive care, a tension I suspect will become increasingly evident over the next decade. (In a nutshell: it makes sense to prevent disease rather than treating it after it develops—but prevention by definition involves healthy people, so the concern —articulated by Nassim Taleb among others—is whether the [often unknown] risk we subject healthy people to exceeds the likely benefit. Eric (#CDoM) Topol Made a related point in this NYT op-ed he wrote about statin use this past March.)

VC Auteurs

Despite their many obvious differences, both McClure and Dyson share a quality I've previously discussed in the context of entrepreneurs—as well as auteurs such as Ira Glass and Woody Allen: the ability to author one's own life.

McClure—combining the urgent upbeat dynamism of Tony Robbins with the savvy earthy critical faculties of David Mamet—comes off as a force of nature, pursuing an ambitious strategy that would seem to require a relentless energy and optimism few could maintain. And while the investment approach certainly has strong mathematical support (as well as eliciting significant real-world skepticism), it seems obvious that he absolutely loves what he is doing, and feels that it's a natural expression of what he most enjoys— his job is his passion.

Similarly, Dyson unapologetically pursues a range of interests and investments—including six months of cosmonaut training in Russia—because it's what she's passionate about, and what she loves to do. Like McClure, Dyson can articulate cogent investment theses, and provide sophisticated justification for supporting the companies she backs, but it's also abundantly clear that she's following her heart, and investing in the ideas, people, and regions that excite her the most.

A critic might scoff that it's inappropriate to place McClure and Dyson on pedestals without more data on their actual success as investors. Perhaps they are simply vanity investors with a gift for good publicity.

My view is somewhat different. I seem to know a lot of investors (including many VCs, surprisingly) who strike me as personally unfulfilled, even if they have managed to do quite well financially. Investing, for most, remains a difficult, strenuous task, and many strive to maximize returns through a highly disciplined process that seeks to be as analytical and depersonalized as possible—and I appreciate the logic behind this.

In contrast, McClure and Dyson seem to view investing as an extension of their personal, entrepreneurial vision, a way to pursue the ideas that most excite and captivate them.

Will their passion and commitment to pursuing these interests lead them to foolishly stick with bad ideas that a more detached investor might avoid or more rapidly exit?

Perhaps. But I can also imagine that their apparent degree of emotional investment might also contribute to the success of their portfolio companies—and all the while, making the journey itself as valuable and as engaging as the ultimate destination.

As Gershwin said, "Nice work, if you can get it." – DS

Why I Disagree With Vinod Khosla About Digital Health—And Hope He Succeeds Brilliantly

At the 2012 Rock Health Health Innovation Summit (where I participated on an angel investing panel with Dave McClure and Esther Dyson), tech VC legend Vinod Khosla expanded in his keynote discussion themes he introduced in previous articles and interviews.

Taken as a whole, Khosla's comments and digital health investments suggest four key theses:

1. Medicine requires disruption;

2. Entrepreneurial technologists focused on consumers are ideally poised to deliver this;

3. Most doctors are so enmeshed and invested in the current system that they are more likely to be part of the problem than part of the solution;

4. In an ideal future state, most care would be delivered by robust computer algorithms ("Dr.A") and doctors would no longer be required.

As Khosla surely intended, these provocative comments have generated a predictable buzz (see this thoughtful piece by Dr. Davis Liu here; this is a useful summary as well).

I've previously discussed what I think Silicon Valley doesn't understand about medicine (here), and why I'd choose to place my bets on innovations seeking to enable rather than replace physicians (here); I won't rehash these arguments.

Rather, I'd like to focus on an important question about the origin of new ideas that's implicit in Khosla's theses: is disruptive innovation most likely to come from within or outside a domain?

While there is a popular, even a romantic view of the naïve outsider wandering into a new area and radically transforming it (similar to Khosla's view of healthcare innovation, as I understand it), most rigorous examples that I've seen describe a very different pattern; domain expertise is often critically required, first to deeply understand the problem at hand and then to come up with an implementable solution—though the solution is often informed by insight gleaned from a different discipline or domain.

Even Khosla doesn't appear to reject domain expertise entirely—while he may view deep experience in medicine as a potential liability, he seems to believe that the most successful disruptors of healthcare will likely have experience in technology and entrepreneurship, and some idea of how to apply this to health.

Coincidentally, investors such as Khosla have the most comfort (and demonstrated success) in identifying promising technology entrepreneurs, but have appreciably less experience navigating the complexities of our existing healthcare ecosystem. Thus, while it may be bold for Khosla to call for a radical reinvention of medicine, it's also convenient, and understandable.

Like other physicians in the valley (e.g.), I disagree with Khosla's perspective, or more accurately, I bring a different set of experiences and biases. Trained as a physician, and working in the medical products industry, it's perhaps not surprising I view deep experience in healthcare and the complexity of the healthcare system as enormously enabling. While Khosla worries healthcare domain expertise may stifle innovation, I see this type of experience as essential, providing the needed foundation for understanding problems and developing workable and relevant solutions.

The beautiful thing about the free market is that these sorts of disagreements don't need to be—and shouldn't be—solved by endless debate, but rather by doing the right experiment, and seeing what sorts of innovations (informed by which investment strategy) actually work and take hold in the real world.

Which brings us to the true problem—and it's certainly not Vinod Khosla. To the contrary, Khosla is doing everything right: he has a passion for health, a thesis for how to develop solutions, and is aggressively investing in this space.

The more serious problem is that most traditional healthcare VCs—those with medical product experience—are effectively not in the game; it's a tough time (especially following the Kauffman report) to be a VC, and a brutal time if you're investing in healthcare, a space now reviled by most LPs (whether this reflects insightful prudence or a trailing edge herd mentality is a subject for another day).

As a result, with a few exceptions, investors who arguably are best suited to identify, evaluate, and cultivate important emerging opportunities in digital health have been sidelined, leaving digital health to the brave tech investors like Khosla with cash to spare, and who are willing—courageously—to explore a phenomenally promising, but also tremendously uncertain and unproven space.

Given the unquestionable need to improve medicine for patients, I hope Khosla succeeds —brilliantly.

But as C.S. Lewis observed, "What you see and what you hear depends a great deal on where you are standing. It also depends on what sort of person you are."

There's no doubt that Khosla is a bold, imaginative, and creative sort of person. But all the same, I'd feel a lot better to see additional investors with deeper healthcare experience and a different set of beliefs get into the game, and take a stand as well. – DS

Digital Health Requires Courageous Investors—And Other Lessons From The Khosla Controversy

As expected, Vinod Khosla's recent comments at Rock Health's Health Innovation Summit have generated a lot of healthy discussion about health, as I wrote in my last post.

It's also clear from the resulting online dialog that there's some basic confusion, as key points have become conflated or confused.

As far as I can tell, no one disputes that healthcare requires significant innovation—that's why digital health has attracted so much attention. There are profound problems with how medicine is practiced, and huge opportunities for improvement, for radically rethinking how we do things.

I do worry that some technologists, including Khosla, have an excessively reductive view of medicine, and don't adequately appreciate the essential humanity, nuance, and complexity that defines a physician's role.

Khosla claims that Google's development of a driverless car is a challenge "two orders of magnitude more complex" than providing the right diagnosis. To me, this highlights what I see as the underlying disconnect—the mischaracterization of the fundamental problem to be solved.

Medicine isn't (only) about inputting symptoms and receiving a diagnosis, it's about trying to elicit symptoms, to understand why a patient is worried or concerned, to appreciate how a particular treatment approach is likely to work in the real world, to provide encouragement as a patient tries to deal with chronic illness.

Doctors could and should do each of these things better (as I've discussed extensively in this space)—and digital health can, must, and ultimately will help.

But I think—and I've seen, from both ends of the stethoscope—the role that doctors, at their best, can play in the integrated tasks of providing diagnosis, explanation, treatment recommendations, prognosis, understanding, support, guidance, and comfort.

While some might prefer a less humanistic, more Spock-like approach to medicine—a computer algorithm (in Khosla's parlance, Dr. A.) that can replace a doctor—most of us would prefer, and benefit from deeply compassionate physicians who are enabled by significantly improved health technologies; certainly this would describe my vision.

A related question is whether the healthcare innovations we need are more likely to come from those with deep experience in healthcare, or from outsiders (say, technologists) who can bring a fresh perspective.

In my last column, I argued that both are essential, but since tech VCs are comparatively flush these days, while traditional healthcare VCs are hurting, tech VCs such as Khosla are playing a disproportionate role in shaping how the space is evolving. It's outstanding that tech VCs are actively investing here, but it would be terrific, and I believe enormously helpful, for more investors with deep health care experience to join the fray as well.

Perhaps the single aspect of the recent online dialog that disturbed me the most was the critique of Khosla expressed by several readers of the wonderful Davis Liu piece (and in response to my last piece as well). Some suggested that since Khosla's results as a leading-edge cleantech investor have been spotty (most comments were less kind), why should we listen to him about health?

I thoroughly reject this—while many Silicon Valley VCs both became successful and remained successful by closely following the crowd, Khosla has demonstrated a remarkable willingness to explore new areas where the need is great, and where success is far from certain. You know, the sort of boldness that VCs tend to advertise but less consistently exhibit.

A key takeaway I had from the Rock Health Summit was that these are very early days for digital health; while the need for better solutions is very high, it's not at all clear what will work, and how anyone will make any money in the process. Not surprisingly, most of the investors represented were extremely early stage, and were involved because they were following their passion, rather than seasoned investors counting on a score.

I understand the reluctance of investors to get involved at this point, but I also believe those who dare will be rewarded—they will have a chance to learn, first hand, what the issues are and where the opportunities lie, and will be optimally positioned so that when the space finally hits its inflection point, and everyone rushes in, they will already be there, deserved beneficiaries of the success they helped create. – DS

Are Successful VCs Lucky Or Good —And Can Health Care VCs Be Either?

I. Taleb: Investors Lucky>Good

A fascinating article by Steven Russolillo in the *WSJ* focused on the skeptical view Black Swan author Nassim Taleb has of investment managers (summarized in this short white paper).

Russolillo reports that Taleb

"says many of the best money managers earn their success based on 'spurious performance' and these folks 'rise to the top for no reasons other than mere luck, with subsequent rationalizations, analyses, explanations and attributions.'

"Once they are at the top, though, they get the bulk of the allocations, creating a 'winner-take-all effect' that causes distortions in the marketplace, he says."

In other words, there will be a Matthew Effect—the rich will get richer.

In his white paper, Taleb argues "an operator starting today, no matter his skill level, ability to predict prices, will be outcompeted by the spurious tail."

Notably, this skeptical view of investing seems to be shared by Daniel Kahneman, expressed in this wonderful *NYT* commentary.

II. Kauffman Foundation: A Handful of VCs Consistently Account For Most of the Returns

A recent, captivating report by the Kauffman Foundation takes a critical look at the venture capital industry, and concludes that the lion's share of returns are generated by a very small number of top-performing firms—the number seems to be between 10 and 50. Most firms (once fees are included) fail to match the returns available in the public market (which the report argues is the relevant comparator).

The report observes, "great VC returns is entirely dependent on which funds you're in, not how many funds. Generating great VC returns requires access to the small group of best-performing funds."

Furthermore, "There is also strong evidence that VC performance is persistent at both the top and bottom." (Of note, the report also presents data suggesting that performance falls as the size of the fund increases, and the best-performing funds seemed to be $500M or less.)

III. Rachleff: Top VCs Good>Lucky

Writing in TechCrunch, Andy Rachleff, Benchmark's highly-regarded founding partner (and now President and CEO of the online financial advisory firm Wealthfront) described what makes VCs successful.

Rachleff noted that in addition to the Kauffman report data, "Cambridge Associates, an advisor to institutions that invest in venture capital, says that only about 20 firms—or about 3 percent of the universe of venture capital firms—generate 95 percent of the industry's returns, and the composition of the top 3 percent doesn't change very much over time."

Rachleff continues, "Those premier venture firms succeed because they have proprietary knowledge of the characteristics of winning companies. Over the years, the knowledge of what it takes to succeed is passed down from partner to partner and becomes part of the firms' institutional memory."

Well, maybe.

Perhaps it's true, as Rachleff's asserts, that top firms continue to succeed because they're smarter. But it's clearly not the only way to explain the data (and may instead offer persuasive support to the notion that every ruling class harbors the myth of its own superiority).

It would seem equally possible that top VCs may be advantaged simply because they are viewed as top VCs, and see more opportunities, can cut better deals, and provide a self-fulfilling signaling advantage to their portfolio companies.

As one TechCrunch commenter observed, "2nd/3rd tier VCs lose not because they lack wisdom, but because they lack deal flow and find it hard to compete against 1st tier brands."

IV. Implications:

While I generally share the skepticism that Kahneman and Taleb so eloquently express, I also strongly believe that some VC investors are sharper and more savvy than others—even though this difference may account for a smaller fraction of their performance differential than they tend to believe.

More importantly, I seriously doubt (and bristle at the notion) that a handful of top players have a lock on the relevant "proprietary knowledge" needed to be successful—this strikes me as the sort of desperate argument that has always been used by the dominant group in power to exclude new arrivals.

I also suspect that the profile of successful companies represents a constantly evolving target, and it isn't always possible to know how the next generation of winners will appear.

Healthcare VC seems like a particular vivid object lesson in the value of VC humility. Many of the top players of a decade ago aren't even around today, and many of those still with us seem to be sitting on distinctly unremarkable portfolios.

Some look at the sorry state of healthcare VC and conclude the category should be avoided—few winners today suggests there will be few winners tomorrow.

But I prefer to believe that the leading healthcare VC firms of the future just haven't yet been identified—perhaps because the characteristics of winning healthcare companies haven't yet been defined. – DS

Digital Health: Almost A Real, Live Business

While the evolution of the digital health ecosystem has seemed at times almost painfully contrived, it's now appears to have reached the point where it requires but a few sprinkles of magic fairy dust to be truly alive.

The basic idea behind digital health is pretty clear: we can (and must) do health better, and technology should be able to help,

There's also an ever-increasing amount of support for early-stage innovators in this space. A remarkably large number of digital health incubators have sprung up around the country, as Lisa Suennen captured with characteristic verve in this recent Venture Valkyrie post.

On top of this, a slew of corporate VCs have now emerged—many from payors, but some from communication companies, and even a few from big pharmas such as Merck—all keen to invest strategically in the digital health space.

Deliberately, many of these large corporations also represent likely buyers for the products or services that will be produced, so it really does seem like an example of the savvy external sourcing of innovation.

So we're good, then—right?

Well, not so fast.

It turns out that many high profile VCs continue to eschew this space, other than perhaps an occasional investment or two. The reason? As one extremely well-regarded VC—with extensive healthcare experience—told me yesterday, "I haven't seen a viable business model yet."

Translation: how do you make (serious) money here? Where's the revenue?

This is a reasonable critique—though one that seems equally applicable to the many tech start-ups that seem deliberately geared to fulfill a niche need at Google or Microsoft or

Oracle, rather than to thrive as a stand-alone company. While not IPOs, a number of these exits have generated sizable returns for their venture backers.

Without question, it would be terrific to see some truly disruptive, stand-alone companies emerge and arise, the Google of Medicine, the Facebook of Health.

I understand and deeply resonate with the urge to reach for the sky, and to build something significant and durable—an aspiration eloquently reflected in a recent NPR profile of former Intel CEO Andy Grove.

In the early days of Intel, NPR reports,

"Grove emphasizes they were trying to create products of value and a company that would last. Today, Grove thinks that many in Silicon Valley are merely hoping to make a quick profit. There are two words that make him cringe: 'Exit strategy,' he says. 'I hate it!'

Perhaps Big VC (a term that seems apropos these days) is smart to wait it out, until the time is right for the next new, new thing. But the question the major funds should be asking isn't whether this moment is perfect, but whether it's good enough.

Visibly, there are important problems that digital health can help solve today, and large corporations—with deep pockets and lots of cash—who seem genuinely interested in seeing these problems solved, and who are looking eagerly outside their own walls for the solution.

We might also reevaluate our view of salvation, and consider the possibility that the next great revolution in health might not arise from a new player appearing heroically upon the scene and changing forever the rules of the game; perhaps part of the problem here is that we've been waiting expectantly for such an arrival.

What if the change we seek is already here, in the form of established players who realize they must rapidly evolve, and profoundly reinvent themselves if they are to survive? What if their corporate venture groups aren't simply *pro forma* gestures towards innovation shaped by cynical management consultants, but serious efforts to scope out the future, and figure out how to adapt to it?

Too much to ask? Try a bit of fairy dust. Perhaps it's time to start believing in digital health.

It's also possible I should watch a bit less Disney with my kids. – DS

Digital Health Companies Must Make Themselves Indispensable To Established Stakeholders

In a post last year that must qualify as an instant classic, my co-author, Lisa Suennen (aka Venture Valkyrie), compared her experiences at the old-school, tragically unhip (e.g.) 2012 HIMSS (Health Information and Management Systems Society) conference and at the "Woodstock for Geeks" (in her words) SXSW conference a few weeks later.

The money paragraph is this one:

"It is an interesting time in healthcare IT and I think that the incredible gulf between HIMSS and SXSW is a perfect metaphor for the challenge. We have to figure out a way to engage legions of young innovators who really understand next generation technology in channeling their energy into healthcare solutions. The old school enterprises who have the biggest presence at HIMSS are unlikely to be the leaders of the future if they don't come up the social networking ubergeek learning curve. On the other hand, too many of the new kids on the block can program a sophisticated piece of software in their sleep while eating a pizza with the other hand, yet don't really understand the intricacies of how money moves through the healthcare system and where all the privacy, security and financial incentive bodies are buried."

I was thinking about this exact challenge when reviewing the originally published agenda for the Real Endpoints Symposium.

The symposium, titled "Disrupting Drug/Dx Reimbursement," features speakers from leading payors (Aetna, Wellpoint, United Health), pharmas (GSK, Merck, Pfizer, AZ, BMS, J&J), and healthcare systems (MSKCC, Harvard Pilgrim) but none of the usual suspects from the digital health startup scene. [Note: several were subsequently invited.]

This is a fascinating disconnect that may also highlight an important opportunity. For all the interest in wellness apps and engaging gadgets, here is where the money is—or at least a lot of it. It's in payors trying to assess value, medical product companies trying to create it, and healthcare systems trying to deliver it.

To be sure, it's a complicated, even byzantine ecosystem, but one that digital health companies would do well to understand and master, and in which to make themselves indispensable, given the abundant opportunities, tremendous resources, and urgent needs of each of the invited stakeholders. I'm not sure who is most in need of some serious SXSW thinking—payors, pharmas, or providers—but it's a safe bet that each could gain appreciably.

The good news is that some digital health companies (though still precious few tech-oriented investors, who have remained generally skittish) are beginning to brave the complexities of what might be called "real health care"; perhaps the mark of their success will be when they start to generate real revenue, begin to have a real impact, and consequently earn their way onto the agenda of a future Real Endpoints symposium.

One final point: many entrepreneurs (and VCs) would contend that they are focusing their health care efforts exclusively on the most important stakeholders of all: patients (or more broadly, consumers). Fair point, and these may be important efforts (or, more frequently, not); but ideally they should complement, not replace, meaningful efforts to enter, and ideally improve, the existing healthcare system. Radical reinvention may be a noble goal, but there's a lot to be said for the adage, "you gotta be in it to win it." – DS

Rock Tease: Investors Flirt With Digital Health But Avoid Serious Commitment

Rock Health released a decidedly mixed report on the current state of Digital Health investing, as the data suggest many investors continue to tentatively explore the sector, but most have yet to make a serious commitment.

Overall, VC funding for digital health increased significantly over the past year, from just under $1B in 2011 to about $1.4B in 2012; 20% of this total was associated with just five deals: two raises for transparency companies, Castlight (targeting employees with high deductible plans looking to manage their costs) and GoHealth (targeting consumers contemplating purchase of health insurance); two raises for referral companies, Care.com (helps consumers find the right caregiver—defined broadly, as needs addressed include eldercare, child tutoring, babysitting, and pet care) and BestDoctors(helps employees find the right doctor), and one deal for 23andMe (a pioneering consumer genetics company).

Not surprisingly, the largest thematic area of investment ($237M) was "health consumer engagement," comprised of companies that—like the first four above—help consumers or employees with health care purchases. "Personal health tools and tracking," the second leading category, captured $143M in funding last year. "EMR/EHR" ($108M) and "hospital administration" ($78M) rounded out the list; the last two numbers seem shockingly low given the apparent size of these markets, and suggest both areas may be perceived as firmly owned by incumbent players, and prohibitively difficult for new participants to enter.

Athenahealth's acquisition of Epocrates highlights the competitive pressures even existing EMR companies face as they struggle for traction in an environment that seems to be increasingly dominated by a few large players, most notably Epic. "Our biggest obstacle," Athenahealth CEO Jonathan Bush told Bloomberg Businessweek, "is that 70% of doctors don't even know we exist." In contrast, I've suggested that a category I'd broadly define as EMR adjacencies may be primed for growth, as VC's Stephen Kraus and Ambar Bhattacharyya have also discussed recently in this intelligent post. The related area of care transitions is also attracting considerable entrepreneurial interest, including current Rock Health portfolio companies WellFrame and OpenPlacement, and TechStars alum Careport; it remains to be seen whether a robust business model will emerge here.

Rock Health's analysis of deals revealed that while 179 different organizations participated in at least one significant ($2M or greater) digital health financing in 2012, the vast majority were single investments; only a handful of organizations invested in three or more digital health companies. This could be because most investors are only willing to dip their toe in, but not make a serious commitment (especially common among traditional tech-oriented investors); in other cases, a commitment to the sector might exist, but suitable investments could not be found (something I've heard from several seasoned healthcare VCs). Or, it could simply reflect where some funds are in their investment cycle.

The most active 2012 investors (3+ digital health investments) break out into two general groups, strategic and traditional. The strategics include a telecommunication company, Qualcomm; the insurer, BlueCross BlueShield; Merck, surprisingly the only biopharma venture group represented in the "active investor" category; and West Health, a nonprofit focused on reducing the cost of healthcare, funded by entrepreneur-philanthropists Gary and Mary West.

The most active traditional VCs include Aberdare Ventures, which has emerged as a highly respected player in the space (partner Darren Hite seems to be emerging as a crowd favorite); NEA, a behemoth (closing a $2.6B fund last July) with long-standing interests in healthcare, life-science, and technology; and Khosla Ventures, reflecting Vinod's much-discussed commitment to this area. Council Capital, a Tennessee-based private equity firm, rounded out Rock Health's list of most active digital health investors.

One conclusion emerging from the investor data is that there certainly doesn't seem to be a single dominant investment firm in this space, or even a handful that stand out significantly above the others. This was reinforced in my mind by an informal, non-scientific survey I recently conducted among a handful of digital health thought leaders, asking who they would designate as the most important digital health investors. The result was a striking lack of any consensus, and no firm emerged as particularly dominant. The distinction "most impactful digital health VC" is clearly up for grabs. I suspect that a few good exits could change the investor landscape appreciably—and intensify the competition. Easier said than done, of course, as "a few good exits" is not a sure thing—a lesson many life science venture firms, in particular, have learned through bitter experience.

Perhaps the most striking, and disheartening, findings in the 2012 Rock Health report involved the digital health companies themselves. The typical digital health CEO, it turns out, looks (to my eyes, anyway) a lot like a typical tech CEO—a male with a bachelors or MBA. Only 7% of digital health CEOs are women, and only 5% of digital health CEOs are MDs; other essential clinical professionals, such as RNs, don't appear to be represented at all. (In contrast, about a third of practicing physicians, and about half of current med school graduates are women—and both fractions are on the rise.) Furthermore, while there seem to be a number of job opportunities now available in digital health, according to the Rock Health Report, the two leading categories are "engineering/IT" (33%) and "business/ops" (32%), again a breakdown that seems grossly similar to what you'd expect from a tech startup, but perhaps not what you might look for in a health company.

Concluding Thoughts:

The view of digital health that emerges from the 2012 Rock Health report is an industry that looks a lot like a (complex) subcategory of traditional tech. This will certainly get us more consumer-facing wellness products, such as diet apps and activity monitors, that tend to amuse for a few weeks but generally have little sustained health impact (see this savvy, critical assessment from AllThingsDigital's Bonnie Cha).

The current thinking in digital health may also be fine for producing the next generation of scheduling software and rating platforms that may help us identify and take advantage of existing medical treatments in a cost-effective fashion, enabling us to optimize what I've described as "attained health"—see here, here, and here.

But at least for the moment, digital health investments seem to fall far short of delivering innovations that meaningfully push the diagnostic and therapeutic frontier. The road from data to clinical impact, as Tory Wolff and I recently discussed, is long and difficult; just as life scientists learned that a gene sequence is not a drug, data scientists are discovering that information is not a cure.

Yet, improved treatments must remain the ultimate goal of digital health; we must aspire to leave our children with something more than just the best practices of today. – DS

Life Science VCs: Definitively Indefinite About Digital Health

Many of the earliest investors in digital health have been tech investors such as Vinod Khosla, who believe that, as Khosla puts it, "mobile devices, big data, and artificial intelligence will disrupt health care," and who presumably hope they can leverage their expertise in these technologies to help identify potential winners.

Life-science investors—in part because they often don't have the money to spend—have moved more cautiously, despite the fact that they arguably have the best understanding of the medical problems to be solved, as well as the most experience working with the relevant stakeholders, from payers and regulators to doctors and patients.

The ambivalence was nicely captured earlier this week by two contrasting reactions from early-stage life-science shops in Boston. In an interview with Xconomy's Luke Timmerman discussing Third Rock Venture's recently closed third fund and plans for the future, partner Bob Tepper was asked about plans to explore healthcare IT and other areas besides drugs and devices. His response?

"Healthcare IT is an area we're looking at a lot. We're intrigued by it. It's a really important area, but I'd say to be fair, we still have to learn a bit more about the right strategies there, and how it's going to evolve. The role of the government in the whole healthcare revamping will impact things significantly in that space. I'd say we're going to do a little more homework in that area and get more expertise, but I certainly think it's a possibility for the future."

In other words, they're still kicking the tires.

On the other hand, PureTech Ventures (technically not a venture fund, but an "institutional entrepreneur") has backed at least one digital health company, Akili (profiled last year by the ever-present Luke Timmerman in Xconomy Here), and just announced they are seeking applications for an entrepreneur-in-residence to help them build a new digital health enterprise.

Clearly, a few life-science VC's, such as Venrock (notably partner Bob Kocher, a driving force behind Castlight Health) seem to share PureTech's evident enthusiasm for digital health and health services. Fidelity Biosciences(disclosure: I spent some time there about eight years ago) and Aberdare Ventures also seem to have moved deliberately into the digital health and health services space.

Yet many others are hesitant to make the leap. As Domain's Nimesh Shah Commented on Twitter, "most digiHC simply disease mgmt or consumer internet w/ HC twist. Few can be real business," adding, "Hype takes you only so far; you need a real biz model 2 win," and observing that healthcare IT "has way more sizzle than steak." Finally, he suggests that the current interest in digital health may be "merely a bubble. All signs are there. Cleantech anyone?"

Perhaps reflecting these concerns, a number of leading life-science VCs (from what I can discern)—including firms with plenty of cash (such as OrbiMed) and with experience successfully navigating early-stage risk (such as Atlas) have to this point generally shunned digital health.

Other firms with deep pockets, such as NEA and KPCB, seem to be cautiously dabbling, but not really jumping in feet first. According to Misfit Wearables Sonny Vu, via Twitter, Kleiner is "watching" six areas: "EMR, home health monitoring, insurance models, chronic disease management, telemedicine, health big data," an everything-but-the-kitchen-sink list that doesn't suggest (or at least reveal) more specific insight.

While digital health is certainly enjoying its moment in the sun (e.g. Eric Topol, California's answer to Cory Booker, on Colbert), the ability to attract at least traditional (vs strategic—see here) venture investors will naturally depend on the exits achieved (though even this need not limit funds that manage their PR correctly—as TheStreet's tart-thumbed Adam Feuerstein commented on Twitter, Third Rock may have more funds than exits).

It's not just the number or size of the digital health exits that matter, but also who drove the investment. For example, a big exit for Castlight, say, would not only increase enthusiasm for the sector, but would highlight the value of deep healthcare experience in identifying and nurturing promising investments. On the other hand, if Practice Fusion manages a big exit, it's likely to be seen as a victory for the tech folks, and a testament to the power of their vision. Of course, many worry there won't be any significant exits at all.

I confess to being an optimist here: while I agree with Shah (and many others) who highlight the absence of clear revenue models in many digital health startups, I remain incredibly excited by the opportunity space here, by the urgent need for impact, and by the value that could be generated by the thoughtful, integrated synergy of tech and healthcare, working together both to build new digital health companies, and also to fund them.

Digital Health: It's On

Digital health has waited—for a very long time—to be taken seriously by investors; I suspect the moment has finally arrived.

To get a sense of why, consider the strategy associated with the recently-announced hire by Aberdare Ventures of Dr. Mohit Kaushal, an appointment discussed intelligently both by my colleague Zina Moukheiber here, and by Brian Dolan of MobiHealthNews here.

"Mo's joining is sort of a capstone of a recent aggressive period of strategic evolution for us," Aberdere's founding partner, Paul Kligenstein told Dolan, who continues,

"Klingenstein explained that Aberdare's investment strategy has changed markedly in recent years, and it's not a simple shift away from traditional life sciences companies or medical device companies in favor of digital health ones. Klingenstein explains it as a shift away from investments in companies that lead to more expensive, incrementally better healthcare to companies that provide 'transformational technology' that 'tie together to drive efficiency in care for the system, for the individual, and for payers.'

"'If you look at our portfolio today it's clear these types of companies cover the gamut: information tools to help people take their drugs, information tools to gather data in doctor's office, sensors that communicate with systems to perform analytics, and information tools to help people do clinical trials to discover drugs better,' he said.

"Klingenstein said their latest investments stand in contrast to the way Aberdare and others investing in healthcare have been doing it for years."

My sense is that Kaushal at Aberdare and Dr. Bob Kocher at Venrock Represent the next incarnation of healthcare venture capitalists—joining a select group of investors including Lisa Suennen of Psilos , Dr. Bijan Salehizadeh of NaviMed, Steven Kraus of Bessemer, Todd Pietri of Milestone, and Jack Young of Qualcomm, who arguably have all been ahead of the curve here (disclosure: I know both Lisa and Bijan), in the same way that Eric Topol and Paul Sonnier have been out in front on the adoption and dissemination side.

Further evidence for digital health's emergence may be found in the announcement—at the high-profile "D-Dive Into Mobile" Conference—of a new digital health company, called

Better, founded by Geoff Clapp (who I also know).

Better—which apparently seeks to help patients access health information, and potentially services, through a relationship with the Mayo Clinic—is significant not so much because of the vision (perhaps promising, though it's far too early to get a sense of whether or not the approach will succeed), but because of its founder—Clapp—and its funder—"Social+Capital Partnership" (S+C).

Clapp, the former CTO of HealthHero, has been what might be described as the unofficial "operations" partner at Rock Health, providing vital mentorship to the many companies associated with this digital health incubator. He obviously has been immersed in the space for quite a while, and his decision to jump into the mix as a founder suggests the opportunity he's identified cleared a sophisticated critical bar.

Meanwhile, S+C—the fund started by former Facebook VP Chamath Palihapitiya—seems to be the Valley VC of the moment, enjoying the sort of buzz most recently experienced by the likes of Andreessen-Horowitz and Founders Fund. It has not shied away from healthcare technology and services, investing in Asthmapolis, Synapse, Glooko, and Flatiron Health.

Notably, S+C recently raised their second fund, and the Mayo Clinic was reported by TechCrunch to be one of their LPs. Palihapitiya's stated investment goal is to create social as well as financial returns, and it's encouraging to see that digital health is now recognized as an area where both may be possible.

It will be even more encouraging when (not "if") the results—measured by both health and dollars—validate this bold, optimistic thesis. – DS

XII.

Innovation

You Say You Want A Healthcare Revolution

A while back I had the pleasure of attending a "salon" type dinner hosted by Xconomy and its chief correspondent and San Francisco editor Wade Roush (graciously sponsored by Silicon Valley Bank and Alexandria Real Estate Equities). The dinner included about 24 people, all of whom in some way had a connection to the emerging field of digital health. In addition to the sponsors, the group featured many CEOs of newly minted companies, some highly experienced and at their second or third rodeo, and some very new to the big desk in the corner. Also present were a few industry thought leader and advisor types, including representatives of Rock Health and Singularity University, as well as a few venture investors, just to be sure all the air would get sucked out of the room. Because the dinner was meant to be off the record, I have not attributed points below to specific individuals.

The theme of the dinner was "The Quest to Disrupt Health Care," and at the beginning of dinner we started around the room to introduce ourselves and to answer the question posed by Wade, which was, "What is the single largest headache you face in your business that, if solved, would lead to exponential growth?" It was a very thought-provoking question. I was struck by the fact that while other topics came up, the one that rang out loud and clear was this: the healthcare industry, particularly that defined by traditional institutions such as payers and providers, is just not interested in or committed to innovation.

It was an interesting perspective to hear from entrepreneurs, who have bet the entire farm in many cases that their newfangled idea will change healthcare, make them rich, and/or make them famous. (FYI: venture capitalists always prefer the ones who want to be rich over those who want to be famous—it's all about alignment of incentives.) In fact, one attendee kicked off the conversation by saying she had recently attended a big conference on innovation that had one session about innovative disruption in healthcare and that no one showed up for it. Instead attendees chose sessions about gaming and social media while the crickets chirped uninterrupted in the healthcare room. Another dinner mate characterized this issue from a different perspective, talking about how the great minds in Silicon Valley need to be focused on changing health care rather than on stealing attention by building things like Twitter and games. Or, to say it in a way people will understand, #getonboardthehealthcareinnovationtrainpeopleorwearedoomed.

There was a lot of talk about how the FDA is limiting innovation, or at least potentially so, through regulatory foot-dragging that makes it far more costly and time-consuming to get products to customers, but that wasn't the crux of the concern (and some of us didn't really agree that was a significant limiting factor in digital health at all). Rather the focus of the conversation was how traditional buyers of healthcare solutions talk the innovation talk, but when it comes right down to it, are not interested in paying for it. One health IT CEO summed it up by saying that the healthcare field is afraid of innovation, resulting in impossibly long sales cycles and chief information officers who are risk-averse because they have had a few bad experiences. There was a discussion about how payers and provider systems in particular will dip their toes in the water with small innovation pilots, but in the end rarely commit to rolling out big new ideas, leaving their co-pilots, the entrepreneurs, high and dry and drifting at sea Amelia Earhart-style.

Extending that thought, one of the field's thought leaders argued that an obsession over who pays and who reimburses for healthcare solutions is limiting the imaginations of entrepreneurs.

You say you got a real solution

Well, you know

We'd all love to see the plan

You ask me for a contribution

Well, you know

We're doing what we can

—The Beatles

Inevitably this discussion about how little true innovation is valued in healthcare led to a corollary discussion about how this manifests itself in a lack of funding for early stage companies that are bringing healthcare innovations to the fore. The entrepreneurs at the dinner were almost universally frustrated in their quest to find conventional sources of financial backing for their ideas. Many of them described a venture capital field that has mirrored the risk aversion of the buyer market, leaving healthcare innovators to max out their credit cards and do damn near everything short of selling pencils on a street corner to find ways to finance their ideas for revolutionizing the universally acknowledged mess of a healthcare system.

Those investors among us who caught the arrows slung by our dinner companions described the conundrum that we face because our own backers, the community of institutional limited partners, is wholly unimpressed with healthcare returns and as a result is uninterested in shifting money away from finding the next Instagram. It is classic trickle-down economics: it's a struggle for VCs to raise investment capital to fund healthcare innovation, so there isn't much to hand out to those seeking it to deliver healthcare innovation. The good news is that we are starting to see the emergence of nontraditional limited partners (e.g., corporations with a strategic interest and socially-oriented non-profit foundations) investing with a combined business and social mission that is squarely focused on improving the healthcare system. But the volume of capital they bring to the market is nowhere near enough to finance the changes in the system we all know we need. While there are still a few healthcare-focused VCs, those targeting seed and early stage investments are a bit like white tigers—a genetic mutation known to exist in nature but rarely seen with the human eye.

It is a worrisome state of affairs, in my opinion, to breed a generation of highly frustrated entrepreneurs who ultimately throw up their hands to go build photo sharing websites, or worse, turn to other countries more eager to fund the healthcare innovation that should be Made in the USA. We are already seeing evidence that innovation leadership is moving offshore to India and China and elsewhere in the medical device industry as similar issues surfaced in that sector. We had better be careful or health care IT will follow behind it, leaving us with Flintstones-era technology and technology-enabled (disabled?) services while we watch Medicare lapse into insolvency, taking the rest of our economy with it.

Revolutionizing the U.S. healthcare system is truly a matter of national economic security. Nibbling at the edges simply isn't going to cut it. We need to fundamentally and profoundly change the way our citizens care for themselves by helping them have access to healthy food choices and preventative health products and services, while ensuring that those who are sick get treated in a way that delivers true value, both in terms of quality and cost. We don't really have the time for incrementalism. Medicare hits the insolvency brick wall around 2024 and it's is estimated that our current trajectory will bring the U.S. from our current $2.8 trillion national healthcare spend to $4.8 trillion by 2020—only slightly more than the likely M&A purchase price of the next Instagram. – LS

Eye On The Prize

There has been a lot of talk in healthcare circles about the concept of "gamification," a super-annoying made-up word that means turning health tasks into games so they are more engaging and people are more willing to do them. People and companies are coming up with all sorts of games for kids with asthma and diabetes to learn good medical compliance and for adults who need the extra incentive to do their exercise and comply with their chronic care regimens, among others. Michelle Obama even sponsored a big contest to foster the creation of games to sponsor healthy eating and virtually every large health insurance company is now offering various forms of incentive game and points programs for taking better care of oneself. You can get frequent flyer points for taking United Airlines and "personal rewards" points, that you can turn into cash, for being insured by United Healthcare.

We Americans just love our games and nothing sells like a healthy competition. Just witness the insanity of prime time television and you will see people attempting feats that they never would have done (losing hundreds of pounds, surviving extreme conditions, baring their souls in front of Simon Cowell) if it weren't for the big juicy cash prize at the end of the rainbow. Vanna, can I buy a vowel?

So it was with this thought in my mind that I recently attended the X Prize Radical Benefit for Humanity (thanks, Qualcomm guys, for inviting me!). The event was a fundraiser/auction for the X Prize Foundation, which describes itself as: "the leading nonprofit organization solving the world's Grand Challenges by creating and managing large-scale, high profile, incentivized price competitions that stimulate investment in research and development with far more than the price itself. The organization motivates and inspires brilliant innovators from all disciplines to leverage their intellectual and financial capital for the benefit of humanity."

The X Prize Foundation made its name in 2004 when it awarded its first $10 million prize to aerospace designer Burt Rutan and former MicroSoft leader Paul Allen for building and launching a spacecraft capable of carrying three people to 100 kilometers above the earth's surface and then repeat the mission within two weeks.   This was the first time in history that private sub-orbital space flight had been accomplished in any significant way without the intervention or funding of government. Interestingly, Dr. Peter Diamandis

(Chair and CEO of the X Prize Foundation), founded the Ansari X Prize after being inspired by learning of the Orteig Prize, a $25,000 challenge sponsored by a rich NY hotelier in 1927. The winner of the Orteig Prize would be the first person to fly nonstop from New York to Paris. Winner: Charles Lindbergh. Spirit of St. Louis, come on down! I guess we Americans have been contest-motivated for a long time.

Today the X Prize has diversified to include not just space travel, but also environmental, energy and, most interesting to me, several life science challenges.

The X Prize benefit in San Francisco was a very swank affair (we're talking sequins, baby) filled with the San Francisco glitterati and me. Ali Velshi, Chief Business Reporter for CNN was the evening's master of ceremonies, doing double duty with movie producer and entrepreneur James Cameron (turns out that, in fact, he IS king of the world). Cameron, an X Prize Trustee, said that "most of humanity's challenges can be solved by small teams using new technologies," and that we are entering a "new golden age of exploration" in which "ideas that could once only be done by government" can be realized by regular people given the right incentives. In fact, hanging prominently in the room where the various current and past X Prize challenges were displayed before the gala dinner began was a sign that really got my attention, "You are what you incentivize."

That is a very interesting thought. It implies that it takes eye-popping financial incentives and somewhat dramatic gestures to spur real breakthrough innovation and that, conversely, without such incentives, profound innovation is unlikely. Let that settle in for a moment, as it is a slightly worrisome thought, at least to me. Considering the unbelievable amount of money that is already spent to spur research and development of new ideas through government, universities, industry and my own field, venture capital, it is interesting to think that it may take a gameshow approach to get truly profound innovation. Ladies and Gentlemen, come on down! You can be the next contestant on The Price is Right if you change the world for the better!

Those of us who have kids are constantly trying to stay "above" the bribery thing, hoping our kids will do what we tell them to do without a financial pay-off. Yet lets be honest, almost all of us succumb to the act of paying the little weasels in cash or TV time or whatever currency moves them to do things they should do just to make us happy (yeah, right). The idea behind the X Prize and many of these other cash-prize contests is, in some way, right up this alley. Yes, some innovation can and will happen on its own, but if you slap $10 million bucks on the table and a short list of seemingly impossible requirements, innovation will show up faster and better and with a cherry on top. Son of a bitch, it seems to work.

The X Prize event got me thinking hard about the recent upsurge I have seen in challenges and prize competitions and the like in the healthcare field. Clearly the healthcare field is broken to the point of disaster and legions industry veterans have done little to fix that. It isn't hard to understand that those who have always done things a certain way are somewhat hamstrung by the fact that they benefit greatly from keeping things the way they are, even if it does not serve the greater good. Their incentive, for better or for worse, is to keep the status quo even if it is everyone's ultimate undoing.

Charging into the void has been a mounting series of cash-prize competitions sponsored by the government, private industry and a variety of nonprofit entities, including the X Prize Foundation. A couple of examples:

- The Office of the National Coordinator for Health Information Technology (ONC) within the Department of Health and Human Services (HHS) has committed nearly $5 million in U.S. government funds to its Investing in Innovation (i2) program, which was formed under the American Competes Reauthorization Act of 2010. The Act authorizes federal agencies to create challenges to further innovation and about 30 such challenges with prize money are in the works. The competitions focus on innovations that support widespread Health IT adoption and meaningful use, ONC's and HHS' programs and programmatic goals, and systems that improve quality, safety, and/or efficiency of health care. The I2 Program is being administered by Health 2.0, which also administers a number of similar healthcare IT prize programs for other organizations (fyi, I'm on the advisory board for the I2 Program). Notably, NASA and the Defense Department have formed challenges similar to ONC.

- Heritage Provider Network, a network of doctors and medical groups in California, is touting its answer to health-care innovation: a $3 million prize to the person who can derive an algorithm to can identify patients who will be admitted to a hospital within the next year, using historical claims data in order to prevent unnecessary readmissions.

- The Center for the Integration of Medicine and Technology (CIMIT) has announced their Fourth Annual CIMIT Prize for Primary Health Care, sponsored by the Gelfand Family Charitable Trust, a $400,000 competition for engineering students to help foster solutions that improve access to medical care, leverage the skill of caregivers, automate routine tasks, increase workflow efficiency, support patients managing chronic disease, increase compliance with care protocols, reduce medical error, or augment the physician-patient relationship.

- Back to the X Prize, they have some pretty amazing activities in process. Medco has sponsored the $10 million Archon Genomics prize that will be won by the team that can sequence 100 human genomes in ten days for less than $10,000 per sample. [This was subsequently cancelled, "outpaced by innovation."] Other prizes are actively in the works to incentivize dramatic advances in the field of predicting/treating Alzheimer's (Biogen IDEC to sponsor) and to build a mobile diagnostic tool for consumers, ideally around a smartphone, that will be capable of accurately diagnosing at least 15 diseases without the intervention of a doctor (Qualcomm is working on this one). Qualcomm told me that their concept, to be named the Tricorder Challenge, is to make the consumer the CEO of their own healthcare. What a great concept. It is worth noting that a kid-oriented healthcare X Prize competition got a troop of 12-year old Girl Scouts $20,000 for inventing a biomedical device that allows children with disfigured hands to write with a pencil or pen just like their friends. You go girl scouts.

This is by no means a complete list of the prizes being offered for people who can come up with dramatic breakthroughs to advance a healthier healthcare system. If you can wrap a game around it and attach a nice cash prize, you too can spur innovation and engagement. And yes, while it makes me somewhat uneasy to think that it's always the financial incentives that get people motivated to make a difference, I think it is rapidly becoming my final answer.

While not quite the same, I lived a recent example of this gamification (aack, I hate that word) thing; I got to serve as "the bachelorette" at San Diego Venture Group's recent breakfast event, entitled The Dating Game: Who Can Best Transform Healthcare, where I got to ask questions of 3 entrepreneurs hidden behind a partition in order to determine which one got to win a "date" with me to pitch their business based on which idea had the most potential. Yeah, I know what you're thinking: second prize is two dates with me. It was a really fun event with around 250 people in the audience, no doubt interested because we just love our game shows and the usual format for such events, a bunch of talking heads on a panel, is oh so yesterday. The only thing missing was the groovy Dating Game music. Note: if you are too young to remember the Dating Game then I do not want to hear from you.

Circling back to the X Prize benefit event, the presentation that really grabbed my attention was the one about the recently awarded Wendy Schmidt Oil Cleanup X Challenge. In this challenge, $1 million was up for grabs for the team able to build a new device capable of massively increasing (by at least 2x) the ability to extract oil from seawater after a spill.

While the third prize winner of this challenge was–and I swear this is true–a bunch of guys from a tattoo parlor that were able to just about hit that 2x mark with their invention, the big winner was Team Elastec, which is comprised of workers from an existing manufacturer of oil spill equipment. They were able to come up with a machine that performed at 4x the industry best, sucking up oil like breadsticks at an Olive Garden. That is pretty awesome, particularly given what happened in the oceans outside Louisiana and Mississippi earlier this year, but it made me wonder why these guys, who are already paid to do exactly the task of building oil clean-up equipment, hadn't innovated to this level as part of their regular jobs. I find it fascinating that it took the X Prize, with its goal to do something the industry veterans thought impossible (hit that 2x improvement mark) in order to get this company to rise to and even blow out, the challenge. Shouldn't they have been doing that anyway to keep their company ahead of the pack? What does this say about American corporate ingenuity?

I think it is this particular example that gave me the most pause in thinking about how much we love our games and need to have the gauntlet thrown down to take on the impossible. We are going to have to figure out how to put some of that drive into our regular everyday culture to stay at the top of the innovation food chain. There isn't always $10 million lying around to foster innovation and it worries me to think that every great breakthrough might have to have a contest attached to it. Another question I have, particularly as I have seen what has come out of some of the healthcare challenges that have already occurred, is whether they spur great businesses or just great technologies. Technology is often critical to the making of a great business, but it isn't enough. There has to be a market willing to buy and a plan to execute. Virtually none of the healthcare challenges I have seen put any value on these latter issues.

Don't get me wrong, I think that the philosophy behind the X Prize and other challenges is really intriguing: by challenging people to do what is believed impossible you make it possible. Certainly the results they and others like them have inspired would suggest they are on to something very real. It would just be great if that drive to reach unparalleled heights of innovation could come from within some of the time and not from the chance to beat out some other guy to get there. Competition can definitely be healthy, but it just feels odd to me to think that is the only way to get big things done. And if competition leads to great research, but not great opportunity to spread an idea far and wide through great business execution, it will be for naught. It would be great to see some of those business-related criteria wrapped into the judging mix.

Anyway, I think the best part of the X Prize benefit evening (other than the fact that I won 4 VIP tickets to see Wheel of Fortune being filmed—I swear this is true and God I love irony), was a poetry slam performance by Sekou Andrews and Steven Connell, who call themselves "motivational poets." They sang/spoke/rapped with unbelievable enthusiasm and skill and got a standing ovation for their piece which was a story about a kid who was told it was impossible to fly so he climbs to the top of a jungle gym in the park and leaps off. Yeah, he gets a bit clobbered when he hits the ground, but the punch line was, "hey, I flew didn't I?" Among the memorable lines from this awesome performance were, "It's my world to change, I don't need you to *let* me," and an admonition to anyone who is told the words "you can't" to respond with the words, "wanna bet?!" You gotta love that spirit, even if it does come in the form of a question, Jeopardy-style. – LS

Using Crowdcasting To Find Treatments For The Paralyzed

An inspirational article from the *New York Times* highlights the intelligent use of open innovation to accelerate (hopefully) drug development—in this case, for the dreadful condition, amyotrophic lateral sclerosis (ALS), also known as Lou Gehrig's disease.

Prize4Life, an organization founded by Avichai Kremer and classmates at Harvard Business School after Kremer was diagnosed with ALS, seeks to accelerate research towards a cure by funding prize-based competitions. Dr. Seward Rutkove, a neurologist at Boston's Beth Israel-Deaconess Medical Center, was awarded a $1M prize by Prize4Life for his development of an approach to more rapidly assess disease progression.

Two features of this accomplishment warrant particular consideration. First, Dr. Rutkove's discovery emphasizes the potential value of open innovation in developing new medicines. Open innovation (as a colleague and I discussed in the *Boston Globe*) describes a set of approaches that seek solutions broadly, rather than from a pre-specified group of solvers, and recognizes that in the words of Silicon Valley Pioneer Bill Joy, "No matter who you are, most of the smartest people work for someone else."

A prize competition is a classic example of a particular open innovation approach called crowdcasting; the idea is to specify the problem to be solved, and then solicit responses from a wide range of potential solvers. Often—although admittedly not in this instance—solvers come from places you might not expect; for example, when Procter & Gamble wanted help developing a particular type of dish detergent, they tapped the pioneering broadcast search platform InnoCentive, to elicit solutions. And they found it—in Perugia, Italy, where Giorgia Sgargetta, a chemist with a home laboratory came up with the solution.

Other well-known open innovation approaches include crowdsourcing (the "wisdom of the crowd" premise that often collective intelligence exceeds that of any individual expert), and swarming (the approach used to develop Wikipedia, and also in programming competitions such as this example from MATLAB).

The real value of open innovation may transcend the specific advances delivered by these approaches—rather, it may be in helping us recognize the limitations of our own knowledge, and to appreciate how much underappreciated wisdom may be out there. Embracing open innovation—even internally(!)—might be especially valuable for big corporations, as it offers the potential to disrupt traditional hierarchies and siloed thinking, and capture the value of the exceptional human capital within large companies that often remains untapped.

The other feature of the Prize4Life award worth pointing out is that it was awarded not for a cure for ALS, but rather for a biomarker, an early read of disease progression. This is important because the ability to rapidly figure out whether or not a drug is working can enable clinical trials that might otherwise be too complicated or expensive for a drug company to pursue. What Prize4Life—and other forward-thinking patient advocacy groups, such as the Michael J Fox Foundation—recognize is both the urgency and complexity of biomarker development. While medical product companies clearly embrace the concept of biomarkers, and while useful biomarkers can dramatically accelerate drug development, the process of identifying—and ultimately qualifying—adequate biomarkers turns out to be a monumental challenge, in many ways as difficult as development of the drugs themselves. While many academic papers report candidate biomarkers, the unfortunate reality is that most are not nearly robust enough for high-stakes decision-making.

Hopefully, Dr. Rutkove's promising biomarker will prove reliable enough to catalyze the discovery and development of new, effective medicines for ALS; Avichai Kremer, and thousands like him, cannot afford to wait much longer. – DS

Medicine's Next Great Challenge: Returning Science To Patients

"You can't improve what you don't measure," first-year MBA students are taught. Yet physicians struggle every day to take care of patients based on remarkably sparse information, a nearly impossible task that has frustrated doctors and patients, and raised healthcare costs for everyone. It doesn't have to be this way—but change will require a more deliberate focus on the real-world patients we're trying to treat.

When you think about great biomedical advances of the modern age, you think of our profound advances in molecular understanding—the precise analysis of DNA, for example, or the study of stem cell biology. The progress we've made in taking science from the patient's bedside to the laboratory bench has been nothing short of exceptional. The problem is that we've had a lot more trouble moving in the other direction: returning science to patients, and translating laboratory results into clinical progress.

We've had a particularly hard time with the final and most important step in research translation—the gap between the clinical practice of medicine and health as it's experienced in real life, every day, by real people. It has become increasingly clear that the next great wave of innovation in medicine will—must—revolve around this gap and how to close it.

Consider your last visit to a doctor—if you can remember that far back. Most likely, your physician took a hurried history, performed a brief physical exam, and perhaps requested several laboratory tests or an imaging study. You may then have been given some advice, likely a prescription as well, and then you are gone, lost to the system until you decide—or need—to return again.

Even if your doctor is an expert diagnostician, and ordered just the right tests, how much did she really learn about you and your health, about how your body and mind were doing during the time since your previous visit? Even she made treatment recommendations informed by the robust clinical studies, does she know how closely you've chosen to follow her advice, or what other activities, behavior, or habits you may have adopted that could be influencing your health?

The limited visibility your physician has into your health has implications for her as well as for you. Without a functional feedback loop, without a way of reliably connecting what she is doing in the office with the results—improved health—she is trying to achieve, she is effectively flying blind. She has no way of figuring out the right interventions for you and other patients, and no way to learn what she's doing particularly well and where she might improve.

This has profound implications for our healthcare system as well: with so much of our GDP devoted to healthcare costs, it's important to figure out how to deliver care—as measured by improvements in the real health of real patients—as effectively as possible, and to ensure that doctors are using the most effective treatment approaches for each patient seen.

Solving these problems will require investment in a concept we call "continuity-inspired medicine" (CIM), an approach to medical research and practice that aims to be closer to the patient in both space and time, and will be built on a foundation of more personalized measurement.

"Measure something," legendary endocrinologist Fuller Albright would admonish his students. As usual, Dr. Albright was onto something: measurement matters, and it's essential that we develop improved approaches that will provide a much fuller understanding of patients in their daily lives, including technologies that can monitor a range of physiological factors, such as blood pressure, oxygen saturation, and glucose level, as well as many other factors we're just starting to contemplate.

We will also need to develop robust approaches that can meaningfully assess psychological well-being and quality of life, and to capture more completely the behaviors that can impact health, including diet and activity level, prescription adherence and subtle habits.

Here's the catch: while everyone wants to be healthy, most of us don't want to spend our time thinking about our health, measuring our health, reporting our health; a key challenge of the new medicine will be coming up with techniques that are not only minimally invasive, but also minimally intrusive. This is a difficult but not impossible task: early examples of this approach include pill bottles that automatically report when they've been opened and activity monitoring using smart phones.

Improvements in measurement (imagine months worth of data summarized on a simple dashboard) will enable providers to understand with much greater precision and nuance the effects of their recommendations and to see what sorts of approaches work best for each patient—the opportunity to personalize therapy based on a patient's distinctive physiological and behavioral characteristics as well as their unique DNA. Better measurements—together with improved, accessible data registries—will also enable the sort of progressive, incremental improvement in health delivery that is nearly impossible without a functional feedback system.

The evolution towards more personalized measurement will also have implications for the private sector, creating exciting opportunities for the entrepreneurs and companies who will develop these novel technologies, methods, and data management systems. A more detailed view of existing medical need will also enable drug and device companies to sharpen their focus, and to develop products in a more efficient and effective fashion.

Creating the personalized healthcare system of the future will require the combined efforts of universities and industry, regulators and entrepreneurs. But more than anything else, it will require an unprecedented level of participation from patients themselves, whose willingness to contribute to this effort and share of themselves will ultimately drive the success of this initiative.

A decade ago, it would have been difficult to imagine such a level of patient participation. But in the era of Facebook, we now understand that not only is possible for medicine to move closer to patient, but patients will increasingly expect it, and demand it.

As usual, it will be our patients who are teaching us—and our responsibility to ensure we are listening. – DS + Dennis Ausiello

Balancing Disruptive Innovation And Progressive Progress In Medicine And Business

How can I change the world? I ask myself this question every day. It's the standard against which I measure myself, and seek to calibrate success. I admire those who've achieved this, and reserved my greatest admiration for those who try. And I know I'm not alone. Recently, however, I've started to wonder whether by glamorizing the Next Big Thing, I—we—have undervalued the importance and the impact of the day-to-day. Have we glorified the virtue of unrestrained ambition while minimizing the worth of structured effort?

* * *

Let's begin with a story I first heard from the late Dr. Judah Folkman, a surgeon and pioneering medical researcher at Harvard. Folkman explained his mission by telling the tale of a man, our protagonist, who was walking by a river when he heard someone call out for assistance mid-stream; immediately, a passerby jumped into the water to rescue the drowning person. A few minutes later, another drowning person called out, and again, a passer-by jumped into and rescued him; it happened a third time as well. At this point, our protagonist, who had been carefully observing the successive rescue missions, started to walk purposefully upstream. "Where are you going," one of the rescuers cried, dripping wet. "Aren't you going to help save these struggling swimmers?" To which our protagonist replied, "I am: I intend to find out who's throwing them in."

Through this parable, intended to highlight the role of the inquisitive physician, Folkman captured the ambition of medical research perfectly: to understand the fundamental basis of illness and use this knowledge to transform medical practice. It seems like a dead-on description of just the sort of disruptive innovation (PDF) Clayton Christensen describes.

I've always found this ideal incredibly compelling; the people I've most admired and wanted to emulate growing up were just these sorts of medical researchers, seeking to use basic knowledge to drive transformative change. And in some cases, these investigators, including Judah Folkman, have been remarkably successful—they set out to revolutionize medicine and succeeded.

Over time, however, I've developed both a greater skepticism of the transformative potential of much of the basic research that I've seen as well as a deeper appreciation for the people who are actually jumping in the water day after day to rescue the drowning swimmers. If you were to add up the contributions of the two groups over the course of a career, I suspect most of the ambitious physician-scientists I know will wind up contributing only marginally (at best) to the practice of medicine, while the clinicians will have steadily (if perhaps incrementally) impacted thousands of lives.

The familiar partitioning in medicine into those who set out to change the world and those who aim to perform their daily tasks with excellence seems intrinsically unhealthy, and to the extent that the medical community has implicitly endorsed this mindset (perhaps as a consequence of what geneticist Richard Lewontin famously described in the *New York Review of Books* as our fetishization of DNA, and by extension molecular medicine and the reductionist approach in general), it has contributed to the problem.

Historically, many of the most important innovations, inside and outside of medicine, have not come from a separate class of researcher-kings, but rather from the men and women in the arena, and in particular from clinicians struggling to understand and help the patients in front of them—something Folkman himself (a practicing surgeon for most of his career) keenly appreciated.

Perhaps, as medicine recognizes the limitations of the preclinical models, and returns the focus of medical science to the patient (see here and here), we will look with greater respect upon those physicians who've never left the bedside—and we'll work intensively to find ways to leverage their knowledge and share the benefits of their experience.

* * *

The tension between self-conscious innovators and incremental executors pervades the business world as well. We tend to embrace the innovators—the entrepreneurs—of course, and thrill to their narrative. I certainly do. But as David Brooks has pointed out in a 2009 op-ed I've often cited and continue to wrestle with (mostly because I believe it's correct but wish it weren't), most successful business leaders aren't disruptive thinkers, nor are they compelling, self-aware protagonists. They're meticulous, methodical, detail-oriented people who seem to genuinely embrace process and highly-structured thinking: I seriously doubt most entered business to make a dent in the universe, but rather because they found a business function they enjoyed, and an environment in which their particular attributes were recognized and rewarded.

Arguably, most current pharma leaders aren't disruptive thinkers, but careful, deliberate, incremental ones; while many critics have blamed this leadership style for the many challenges the industry faces, I've started to wonder if you could construct an equally powerful argument that this careful, incremental thinking has also permitted the industry to continue to survive financially in the near-absence of any profound, disruptive innovation, and in a global environment that's increasingly sensitive to rising healthcare costs.

I suspect that, just as in medicine, the distinction between deliberate innovator and dutiful incrementalist may be overstated in business as well. While we celebrate (as we should) the self-described entrepreneurs, we may not give adequate credit to those who've managed to get a large organization to pivot in a useful and impactful fashion—and pivot not because these leaders were determined to change the world, but because it seemed like the right business decision at the moment.

Similarly, we adore the out-of-the-box entrepreneurs, yet tend to under appreciate the amount of tedious and, yes, deliberate work that's often required to go from an original inspiration to a successful business—a point Mullins and Komisar emphasize in their well-grounded book, *Getting to Plan B*. Even the success of Apple depended not only on the inspired vision of Steve Jobs but on his relentless execution, and mind-numbing attention to price, timelines, and detail.

Perhaps the lines between these two models will continue to blur. Certainly, deliberate leaders can discern the appeal of a broader purpose; I'm not aware of a single CEO that hasn't tried to cast their work—whether selling soup or servicing widgets—in a more mission-oriented light; they've seen the way business-school graduates flock to companies that have defined themselves as innovators in this fashion. Conversely, I suspect that the venture community will continue to prize not the entrepreneur with the boldest dream but rather the team that seems most likely to execute against a compelling vision.

* * *

It seems strange to segregate business achievement into two extreme phenotypes—disruptive entrepreneur and process-hound—but I suspect there's a good reason for this: certainly in biopharma, and I suspect in most other areas of business, success requires managing an overwhelming amount of uncertainty, and dealing with a shocking number of unknowns. As Daniel Kahneman discussed in the *New York Times* (in a piece adapted from his current, long-awaited book, *Thinking Fast and Slow*), a lot of the decisions you need to make in the course of running an enterprise are not rational, not what might be termed evidence-based. Everything from deciding who to hire to knowing what product to work on or what strategy to deploy—if you look carefully at the data, and are honest, there's really little basis for decision making at all. Thus, if you try to look at a business rationally, you'd freeze, paralyzed by the disconnect between information available and choices that you need to make.

My hypothesis is that there are two principle ways of dealing with this problem: the process method and the entrepreneur method. The process method—which is what most management consultants, investment banks, and CEOs do, is to essentially borrow a technique from economics: they assume a can opener. That is, everything would work so much better if you could believe in projections, in spreadsheets, in detailed methodologies for acquiring talent and developing forecasts—and so you go ahead and believe in them. While most leaders attach the requisite qualifiers (my favorite from consulting is "directionally correct"), my experience is that most senior managers believe in the system, believe in the process—they're not suspending disbelief, they believe. Because once you believe, everything starts to move, everything starts to progress—the whole system works. And since everyone else is doing basically the same thing, even if you are entirely wrong, at least, as was the case with stock analysts projections (see my review of *The Black Swan*, here), you won't be alone.

The entrepreneur method, by contrast, relies on the conviction of a motivated leader to believe that they can change the world, screw whatever the data might say. The analogy in medicine is the so-called "clinical champion," as described in this wonderful classic article (abstract only) by Flowers and Melmon. These advocates have in their corner many well-studied examples of disruptive innovation.

Unfortunately, these two worldviews are frequently at odds. As Clayton Christensen and his colleagues have shown (PDF), the benefits of disruptive innovation are systematically undervalued by just the sort of analyses generally used by process hounds, and by definition are initially more expensive than conventional approaches. Thus, disruptive innovators have a difficult task in most organizations, and I'm aware of very few examples where success has extended much beyond a commitment on a press release (an actual outcome I recall from my consulting experience).

Conversely, disruptive innovators might enjoy positioning themselves as fighting the system—but not only does success require remarkable attention to detail that generally includes tenuous revenue projections and market forecasts, but if you're successful, you then need to scale, and, pretty soon, you may find yourself in need of just the sorts of the processes and approaches you have to this point conveniently despised.

In my view, this tension is not just inescapable, but also healthy. My heart, of course, remains with the disruptive innovators: I continue to wake up every day and ask how I can change the world. But with experience, I've also developed a more nuanced and considerably more expansive view of what real change requires, and recognize the range of talents and perspectives that must be integrated for durable change to be achieved. – DS

Do Something Really Innovative In Health: Crowdsource Problems, Not (Just) Solutions

Businesses exist to solve problems, right? Certainly, this is the heart of the classic entrepreneurial model: you become obsessed with a particular problem, and create a business to solve it. Example: eBay was created by Pierre Omidyar to solve a perceived problem with inefficient markets, and since its inception has generally focused on doing exactly this.

Most enterprises are not blessed by such a coherent focus, at least not for long. More often, organizations—including university research labs as well as for-profit businesses—have a point at which they realize that their challenge has changed, and the problem they thought there were going to solve has shifted or even completely disappeared. The team —often an impressive group of people representing a wide range of capabilities—is then left to figure out what to do.

While disbanding is always an option, it rarely seems to happen, at least volitionally. Businesses, projects, academic enterprises—all are obsessed with their own survival, which rapidly becomes the defining mission. As a result, the organization urgently tries to figure out a way to pivot, a way to apply established resources in a different, useful way as it searches for a purpose to justify its existence. Very often, the question becomes: what should we do—what problem should we solve?

This desperate struggle for survival isn't necessarily a bad thing—in fact, the very urgency of this existential dilemma is arguably responsible for some of history's most important advances, whether the crisis is faced by a small tech company that's constantly shape-shifting as it tries to stay solvent or by a seventh-year PhD student whose first several projects crashed and burned and is desperate to find some way to graduate.

The constant need for businesses to adapt and survive rather than move towards a single fixed vision may help explain the David Brooks observation that continues to trouble me:

most successful CEOs are not about self-actualization but good execution—they are diligent managers seeking to survive rather than inspirational leaders striving to fulfill a deep vision (it's also why we're so entranced with the rare visionary leaders like Branson, Jobs, and I'd add Howard Schultz), who offer so much more than simply responsible stewardship.

While biopharmaceutical companies may be thought of as mission oriented, they are almost certainly the poster children for adaptation.

Biotech start-ups are known to rapidly lurch in different directions in response to changing data—genomics platform companies become oncology products companies, for example.

Perhaps less well appreciated is that big pharmas (many of which began as chemical companies) are beset by the same dilemma: at a fundamental level, they often do not have a clear sense of what it is they should work on, or how they should do it—therapeutic areas, disease areas, organ systems, severity of illness, location of patients—what to do?

The need for focus was perhaps best captured by a consulting project I once worked on: the goal was to construct, for a large pharma client, a rank list of all human ailments, from 1 to the end, based on some weighted integration of a large number of factors (number afflicted, burden of disease, generic presence, etc.). Presumably, this master list would help the client prioritize opportunities; I'm not sure whether it was actually useful.

In most businesses, of course, you identify a customer need (via market research, intuition, or some combination), then go out and design a product to address this; at some fairly coarse level, this is how biopharmas work: you create a "target product profile" (TPP) that supposedly represents where you think where a new product could be useful, and then you seek to deliver against this TPP. Problem is—funny story—biology is pretty damn complicated, and you can't generally order up therapies along predetermined lines. (Even if you succeed, forecasting turns out to be pretty damn fragile.)

The irony is that if you could actually design biopharma solutions as easily as this, I doubt that at least in the short-term there would be nearly as much obsessing about the nuances of these profiles—rather, we'd be out there developing outright cures for pancreatic cancer, Alzheimer's Disease, brain tumors, etc., rather than debating how slight a change in progression-free-survival should be targeted by the next oncology drug.

Nevertheless, even with the complexity of biology, there are still a wide range of diseases (including, aspirationally, the ones above), and certainly aspects of diseases (such as bothersome symptoms, existing therapies that are unpleasant or difficult to take, or to remember to take), that industry can tackle effectively—if only there was a better sense of where to look.

Increasingly, open innovation is invoked as the Big Answer—we constantly hear about communities of solvers out there to work out our most pesky problems.

But that's not our biggest problem right now: most companies have excellent solvers: the issue is figuring out the right questions. I suspect what's needed most (as I've previously discussed) is more "field discovery"—the granular input of the patients and physicians who are trying to cope with some real-world aspect of an illness—challenges that in many cases medical product companies, or digital health companies, could effectively address, if only they realized these problems existed and could be adequately defined.

This challenge—which, as I've discussed with Halle Tecco, founder of the non-profit SF incubator Rock Health, is also endemic is the digital health space—is fundamentally an issue of asymmetric information: the people who know what the problems are usually aren't the people best equipped to develop and design the solutions (whether a drug, a device, or an algorithm or therapeutic approach), and as a result, you have solvers solving problems that often not germane (a huge problem in the technology area, as I've written, and also a problem in biopharma, where the bench scientists developing new treatments often have minimal understanding of the clinical entity they are targeting). You also wind up with frustrated patients and physicians who constantly encounter problems they are unable to solve.

The idea of bringing together stakeholders is a classic approach that was pioneered at Stanford to unite engineers, physicians, and business people to generate more useful devices, and more recently (as I've discussed here) has been used to work on health system problems as well. The question is whether a more general approach could be developed that might enable the more efficient surfacing of problems, and more effectively and efficiently bring the right solvers to bear to address it.

Critically, such an approach should be not just participatory but iterative and interactive, so that questions can be refined, and potential solutions discussed and prototyped.

Developing this sort of platform is an effort I expect to be working on with Halle and her Rock Health colleagues in the coming months; it's a tough nut to crack, but I think if progress can be made here, there's a huge opportunity for benefit, as right now there are thousands of solvers who could easily impact the right problem, and there are millions of stakeholders who could identify and help characterize specific health problems in need of a solution. Something's gotta give. – DS

Entrepreneurs Are Drawn By Vision; Managers Are Driven By Process; Transforming Healthcare Will Require Both

The much-anticipated Facebook IPO stimulated a healthy national discussion about the nature of innovation and the role of entrepreneurship.

An outstanding op-ed by Rich Karlgaard in the *WSJ* focused squarely on the key question raised by the valuations of contemporary Silicon Valley innovation success stories such as Facebook, Instagram (and we could include Pinterest), and basically asks whether these companies have generated light or merely heat—in a world with real problems, are we just getting mindless apps? As one self-described manifesto put it: "We wanted flying cars. Instead, we got 140 characters. What happened to the future?" (See here for the back story, via the *New Yorker*).

Karlsgaard's response: the future is on the way. Leading-edge innovators, we are assured, have already moved on, and are earnestly focusing on the just the sort of problems—manufacturing, energy, transportation (and I'd add healthcare)—that urgently require imaginative solutions.

While I'm not sure every leading-edge investor would agree that social networks are over —see this recent *WSJ* interview with Benchmark's Bill Gurley, an investor in Nextdoor and Edmodo –I suspect Karlsgaard is spot on in his assertion that revolutionary innovation, when it arrives, is almost certain to be delivered by an upstart entrepreneur.

In my view, the defining characteristic of entrepreneurial organizations is that they are built around a compelling narrative—they were created to answer a question, solve a problem, meet a need, and—at least at the early stages—attract people largely on the basis of this vision.

Listen to almost any seminar from the wonderful Stanford Entrepreneurial Thought

Leader Seminar Series, or consider this Quora post (via *TechCrunch*) from an engineer, Robert Cezar Matei, explaining why he declined an offer from Instagram to work at Quora:

"I ended up going to Quora, because I was even more passionate about the vision and the role. I had a chance to help build what could become the platform for all human knowledge, which I thought could be a revolution on the same level as Google. Little else mattered in the end."

Matei's ambition, like so many drawn to startups, is to make a dent in the universe.

Matei's mindset, attitude and expectations seem strikingly different from those of most employees at most conventional companies.

I've come to believe that this lies at the heart of our innovation culture: entrepreneurial companies are drawn by vision, while conventional companies are driven by process.

Sure, conventional companies tend to have a well-crafted Mission Statement, Core Values, perhaps even a Credo—but these carefully-polished words tend to be irrelevant at best, and more typically, painfully ironic to the employees grinding out the day-to-day work.

At conventional companies, the successful employees tend to be responsible, professional, competent, and typically focus primarily on their specific assignments, their obligatory deliverables, their small circle of colleagues who either enable or obstruct them, and spend little time if any thinking about their company's overall mission, whatever it might be.

While entrepreneurial companies are brought into existence with much difficulty and through the exercise of considerable will explicitly in order to create something new, different, or qualitatively better, most conventional companies thrive through incremental change, and eventually exist simply to exist. Their size, mindset, and the realities of internal politics (as Dave Chase Points out eloquently here) don't allow for really profound innovation. It's just not what conventional companies do. Moreover, from what I've seen, most people who've remained and climbed the ladder at conventional companies have succeeded by accepting and working within the system (however flawed), rather than by radically reinventing the system or working around it.

It's not surprising, then, that as David Brooks has pointed out (and as I have occasionally discussed—see here and particularly here)—most leading CEOs turn out to be diligent managers, rather than inspirational visionaries. Most business succeed by doing things slightly better, or slightly differently—by making incremental, evolutionary changes—though often invoking the language of innovation and entrepreneurship. (Not surprisingly, there's now an entire Steve Jobs section at Successories—as I discuss here).

Can conventional companies change significantly, think differently? In general, I've come to believe the answer is no. Profound change is far more likely to originate not from a process-laden organization leveraging scale but rather from an impassioned, narrative-driven company, formed around a compelling idea that's engaged the mind and spirit of small number of highly motivated people, viscerally driven to pursue this vision.

To be sure, the fact that a small group of people are impassioned about an idea doesn't mean it's a good idea, much less a compelling business; there are a lot of dumb ideas out there, and a lot of would-be entrepreneurs passionately pursuing them.

Moreover, even the best and most ideas require scale, resources—and yes, eventually reproducible, well-executed processes—if they are ultimately to have the world-changing impact their originators envision. This lesson is one many young founders have learned the hard way.

For industries that urgently need to move in new directions—and health care stands out in my mind front and center here—the great new ideas are almost certainly going to arise from the next generation of entrepreneurs. The conventional companies that continue to succeed in these areas will be those wise enough to recognize their own limitations, and prescient enough to adapt through acquisition—acqui-pivot?—before it's too late.

Will entrepreneurs save healthcare?

If not us, who? If not now, when? – DS

Health = Potential x Attainment: Two Important, Often Distinct Opportunities For Entrepreneurs

In simplest terms, health can be thought of as the product of our "Potential Health" (the best health available to us if we saw the best doctors and received optimal therapy) multiplied by our "Attained Health" (how close we get to achieving this ideal).

That is: Health = (Potential Health) x (Attained Health).

The Supreme Court decision upholding key provisions of the ACA is likely to mark a key inflection point in a vital national discussion about how we think about these two important, and often distinct, health parameters.

For at least the last fifty years, most of our efforts have focused on maximizing our Potential Health. To this end, there was considerable interest in medical research exploring the molecular basis for diseases that make people sick, based on the assumption that this would lead to improved treatments for these patients.

For example, pancreatic cancer is a uniformly terrible disease, with a miserable prognosis no matter what doctor you see. A treatment that offered significant benefit to these patients could be described fairly as increasing our Potential Health.

More recently, we have started to place much greater emphasis on our Attained Health—the health individual Americans actually achieve (as a fraction of our ideal or potential health).

According to many health policy experts, there's a large discrepancy between the best care available and the care many patients receive, and consequently a profound need for research into approaches that will close this gap. The hope is that by improving access to care, and by ensuring the care provided is in accordance with the best medical evidence, our Attained Health can be significantly improved.

While there's little argument that improving both Potential and Attained health is important, many health policy experts (generally proponents of the ACA) contend that if we want to improve overall health, we'll get much more bang for our buck (i.e. better value) by focusing more of our attention—and especially our limited resources—on improving the Attained Health component, rather than pouring time and money into tweaking the Potential Health component—usually (it is often asserted) with little discernible success.

To appreciate what this is likely to mean for healthcare innovation, consider these comments from a key ACA architect, and current VC, Bob Kocher:

"As a venture capitalist, today's [Supreme Court] ruling creates an even greater opportunity to invest in innovative companies focused on bending down the cost curve, improving outcomes and creating more effective health care marketplaces. As we expand coverage, we will need more tools to help consumers shop for care, suppliers to redesign their products and services to be more productive, and innovators to reimagine how to engage doctors and patients in preventing complications and exercising value-consciousness."

This captures beautifully the ambition, language, and rhetoric of Attained Health—and the contrast with Potential Health couldn't be more striking.

In the giddy heyday of molecular biology, when Genentech and Amgen were founded, VCs used to talk about curing disease and saving lives. Still today, Genentech asserts that "One of the goals we strive toward every day is to find a cure for cancer." Meanwhile, Amgen's stated goal remains "to serve patients by transforming the promise of science and biotechnology into therapies that have the power to restore health or even save lives."

To be sure, many Attained Health proponents would contend that biopharma has enjoyed only limited success in its mission, producing what are often very expensive drugs that in many cases appear to offer only limited benefit. Sure, these critics agree, curing cancer is great—if you can do it; but if you're just talking about adding a few weeks at most, wouldn't the resources be better spent somewhere else?

Like many of us, I suspect, I feel more than a little torn; I agree with Kocher that there is a profound need for entrepreneurial innovation in what I'd call the Attained Health space, and have discussed this opportunity at length (see here, here, here, and here, for example).

At the same time, as I've also highlighted before (see here in particular, also here, here, and here), there's a real danger that in focusing so intently on attainment, and on measurements of communal health, we may overlook the need and the value, of pushing the edge of Potential Health as well—in the research we support, in the companies we nurture, and most importantly, in the patients in our trust. A compassionate commitment to Potential Health is what each individual patient is owed; this promise also reflects the relentless, innovative spirit that has propelled our nation's biomedical enterprise forward, and enabled it to achieve such worldwide prominence.

If you have pancreatic cancer today, you might be reassured by the promise of value-conscious care—but what you really need, and deserve, is an effective cure—and an innovative biopharma company able to deliver it.

Let's work towards ensuring that our healthcare innovation ecosystem evolves in a fashion that supports entrepreneurship in Potential Health as well as Attained Health, and ultimately identifies powerful new ways to elevate both. – DS

Better Than Pandora For Cats: Why LPs May Be Giving Health VCs Another Look

Health VCs: Desperate...

As a tech VC recently told me, refuting the latest flimsy rumor of a huge tech-dominated fund contemplating significant new investment in life science, "Wow, you healthcare guys are really desperate for some good news!"

It's true; not only are LPs looking ever more critically at VC as an asset class—especially since the publication of the Kauffman report—but the life science sector, in particular, has been devastated, and health VCs have been hurting. (See this fascinating Xconomy profile of Avalon's Kevin Kinsella and discussion of the current sorry state of healthcare VC.)

Part of the issue, as Bruce Booth and Bijan Salehizidah have described previously, and as Sarah Lacy summarized nicely in PandoDaily, is that the return profile of life science venture investments looks very different than tech in general, and consumer web (the focus of Lacy's article) in particular.

The sex appeal of tech investing is that a relatively small initial investment can blossom very quickly to yield huge returns; the catch, of course, is that this happens very rarely, and much like at a casino, and the tremendous attention lavished upon these winners can almost make you forget how infrequently they occur.

Life-science investments, by contrast, tend to be very different in nature—it traditionally takes a long time and a lot of money (especially vs consumer web) to reach a value inflection point, and even then (i.e. at early clinical stage of development), you usually only get a fraction of your potential value given (a) the large amount of undischarged risk that remains, and (b) current market dynamics, which generally favor the relatively few, deep-pocketed buyers rather than the comparatively large number of sellers, in large measure attributable to the inordinate time and cost of most late-stage drug development.

Some have suggested that venture funding isn't really suitable for the product development cycle in the life sciences, and that it's really geared towards tech applications where a relatively small amount of venture funding can quickly and adequately propel a concept to the point when you can tell whether it's going to work. Product development times in biopharmas, by contrast, are far longer.

However, with the evolution of ultra-lean, capital-efficient biopharma startups (and virtual startups) targeting compelling indications of interest to regulators (highlighted in the PCAST recommendations), an influx of capital available from corporate (generally pharma) VCs, and the legitimate possibility of a (somewhat) early liquidity event of some kind (rarely via IPO, more generally via acquisition by a larger biopharma), a path forward just might be possible.

What are the data suggesting that LPs have decided to give life science another chance? As far as I can tell, the evidence consists of:

(1) This article from Reuters, reverberating on Twitter, pointing out that several health care funds are out raising money, and that venture investment in biotech in 2011 was higher than 2010.

(2) A report from an accounting firm (press release here, nice summary from FierceBiotech here) reporting an increase biotech R&D spending and hiring in 2011 compared to 2010; most of this is occurring in the large biotechs—the small ones report a slight continued contraction.

In other words: 2011 was less bad than 2010—and it's always pretty easy to fit a trend line to a pair of data points.

... But Also Serious

While I'm not yet convinced that LPs have really had a change of heart and decided to embrace life-science, and health care more generally, I believe that the VCs managing to raise significant funds today have an excellent chance at superior performance, especially if they move beyond life science and embrace digital health—or rather, digital medicine (a distinction I first heard from AliveCor founder Dr. David Albert).

As Lacy—one of the Valley's leading tech journalists (see here for a particularly outstanding example of her work)—astutely (some will say unfairly) observed, much of the activity in "digital health" involves creation of fairly trivial apps or other enterprises that could fairly be characterized as "consumer web."

While some of these approaches may be impactful, most seem to lack a measure of gravitas and rigor, as I've argued previously—see here, here, here,here, and here, and references therein.

It's just possible that "Pandora for cats" may ultimately prove less compelling than solutions for patients.

There would seem to be an incredible opportunity for the serious application of emerging technologies to healthcare, in a ways that seek to engage rather than circumvent the health care systems and its many stakeholders.

The fundamental issue, to my mind, is that most tech funds, and especially funds focused on consumer web (to continue with Lacy's premise), are scared to death of getting enmeshed in a system with which they are unfamiliar, but which is laden with risks they accurately perceive. Most tech VCs I know would love "to do something" in health, but in practice find it very difficult to convince themselves it's worth it to pull the trigger—especially for opportunities embedded within the healthcare system and thus outside their traditional comfort zone.

The best digital medicine investors—as I continue to argue—are likely to come not from the tech world but from the healthcare world, and have deep experience in medical products (either drugs or devices). Such investors are likely to have the best understanding of the complex interactions and needs of the various players, and to best appreciate the current pain points—as well as the emerging problems to be solved, as physicians, patients, payers, and medical products companies struggle to adjust to a rapidly-changing world.

I appreciate the appeal of a mixed health/tech fund (an approach Lacy rejects), and Bruce Booth has presented data suggesting that historically, biotech investments made by diversified funds exceeded those from health care-only funds. If a health-focused VC is contemplating technology-oriented investments, the in-house tech expertise—and education of the health team—would seem helpful.

In practice, however, I can easily imagine the tech expertise coming from other, tech-oriented VCs—in which case the diversification would be achieved at the board level, rather than at the level of the individual investor. This assumes, of course, that tech VCs would be willing to invest in such health opportunities—though I'm hopeful that energetic participation in digital medicine from a resurgent life science VC investor base could provide useful reassurance.

This is an optimistic picture, to be sure, but one that offers exceptional upside, tremendous reward—for the LPs who embrace this vision, for the VCs who execute upon it, for the entrepreneurs who drive it, and especially for the patients, who ultimately stand to benefit from the offerings of entrepreneurial companies created by a thriving healthcare sector. – DS

My 2012 Digital Health Awards: Company, Person, Book Of The Year

The year 2012 in digital health whiplashed between a broader appreciation of the promise of digital health and an increased recognition of just how difficult it is, meaningfully and measurably, to improve health and drive revenue. My selections for the year's digital health awards capture important aspects of the evolving landscape, and also highlight where future opportunities for innovation might lie.

Digital Health **Company of the Year: Epic Systems**

Epic is the EMR company that everyone loves to hate, and that has clearly emerged as the go-to EMR platform for large hospital systems—a great segment to dominate, given the progressive consolidation of physician practices, as discussed recently in the NYT. (Tory Wolff and I discussed Epic at length this year, see Part 1 and Part 2.)

To technologists in Silicon Valley, Epic epitomizes everything that's wrong with modern medicine—it's inelegant and clunky, it delivers a user experience many physicians view as awful, and worst of all, it's a closed, highly proprietary system. I imagine struggling EMR companies must regard them the way SNL's Jon Lovitz's Dukakis looked at Dana Carvey's Bush and said "I can't believe I'm losing to this guy!"

Yet Epic seems to be growing ever-more dominant, while the rest of the field remains highly fragmented, and it's important to understand why.

Quite simply, Epic figured out that what their customers needed—in this case, a way to connect the various parts of their system, so that established physician groups and hospital functions can reliably communicate using a common platform, and share patient data.

The appeal of Epic isn't that its solution is especially elegant, but simply that it works. Epic has a reputation for "flawless implementation" (a phrase I've heard multiple times), and while that's surely an exaggeration, Epic clearly places significant emphasis on the nuts-

and-bolts of the installation, working intensively with each individual client, in a highly customized fashion, holding the client's hand throughout the process.

The key lesson, in my mind, is the importance of understanding Dave McClure's brilliant maxim, "your solution is not my problem." Hospitals systems want a solution that reliably solves their most immediate, most pressing problem: basic connectivity—and this is what Epic effectively delivers.

There are a slew of remaining problems that Epic doesn't effectively address (or as I like to call them, opportunities), functionalities that sit around the EMR, from improved input of data to more sophisticated analysis of the data that's already been acquired, to the improved ability of care providers to have the relevant information at their fingertips, clearly and accurately presented, whether the provider is at the bedside, the clinic, or at home in the barcalounger.

Going forward, a critically important question is the degree to which such innovation can be developed outside of Epic, which obviously would like to offer these functionalities itself. I am inspired by Leigh Drogen's "Law of Unbundling" (h/t to Bijan Salehizadeh for putting me onto this), which basically asserts that at least on the internet, companies that try to win by bundling everything (examples cited include AOL, Craigslist, Facebook) get disrupted as customers realize they have other options, and can get better results from a series of other sources.

The fascinating question is whether Epic will be able to exclude all competitors while improving its own adjacent offerings or whether competitor products will prove so compelling to customers that Epic will be forced to at a minimum accept them, perhaps embrace them (e.g. facilitate development of ecosystem), or if necessary, acquire them.

Digital Health Person Of The Year: Vinod Khosla

Starting with his notorious "Do we need doctors or algorithms" post in TechCrunch in January, continuing with his much-discussed interview this summer at the Rock Health Digital Health Summit, and culminating in his just-posted white paper, "'20% doctor included': speculations & musings of a technology optimist," Vinod Khosla has brought his boldly disruptive spirit—and real investment capital—to digital health. (See here and here for my discussion of the controversy.)

His argument, in essence, is that data and computers should enable significantly better health decisions; he writes,

"Computers are much better than people at organizing and recalling information. They have larger and less corruptible memories, remembering more complex information much more quickly and completely, and make far fewer mistakes than a hot shot MD from Harvard. *Contrary to popular opinion, they're also better at integrating and balancing consideration of patient symptoms, history, demeanor, environmental factors, and population management guidelines than the average physician* (emphasis added)."

In Khosla's future, computers will eventually do almost all the work, with providers relegated perhaps to facilitating the information exchange between patient and computer—sort of like the way an attendant at PepBoys will hook up a computer to your car to figure out why the "check engine" light is on.

I continue to believe Khosla fundamentally underestimates and undervalues the degree to which the practice of medicine is (or at its best, can be) fundamentally more humanistic, relationship-oriented than he recognizes, and also far less transactional, the data and distinctions far less discrete. Consequently, I am intrigued by opportunities that use technology to enhance, not effectively replace, the provider/patient relationship (approaches that most easily lend themselves to either an ACO/capitated environment or concierge care, and work less well in context of traditional fee-for-service).

At the same time, Khosla is absolutely right about the extent to which existing data are profoundly underutilized—and about what an opportunity fixing this would present, from both a health and economic perspective. This is arguably where there's the single greatest opportunity for value capture in the digital health space.

While predictive analytics may change the way we think about risk and disease in the future, I suspect there's a tremendous amount of value to be captured from basic descriptive analytics—from "simply" (as if) putting together a coherent, accurate, comprehensive timeline of a patient's health experiences and expenses over the years, and comparing it to some basic standards.

Steward's de la Torre seems to share this perspective as well, telling Fortune,

"From an IT perspective, health care is at least 15 to 20 years behind the rest of the world. It's amazing to me that Wal-Mart can tell you where one T-shirt is in one of its factories or warehouses at any point in time, but we don't even know if a patient had an MRI or a CAT scan, a test that costs $1,000-plus, in the past few months. That's how far behind our IT systems are."

While I may not share de la Torre's apparent enthusiasm for the strict institution of so-called "best practices" (see this useful, cautionary discussion by Groopman and

Hartzband) I certainly believe in avoiding "worst practices," and making sure providers don't do things that are manifestly wrong (whether by accident or by ignorance). As Ashish Jha has argued, there's a lot of good we can do—and money we can save—simply by reducing medical errors.

Furthermore, while it's tremendously exciting to contemplate the use of sensors, activity monitors, and other approaches to provide rich new phenotypic information (and I love the science here), it's critically important to develop a clearer sense of the information we already have, and to better understand what care actually looks like today.

If I were a harried hospital executive facing the (false) choice between (Option 1) the ability to layer into my system new, elaborate cutting-edge sensor data or (Option 2) improved visibility into basic data that exist (or should exist) today, I'd pick Option Two in a heartbeat—it's hard to move forward and improve processes intelligently without a clear understanding of where you're starting from.

As an inquisitive physician passionate about advancing standards rather than simply maintaining them, however, I'd look eagerly to the dense phenotyping possibilities enabled by Option 1. (This is also exactly what we're pursuing in the MGH/MIT CATCH digital health initiative [Disclosure: I am a SF-based co-founder]).

Digital Health Book Of The Year: "Why Nobody Believes The Numbers," by Al Lewis

Disease management and wellness programs (two related but distinct category of offerings) typically describe both health goals and financial goals. The inconvenient truth, as Al Lewis, a leading figure of the disease management movement, explains, is that far too often, we use faulty techniques to assess the performance of these programs, resulting in essentially cooked data that, well, nobody believes. As Fielding Mellish might say with only slight exaggeration, it's a travesty of a mockery of a sham. (See here for my recent discussion of corporate wellness programs.)

Lewis isn't suggesting that disease management can't reduce costs—in fact, he argues explicitly that it can—only the reduction takes much longer, is far less dramatic, and is appreciably more difficult to achieve (on those occasions when cost savings are actually achieved) than most vendors typically acknowledge.

This is an important book (albeit oddly overpriced, and also poorly rendered on the Kindle, so avoid the digital version) because it explicitly addresses one of the most significant hurdles in healthcare in general, and digital health in particular: credibly demonstrating that a particular intervention delivers return on investment.

I am reminded of a question Stanford professor Arnold Milstein asked me a while back when we were walking around campus. "Can you think of a healthcare technology that has reduced net costs to the system?" he asked me. He acknowledged vaccines would qualify, but beyond that, it's pretty tough going—and it strikes me this is a challenge faced by all new offerings in healthcare, including disease management and wellness programs.

One response to this challenge is to point out that what really matters is the value over time, something especially relevant to the consideration of new technologies. As Gottlieb and Makower recently discussed, and as Clay Christensen has famously argued, disruptive technologies often start off as extremely expensive, but over time, can become dramatically less so, thus evaluating a new technology by original cost can be both unfair and misleading.

Nevertheless, it's today's cost that matters most to potential purchasers, which leads to the phenomenon Lewis describes of using faulty metrics to artificially demonstrate benefit. For example, comparing the performance of program participants to a group who didn't opt-in can lead to "success" that seems attributable to the program but more likely reflects the differential motivation of the starting populations.

While the fragility of ROI claims for disease management and wellness programs likely comes as no great shock to potential purchasers of programs (as Lewis's title suggest), it's important that entrepreneurs in this space appreciate the magnitude of the challenge as well, and understand what they're getting into. There are far too many South Park underpants gnomes business plans around (Step 1: Offer behavior app, invoking BJ Fogg; Step 2; Step 3: Profit), and comparatively few robust demonstrations of value delivery here.

Fact is, it's inherently quite difficult to come up with an innovation that improves health in a significant, measurable, and durable fashion, and it's extraordinarily difficult to improve health to the degree that you actually reduce costs.

Without question, robustly modifying behavior remains one of the greatest opportunities for digital health; but achieving this to the extent that you actually reduce healthcare costs represents a far more difficult task than most entrepreneurs initially recognize. – DS

Academics Embrace Digital Health: Bringing Medicine And Participation To Medicine

I was thrilled to read about UCSF's newly-created Center for Digital Health Innovation (CDHI), an effort to organize and catalyze the university's efforts and activities in this vital, emerging space.

This initiative seems to be driven by much the same spirit that led a group of us to establish the Center for Assessment Technology and Continuous Health(CATCH) at MGH and MIT: the recognition that health care faces unprecedented challenges—challenges that emerging technologies and approaches to information can, must, and will help address.

If I had to distill the opportunities of digital health in medicine down to two themes, I'd nominate "Measurement" and "Participation."

Measurement refers to our increased ability to measure both people and process. Technologies permit us to understand both health and disease with far greater granularity, and in a continuous rather than episodic fashion, affording comprehensive understanding, and ideally enabling the sort of precision medicine for which UCSF Chancellor Susan Desmond-Hellmann has so passionately advocated. CATCH Director Dennis Ausiello and I have argued that phenotype is the new genotype, and that integrating the two may be especially powerful (and very challenging). Such integration has also been effectively championed by Eric Topol, Director of the Scripps Translational Research Institute and author of digital health's defining book, *The Creative Destruction of Medicine*.

Technology also provides us the means to study the delivery of care, to critically evaluate quality and cost, and to identify opportunities for improvement. While medical research has not always paid adequate attention to these sorts of systems issues, healthcare's apparent movement away from fee-for-service to some sort of value-based approach has highlighted the need to figure these questions out.

Participation is the second great theme of digital health, and emphasizes technology's tremendous democratizing potential. While I don't see doctors becoming obsolete, they will need to recalibrate themselves to a world of informed, involved patient and patient communities—and see this evolution for the enormous opportunity it unquestionably is.

Participation also involves the important subject of behavior, which is critically linked to health. Technology can provide new opportunities to better understand behavior patterns, and ideally, novel approaches to motivate and sustain behaviors that are more healthful. Many nascent digital health companies focus on these challenges.

None of this will be easy. Arguably our most significant learning thus far from keeping score has been how incredibly difficult it is to durably improve health(much less to do so in a way that reduces total costs—my "Milstein Metric," and, the goal to which many aspire). Elegant gadgets and inexpensive apps won't offer a magic answer, and engagement, as my favorite digital health provocateur Al Lewis points out, is not a panacea (though, like David Chase, I'd argue it's more important than Lewis lets on).

In the end, we are likely to be propelled less by all the goodies a technology-enabled future might offer, and more by the growing, technology-enabled concern about the level of care we now receive. Digital health approaches, including sophisticated analytics, will not only capture practice variation, but can help guide us to more effective solutions.

A striking feature of both CATCH and the CDHI is the explicit recognition of the translational value of public-private partnerships, and of the need to capture and nurture the development of promising but preliminary ideas from providers in the trenches.

As the newly-designated director of the CDHI puts it,

"UCSF faculty and students are among the most creative and accomplished that you can find. Add to that the proximity to Silicon Valley, and you have the ideal environment for digital health innovation. Previously, faculty struggled to bring promising concepts to fruition due to lack of resources or technical or business expertise. Now, the CDHI will provide the administrative, financial, and technical resources, as well as the guidance and connections to create the public-private collaborations and partnerships needed to bring these exciting projects to market. Great ideas will no longer die on the vine."

Although perhaps less obvious, organizations such as CATCH and the CDHI are also likely to provide technologists with more opportunities to connect with physicians, and to develop a more nuanced appreciation of the challenges they face. I've unsparingly pointed out that many brilliant and bold tech innovators don't seem to know what they don't know about medicine and health. At the same time, many are passionately interested in using their resources and know-how to improve health. Thus, CATCH and the CDHI may offer ideal settings in which important knowledge and cultural differences could be bridged, new understanding forged, and original ideas hatched and productively evolved.

The future of medicine and healthcare—as well as the future of medical products companies (whether or not they fully realize it)—is likely to increasingly depend upon the extent on our success in improving measurement and fostering broader participation.

Hopefully, initiatives such as CATCH and the CDHI will provide the nidus for digital health innovation within the trusted confines of premier academic medical institutions—and achieve results that extend far beyond. – DS

XIII.

In Conclusion

Thank goodness for the innovators and entrepreneurs, those brave souls who remain undaunted by the many structural challenges and obstacles that comprise our healthcare system, and who are working so hard to improve it. Will the enlightened application of digital health technologies make our healthcare system better? Only time will tell. But it is gratifying to see the drive of those who feel passionate about making healthcare a system that delivers real value to its participants, particularly the patients and families most affected by illness.

Hopefully our next generation of citizens will live healthier lives than their predecessors, in part as a result of the efforts of those who have committed themselves to digital health innovation.

In healthcare, we confront a complex set of problems, and we must do all we can to encourage new ideas, new technologies, and new methods that foster positive healthcare engagement and deliver better outcomes. Our economy depends on it. Our lives depend on it.

As "digital health" and "healthcare" become indistinguishable through the passage of time and growing comfort with technology, we look forward to continue musings on the field and particularly the opportunity to report on its successes.

XIV.

Acknowledgments

David Shaywitz:

I'm particularly grateful to MGH's Denny Ausiello, for his mentorship, wisdom, vision, and advice over the last 15 years.

I've benefited enormously from the editors I've been fortunate to work with over the years, including particularly Susan Chira at the *New York Times*, Fred Hiatt at the *Washington Post*, Erich Eichmann at the *Wall Street Journal*, and Marjorie Pritchard at the *Boston Globe*.

I am appreciative of the advice and guidance I've received from Matt Herper and Zina Moukheiber at *Forbes*, and from Alexis Madrigal and James Hamblin at *The Atlantic*.

For their early encouragement of my writing, I'm grateful to Margaret Turner, Jim Bucar, and especially the incomparable Toni Giamatti at Hopkins School, to Mark DeLong at the summer Talent Identification Program (TIP) at Duke University; and to Cheryl Armstrong, my expository writing instructor at Harvard.

On the digital health front, a special thank you to UCSF's treasure, Aenor Sawyer, and to my remarkable, insightful, savvy, and very funny co-author Lisa Suennen.

I've been especially fortunate to work in a company supportive of these orthogonal efforts, and of orthogonal thinking in general; both Mathai Mammen and Rick Winningham stand out for their imagination and breadth of vision.

I've been beyond blessed to grow up in a family where the inspiration was matched only by the boundless support and effusive warmth that characterized each day, and continues to be a vital part of my life.

I've also been unreasonably blessed with the three most wonderful girls in the world, who, together with my wonderful wife, infuse each day with love and meaning.

Lisa Suennen:

I have been very lucky in my career to have some truly great mentors and colleagues who pushed me to learn and take chances and grow.

Most important among these has been my father and business partner, Dr. Albert Waxman, who always sees the possible in every opportunity. I have tremendous gratitude also to Dr. Shannon Kennedy and Jennifer Jones, both former bosses and now colleagues and friends without whom I would not have the impetus or confidence to speak and write publicly the way I do.

On the healthcare front there are too many great old and new friends to name, but those of you who have supported my efforts to try new things and who have tolerated my occasionally extreme candor and offbeat sense of humor know who you are. You have dedicated your careers to doing well by doing good in the world by choosing healthcare over seemingly more glamorous fields and that is something of which to be proud.

In my digital health journey I was so lucky to meet David Shaywitz, my co-author, and find in him a mutual love of story-telling as well as a healthy skepticism about the goings-on in our overlapping worlds. Plus we both love baseball.

I must thank Tracy Dayton and Lynne Esselstein for being my best friends, partners in crime and cheerleaders at all times.

And of course I must thank my husband and daughter and the rest of my family for giving me a warm, loving place to come home to and always encouraging me to be my best.

David Shaywitz

David Shaywitz is a graduate of Harvard College (summa cum laude), and received his MD from the Health Sciences and Technology program at Harvard Medical School and MIT, and his PhD from the Department of Biology at MIT. He trained in internal medicine and endocrinology at MGH, conducted his post-doctoral research in the Melton lab at Harvard, and served as a Venture Fellow at Fidelity Biosciences in Cambridge, MA. He gained experience in clinical drug development at Merck, and in strategy at the Boston Consulting Group. He is currently a strategist and product developer at a biopharmaceutical company in San Francisco. Passionate about the promise of digital health, he is also a co-founder of the MGH/MIT-based Center for Assessment Technology and Continuous Health (CATCH) digital health initiative that seeks to use better patient measurement to improve care and drive science. He blogs about medical innovation and digital health for Forbes.com and TheAtlantic.com. He is also an adjunct scholar at the American Enterprise Institute.

Lisa Suennen

Lisa Suennen is a Silicon Valley-based founding partner at Psilos Group, a healthcare venture capital and private equity investment firm with a specific focus on companies that have demonstrated how to improve quality while reducing costs. Lisa has spent nearly 30 years working in the healthcare and tech industries and currently sits on the boards of several private and public healthcare companies. She also serves on the Qualcomm Life Advisory Board and the Dignity Health Foundation Board and has served as a health technology advisor to the White House Office of the National Coordinator. Lisa is also deeply involved with her alma mater, UC Berkeley, where she is vice chairman of the Institute for Governmental Studies and teaches the healthcare venture capital course in the Haas School of Business. Her wildly popular, irrepressibly candid "Venture Valkyrie" blog has become an institution within the healthcare and venture capital communities.

About the Publisher

Hyperink is the easiest way for anyone to publish a beautiful, high-quality book.

We work closely with subject matter experts to create each book. We cover topics ranging from higher education to job recruiting, from Android apps marketing to barefoot running.

If you have interesting knowledge that people are willing to pay for, especially if you've already produced content on the topic, please reach out to us! There's no writing required and it's a unique opportunity to build your own brand and earn royalties.

Hyperink is based in SF and actively hiring people who want to shape publishing's future. Email us if you'd like to meet our team!

Note: If you're reading this book in print or on a device that's not web-enabled, **please email** books@hyperinkpress.com with the title of this book in the subject line. We'll send you a PDF copy, so you can access all of the great content we've included as clickable links.

Made in the USA
San Bernardino, CA
05 May 2015